EXPAND YOUR VOCABULARY WITH SHORT STORIES

Over 300 Engaging Stories To Help You Learn English Words

Spencer Donahoe

Copyright © 2025 Spencer Donahoe

All rights reserved

No part of this book may be reproduced, or stored in a retrieval system, or transmitted in any form or by any means, electronic, mechanical, photocopying, recording, or otherwise, without express written permission of the publisher.

CONTENTS

Title Page
Copyright
Introduction   1
Nature   3
History   49
Space   75
Science   100
Food   131
Geography   165
Legends and Myths   201
Extraordinary People   242
Strange Events   258
The Everyday World   273
The Journey of Vocabulary Learning   323

INTRODUCTION

When vocabulary is learned in context, it becomes part of a deeper understanding of language. For English learners, especially, vocabulary can often seem overwhelming, with words having different meanings depending on the situation. By learning words within interesting stories, learners get to see how these words are used, making them more memorable and practical.

Contextual, immersive vocabulary learning, as demonstrated throughout this book, provides an opportunity to understand a word's nuances and applications in real-life scenarios. Imagine learning the word "nascent" while reading about the early development of wasps. By encountering the word in the setting of interesting natural examples, it becomes much easier to understand how the word might apply to other situations, such as a nascent idea or project.

When words are embedded in stories, they are tied to something tangible. Stories bring emotions, curiosity, and connection. This is why context-based learning has such a profound impact—it connects words to experiences, making them much more likely to stick with us.

Vocabulary Builder's Purpose

This book was designed with a clear purpose: to help English speakers build and expand their vocabulary by learning it through the lens of true stories. By offering brief stories across a wide range of topics—nature, history, space and science— readers are invited to explore new words in an enjoyable way with their vocabulary broadening as they read. We start with a range of stories about nature and then a host of different educational themes follow later in the book.

Whether you're reading about the mysterious nature of fig wasps, the historical significance of the Library of Alexandria, or the culinary history of chocolate, you will be presented with key words that come alive in context. Each story is followed by a list of vocabulary words and their definitions, allowing you to immediately understand the meaning and application.

This book is an opportunity to learn words in a way that is engaging, memorable, and immediately useful. With over 300 short stories, you will not only be able to grow your vocabulary but will also gain a richer understanding of the world.

The beauty of this book lies in its flexibility. You can read it in sequence, or pick and choose stories from different sections depending on your interests. Each section introduces you to a unique theme, with stories that range from the mysteries of space to the wonders of ancient civilizations. After reading the story, take a moment to review the vocabulary list, reading through each word's definition and reflecting on how it was used in the context of the story.

This approach ensures that learning vocabulary becomes an immersive, enjoyable experience—where each story not only teaches new words but also offers an opportunity to engage with the world in a way that traditional textbooks can't. Let the adventure of learning new words begin, and you'll learn more about the world at the same time!

NATURE

How Octopuses Use Tools to Outsmart Predators

Octopuses are among the most intelligent creatures in the animal kingdom, known for their ability to solve complex puzzles and use tools in ways that rival some of the most advanced mammals. In the wild, octopuses use a variety of objects to protect themselves from predators. One particularly fascinating example is their use of coconut shells. The octopus will carefully collect the shells, position them around itself, and hide inside them, effectively creating a mobile shield. Not only do these tools provide protection, but they also help octopuses camouflage, making it difficult for predators to detect them. Researchers have even witnessed octopuses carrying tools with them, showcasing their foresight and understanding of future threats. This behavior is especially impressive because it indicates that octopuses not only react to immediate dangers but can also plan ahead, demonstrating a level of cognitive ability that is rare in the animal kingdom. The ability of octopuses to use tools highlights their adaptability and cleverness in the face of danger, making them one of the most resourceful creatures in the ocean.

Key Vocabulary:
- **Ingenious**: Clever and resourceful; characterized by originality and inventiveness.
- **Camouflage**: The use of color, patterns, or objects to blend into the surroundings, making something hard to see or detect.
- **Foresight**: The ability to predict or plan for the future,

showing insight or planning ahead.
- **Predators**: Animals that hunt and eat other animals for food.
- **Adaptation**: A change or process by which an organism becomes better suited to its environment.

The Hidden Life of a Fig

Inside every fig, a microscopic drama unfolds. A female fig wasp, no larger than a grain of sand, squeezes through a tiny opening at the bottom of the fig, called an ostiole. Once inside, she loses her wings and antennae—a necessary sacrifice for her species' survival. She moves through the labyrinth of nascent flowers, carefully pollinating them. Some flowers will become seeds, while others will host her eggs. After laying her eggs, the male wasps, ephemeral in nature, mate with the females before chewing escape tunnels, dying shortly after. The fertilized females, now laden with pollen, escape through these tunnels, ready to continue the cycle of life. The fig, in turn, begins its syconium stage, ripening into the sweet fruit we recognize. The entire process takes place within the fig, which serves as both the nursery and the food source for the wasps. This unique relationship between the fig and the wasp is one of nature's most intricate examples of mutual dependence and survival.

Key Vocabulary:
- **Ostiole**: A small opening or pore, specifically the tiny entrance in a fig fruit through which wasps enter.
- **Nascent**: Just coming into existence; beginning to develop. Often used to describe things in their early stages of formation.
- **Ephemeral**: Lasting for a very short time; transient. In nature, it often describes organisms or phenomena that are extremely short-lived.
- **Inexorable**: Impossible to stop or prevent; relentless. Describes processes that continue despite any attempts to

halt them.
- **Syconium**: A specialized structure unique to figs, where the flowers and seeds develop inside a fleshy vessel that becomes the fig fruit.

The Jellyfish That Lives Forever

The Turritopsis dohrnii, also known as the "immortal jellyfish," has an extraordinary ability that sets it apart from most other creatures: it can live forever. When this jellyfish encounters physical damage, environmental stress, or even illness, it has the remarkable ability to revert to its earliest developmental stage. Through a process called transdifferentiation, the jellyfish's cells transform into a different type, essentially reversing its aging process. This means that instead of dying of old age, the jellyfish can regenerate itself and start its life cycle over again. While the "immortal" jellyfish can theoretically live indefinitely, it is not invincible. It can still fall prey to diseases, predators, or environmental changes. However, its ability to reverse the aging process makes it a unique and fascinating subject for scientific study. Researchers are particularly interested in understanding how this regenerative process works, as it may hold clues for medical advancements in human aging and cell regeneration. The jellyfish's ability to defy the natural order of life and death offers a glimpse into the potential future of biological immortality.

Key Vocabulary:
- **Transdifferentiation**: The process by which one type of cell changes into another, often reversing the aging process.
- **Immortal**: Unable to die; living forever.
- **Succumb**: To give in or yield to something overpowering, such as disease, temptation, or age.
- **Invincible**: Too powerful to be defeated or overcome.
- **Prey**: Animals that are hunted or eaten by other animals.

How Trees Communicate Through Underground Networks

Beneath the surface of forests lies an intricate communication system that connects trees through fungal networks. Think of it as the "Wood Wide Web," this underground system allows trees to exchange vital resources like water and nutrients. It also enables trees to send chemical signals to each other, alerting them of dangers such as disease or insect infestations. The mycorrhizal fungi act as conduits, linking the roots of different trees, allowing them to share resources and protect one another. Older, more established trees may even send nutrients to younger saplings, helping them grow stronger in the competitive environment of the forest. The communication between trees goes beyond just survival; it also strengthens the ecosystem as a whole. By sharing resources, trees ensure that the entire forest can thrive. This network also plays a critical role in maintaining biodiversity by fostering cooperation over competition. The underground world of trees is a hidden, yet essential, part of how forests function and survive.

Key Vocabulary:
- **Symbiotic**: A mutually beneficial relationship between two organisms, where both parties gain from the interaction.
- **Fungal**: Relating to fungi, which include organisms like mushrooms, molds, and yeasts.
- **Nutrients**: Substances that provide nourishment essential for growth and the maintenance of life.
- **Infestation**: The presence of a large number of pests or harmful organisms in a place, often causing damage.
- **Interconnectedness**: The state of being connected with each other, forming a network or system.

The Bird That Can Mimic Any Sound

The lyrebird, native to Australia, is one of the most impressive mimics in the animal world. With an astonishing ability to imitate almost any sound, the lyrebird can mimic the calls of other birds, chainsaws, car alarms, camera shutters, and even human voices. Male lyrebirds often use their vocal talents to attract mates by showcasing their remarkable range of sounds, creating an intricate performance that includes both natural and artificial noises. Some lyrebirds have even been known to incorporate sounds from their environment, like construction equipment, into their songs. The ability to mimic sounds so precisely serves a dual purpose: it demonstrates the bird's fitness as a mate and helps it blend into its environment. This mimicry shows the bird's adaptability and its keen listening skills. While lyrebirds primarily use their vocal abilities to communicate with each other, their skill in replicating the world around them is an extraordinary example of how animals can use mimicry not just for survival, but for social interaction as well.

Key Vocabulary:
- **Mimic**: To imitate or copy the actions, sounds, or behavior of someone or something.
- **Prowess**: Exceptional skill or ability, often in a particular field or activity.
- **Astonishing**: Extremely surprising or impressive; difficult to believe.
- **Adaptability**: The ability to adjust or change in response to new conditions or challenges.
- **Vocal**: Relating to the voice or speech.

The Mystery of Bioluminescent Mushrooms

Bioluminescence, the ability of organisms to emit light, has captivated the imagination of scientists and artists alike for centuries. The phenomenon, commonly observed in fireflies and deep-sea creatures, extends to a surprising member of the fungal kingdom—bioluminescent mushrooms. These radiant organisms glow in the dark, casting an ethereal light through the shadowed forest floor. The mystery of their luminescence lies in a biochemical reaction that occurs within their cells, wherein an enzyme called luciferase interacts with a substrate, luciferin, to produce light. But why do these mushrooms shine? Some scientists theorize that the glow acts as a lure, attracting nocturnal insects that help spread the spores, ensuring the mushroom's reproduction. Others suggest that the glow may deter herbivores, signaling the presence of potentially harmful compounds. Interestingly, bioluminescence in fungi is not a uniform trait—only certain species exhibit it. One of the most well-known examples is the Armillaria mellea, which lights up the forest floor with an otherworldly greenish hue. The mystery of these glowing mushrooms is not just a matter of scientific intrigue but a reminder of how nature's wonders continue to defy easy explanation, leaving us in awe of its endless complexity and beauty.

Key Vocabulary:
- **Bioluminescence**: The production and emission of light by living organisms, typically through chemical reactions.
- **Ethereal**: Extremely delicate and light in a way that seems too perfect for this world; otherworldly.
- **Enzyme**: A protein that accelerates or catalyzes a chemical reaction in living organisms.
- **Substrate**: A substance or layer that something else is built upon or interacts with, especially in a biochemical process.
- **Herbivores**: Animals that feed primarily on plants.

How Ants Build Living Bridges with Their Bodies

Ants are not only industrious but also remarkably resourceful, exhibiting an astonishing ability to create living structures out of their own bodies. Known as "living bridges," these remarkable constructions are formed when ants link their bodies together to span gaps, allowing the colony to traverse difficult terrain. This behavior has been observed in various species, such as the Azteca ants, which utilize their strong mandibles and cooperative instincts to create a temporary bridge across gaps or obstacles. Each ant in the bridge plays a crucial role, with some serving as the foundation, while others climb on top, adding layers to the structure. The design is remarkably efficient, as the ants communicate through chemical signals to coordinate their efforts. The living bridge can be disassembled when no longer needed, with the ants simply releasing their grip and moving on. This extraordinary display of teamwork and problem-solving not only helps the ants overcome physical challenges but also showcases their ability to adapt and work together in ways that are far beyond mere survival instincts. The phenomenon of living bridges highlights the complexity of social behavior in insects, offering valuable insights into collective intelligence.

Key Vocabulary:
- **Industrious**: Hard-working and diligent, often referring to those who are constantly engaged in productive work.
- **Resourceful**: Able to find clever and quick solutions to problems, often using limited resources.
- **Mandibles**: The paired appendages in certain insects, used for grasping, chewing, or cutting.
- **Coordinated**: Well-organized and functioning together in harmony.
- **Collective Intelligence**: The shared or group intelligence that emerges from the collaboration and cooperation of many individuals.

The Butterfly That Pretends to Be a Poisonous Snake

The world of mimicry in the animal kingdom is filled with astonishing examples of deception and adaptation, and one of the most intriguing is the butterfly that mimics a poisonous snake. The Batesian mimicry exhibited by the Malaysian swallowtail butterfly (Papilio garamas) is a prime example of how creatures evolve to deceive their predators. This butterfly's wings are adorned with patterns that closely resemble the markings of a venomous pit viper, a deadly snake found in the same regions. When threatened, the butterfly spreads its wings wide, revealing these snake-like patterns in an attempt to scare off potential predators. The mimicry works because predators, particularly birds, learn to associate the distinctive patterns with danger, avoiding the butterfly as they would a real snake. This behavior is not only a defense mechanism but also an evolutionary strategy that ensures the butterfly's survival. What makes this mimicry even more fascinating is that the butterfly itself is harmless, relying on the learned fear of its predators rather than any actual venomous traits. This example of evolution through deception highlights the ingenuity of nature's designs and its ability to craft elaborate survival strategies.

Key Vocabulary:
- **Batesian Mimicry**: A form of mimicry where a harmless species evolves to resemble a dangerous or venomous species to avoid predation.
- **Venomous**: Capable of injecting venom, typically through a bite or sting, causing harm or death to another organism.
- **Adorned**: Decorated or embellished with something, especially to enhance appearance.
- **Deception**: The act of misleading or tricking others, often to gain an advantage or avoid harm.
- **Evolutionary Strategy**: The methods or adaptations that organisms develop over time to increase their chances of survival and reproduction.

Why Some Animals Can Regrow Entire Limbs

The ability to regenerate lost body parts is a remarkable feature found in several species, ranging from starfish to salamanders, and it holds a profound mystery for scientists. In particular, the axolotl (Ambystoma mexicanum), a type of salamander, is famous for its incredible regenerative abilities. When an axolotl loses a limb, it can grow it back fully, complete with bones, nerves, muscles, and skin. This process is a form of biological alchemy, whereby the cells at the site of the injury transform into a structure known as a blastema, which is capable of developing into all the tissues necessary for limb regeneration. This phenomenon is not limited to just limbs; axolotls can also regenerate their spinal cord, heart, and even parts of their brain. The regenerative powers of the axolotl have captivated researchers, who study the process to unlock the secrets of human regeneration. Understanding how these creatures are capable of such feats may one day lead to breakthroughs in medicine, particularly in fields related to wound healing, tissue repair, and even the regeneration of human organs. The axolotl, with its regenerative prowess, serves as a beacon of possibility in the world of biological research.

Key Vocabulary:
- **Regeneration**: The process of regrowing lost or damaged body parts or tissues.
- **Blastema**: A mass of undifferentiated cells capable of developing into new tissues, often involved in regeneration.
- **Alchemy**: A seemingly magical process of transformation or creation, often associated with ancient practices of turning base materials into gold.
- **Prowess**: Exceptional skill or ability, especially in a particular field or activity.
- **Feats**: Achievements or accomplishments, especially those requiring great skill or strength.

The Fish That Uses Electricity to See in the Dark

In the abyssal depths of the ocean, where light fails to penetrate, some species have evolved extraordinary abilities to navigate and hunt. The electric eel (Electrophorus electricus) is one such creature, using electrical fields not only for hunting but also for echolocation in the pitch-black waters. Unlike most fish, the electric eel generates powerful electric charges —up to 600 volts—by passing them through specialized cells known as electrocytes. These shocks are used to stun prey and deter predators, but they also serve a more fascinating function: the fish uses the electric pulses to "see" in the dark. By emitting low-frequency electrical signals, the eel creates a sort of sonar system, allowing it to map out its environment and detect objects, even in the absence of visible light. This ability to navigate through a world without sight is a prime example of nature's ingenuity. The electric eel's use of electricity as a tool for survival opens up an entirely new perspective on how creatures adapt to extreme environments. It also challenges our conventional understanding of sensory perception, highlighting the potential for other species to employ senses and techniques entirely different from our own.

Key Vocabulary:
- **Abyssal**: Referring to the deepest part of the ocean, often characterized by complete darkness and extreme pressure.
- **Electrocytes**: Special cells in certain animals that generate electrical charges, used for various functions such as navigation, hunting, or defense.
- **Echolocation**: The process of using reflected sound waves to detect objects and navigate through an environment, typically used by bats and dolphins.
- **Sonar**: A method of using sound waves to detect objects and measure distances, particularly underwater.
- **Ingenious**: Clever, original, and inventive, often in ways

that are surprising or unique.

How Bees Recognize Human Faces

Bees, though diminutive in stature, exhibit a level of cognitive sophistication that continues to baffle scientists. One of the most intriguing qualities they possess is the capacity to recognize and remember human faces, a trait once thought to be exclusive to higher mammals. This remarkable skill stems from their complex visual processing systems, which allow them to distinguish between different human faces in a manner akin to the way humans recognize each other. Unlike most insects that rely primarily on scent for identification, bees employ their keen vision to process facial features. The process involves a form of facial recognition that mirrors the human brain's method of identifying faces, where key features such as the eyes, nose, and mouth are integrated into a cohesive image. In studies, bees have been shown to learn and recall images of human faces, associating them with rewards such as sugar. This capacity for face recognition is not merely a curiosity; it plays a crucial role in their survival. It allows them to navigate their environments more effectively, discerning between various human faces that may represent danger or opportunity. In a world dominated by advanced technology, the humble bee reminds us of nature's quiet intelligence and the complexity of even the smallest creatures.

Key Vocabulary:
- **Diminutive**: Extremely small or tiny in size.
- **Cognitive**: Related to mental processes such as thinking, memory, and perception.
- **Visual Processing:** The method by which the brain interprets visual stimuli to form a coherent image.
- **Cohesive**: Forming a unified or connected whole.
- **Discerning**: Having or showing good judgment or insight, especially in perceiving differences.

The Plant That Traps and Digests Small Animals

In the world of carnivorous plants, few exhibit the cunning sophistication of the Nepenthes, a genus renowned for its ability to trap and digest small animals. This plant, often referred to as the "pitcher plant," is equipped with a uniquely structured leaf that forms a deep, tubular cavity filled with digestive enzymes. The plant lures its prey, typically insects, with nectar secretions on the rim of its "pitcher." The nectar's sweet aroma is irresistible to the unsuspecting creatures, leading them to the slippery edge of the pitcher. Once the prey enters the plant's funnel-shaped structure, it is unable to escape due to the plant's waxy, slick surface. The victim then falls into the liquid at the bottom of the pitcher, where it is swiftly consumed. The digestive process is both enzymatic and microbial, with bacteria playing a significant role in breaking down the prey into its essential nutrients. This carnivorous behavior is not a mere survival tactic but an adaptation to nutrient-poor environments. In areas where the soil lacks essential minerals, the Nepenthes supplements its diet with animal matter, showcasing the adaptability and ingenuity of nature's designs.

Key Vocabulary:
- **Cunning**: Skillful in achieving one's goals, often through cleverness or deceit.
- **Sophistication**: The quality of being intricate or advanced in design or complexity.
- **Tubular**: Shaped like a tube; hollow and cylindrical.
- **Irresistible**: Too attractive or appealing to be denied or avoided.
- **Enzymatic**: Pertaining to or involving enzymes, which catalyze biochemical reactions.

The Secret of the Deepest-Living Fish Ever Found

Deep within the abyssal zones of the ocean, where light is a distant memory and pressure mounts to crushing extremes, a remarkable fish species has adapted to thrive. The Mariana snailfish (Pseudoliparis swirei) holds the distinction of being the deepest-living fish ever discovered, residing at depths of over 8,000 meters in the Mariana Trench, the deepest part of the Earth's oceans. This species has evolved an array of extraordinary adaptations to survive in such an inhospitable environment. The snail fish's body is semi-translucent, an adaptation that helps it withstand the profound darkness of the deep sea. Its skin, lacking scales, allows it to move more fluidly in the dense, high-pressure water. Moreover, the fish's metabolic rate is incredibly low, enabling it to survive with minimal energy consumption. Scientists have only recently begun to understand the remarkable resilience of the Mariana snailfish, as it defies the conventional limitations of life on Earth. It represents the cutting edge of evolutionary adaptation, demonstrating the tenacity of life in the most extreme conditions. The discovery of this fish not only pushes the boundaries of our understanding of marine biology but also reminds us of the uncharted wonders still lurking in the deepest corners of our planet.

Key Vocabulary:
- **Abyssal**: Referring to the deepest parts of the ocean, characterized by extreme conditions such as darkness and pressure.
- **Semi-translucent**: Partially transparent, allowing some light to pass through.
- **Inhospitable**: Harsh and unfriendly to life or growth, often referring to extreme environments.
- **Metabolic Rate**: The rate at which an organism's body processes energy, typically in terms of consumption and expenditure.
- **Resilience**: The ability to recover from or adjust to adverse conditions.

Why Crows Hold Funerals for Their Dead

Crows, with their remarkable intelligence and complex social structures, engage in behaviors that are often regarded as eerie or mysterious. One of the most fascinating aspects of their behavior is their practice of holding "funerals" for their dead. When a crow dies, its fellow crows may gather around the body in a solemn display, often vocalizing and circling overhead. This behavior is not merely an instinctual reaction to death but rather a learned social ritual. Researchers believe that crows hold these funerals as a means of processing the loss of a group member and communicating the presence of potential threats. The gathering also serves as a way to reinforce social bonds within the group and allow for collective mourning. In some cases, the crows will even carry the body of their deceased companion to a secluded location, further suggesting a form of respect or reverence. What makes these funerals particularly intriguing is that they may also serve a practical purpose. The presence of numerous crows can send a warning to potential predators, signaling that the area is being watched and protected. This behavior not only showcases the intelligence of crows but also the depth of their social interactions, emphasizing the complexity of their emotional and cognitive lives.

Key Vocabulary:
- **Solemn**: Serious, earnest, and marked by a sense of reverence or respect.
- **Vocalizing**: The act of producing sounds or calls, typically used for communication.
- **Ritual**: A set of actions or behaviors performed according to a prescribed order, often with symbolic meaning.
- **Reverence**: Deep respect or awe, often associated with ceremonies or rituals.
- **Cognitive**: Pertaining to the mental processes involved in perception, memory, and reasoning.

The Incredible Migration of the Monarch Butterfly

The migration of the monarch butterfly is one of nature's most awe-inspiring phenomena, a journey that spans thousands of miles and defies the limits of what we once thought possible for such small creatures. Every year, millions of monarchs embark on a perilous trek from North America to the remote forests of central Mexico, where they will spend the winter. This migration, which can exceed 3,000 miles, is driven by an intricate set of environmental cues, including temperature and daylight length. What makes the journey particularly extraordinary is that the butterflies' migratory path is not learned by individual monarchs, but rather passed down through generations. A single butterfly may never complete the journey, but its descendants will continue the trek, guided by an innate compass that leads them to the same forest year after year. Along the way, the monarchs face numerous dangers, including extreme weather, predators, and a lack of food sources. Despite these challenges, they manage to navigate with remarkable precision, arriving at their destination with astonishing accuracy. The incredible migration of the monarch butterfly is a demonstration of the resilience and determination of these creatures, as well as the intricate, interconnected systems of nature that enable such feats.

Key Vocabulary:
- **Awe-inspiring:** Causing a sense of wonder or admiration due to grandeur, beauty, or complexity.
- **Perilous**: Involving danger or risk; hazardous.
- **Intricate**: Very detailed and complex, with many interconnected parts.
- **Cues**: Signals or prompts that help guide behavior or actions.
- **Resilience:** The ability to recover from setbacks or endure challenges.

How Dolphins Use Bubbles to Catch Fish

Dolphins, often heralded as among the most intelligent creatures of the ocean, display an extraordinary level of ingenuity in their hunting techniques. One of their most fascinating strategies involves the use of bubbles to capture prey. Known as "bubble netting," this method sees dolphins create a dense cloud of bubbles by expelling air from their blowholes. These bubbles serve multiple purposes: they disorient fish, confuse their prey, and help corral it into tight, concentrated groups. The dolphins then swim around the cloud in coordinated fashion, trapping the fish in an ever-decreasing circle. By creating this natural barrier, they force their prey toward the surface, making it easier to capture. This technique is not only a testament to the dolphins' cognitive abilities but also to their capacity for cooperation. Dolphins often engage in this strategy in groups, communicating with each other using complex vocalizations and body movements to ensure its success. This level of social hunting, coupled with their use of environmental tools like bubbles, showcases dolphins as not just predators, but as master strategists in the wild. The use of bubbles illustrates the complexity of their underwater life, highlighting a remarkable marriage of intelligence, communication, and problem-solving that only the most evolved of animals could execute.

Key Vocabulary:
- **Heralded**: Praised or acclaimed, often in a formal or public manner.
- **Ingenuity**: The quality of being clever, inventive, or resourceful.
- **Corral**: To gather or move into a confined space.
- **Disorient**: To confuse or make uncertain, particularly in relation to direction.
- **Cognitive**: Pertaining to mental processes like perception, memory, and reasoning.

The Lizard That Shoots Blood from Its Eyes

In the arid deserts of North America, there exists a lizard whose defense mechanism is as dramatic as it is peculiar. The horned lizard, a small reptile known for its spiny appearance and docile nature, has developed an extraordinary means of protection: it shoots blood from its eyes. When threatened by predators, this lizard has the uncanny ability to rupture the blood vessels in its ocular region, causing a stream of blood to shoot forth with remarkable force. This peculiar tactic serves multiple purposes: it confuses and repels would-be attackers, while also startling them with the blood's pungent scent. The blood is not only a visual deterrent but also a potential irritant to the predator's senses, increasing the lizard's chances of escape. Though the act itself seems grotesque, it is a highly effective strategy in the harsh environments the lizard inhabits. It is an example of the lengths to which animals will go to defend themselves and ensure their survival, illustrating nature's penchant for unusual and often grotesque forms of defense. The bloodshot spectacle serves as a reminder of the incredible adaptability and resourcefulness of even the most unassuming creatures.

Key Vocabulary:
- **Arid**: Dry, often used to describe hot, barren regions with little moisture.
- **Docile**: Calm, submissive, and easily managed or taught.
- **Ocular**: Pertaining to the eyes or vision.
- **Pungent**: Having a strong, often unpleasant odor or taste.
- **Grotesque**: Odd or unnatural in shape, appearance, or character, often in a way that is disturbing.

Why Some Frogs Can Freeze Themselves and Survive

The ability of some frogs to survive freezing temperatures is one of nature's most astonishing feats of biological adaptation. Known as "cryopreservation," certain species of frogs, like the wood frog (Rana sylvatica), are capable of surviving the freezing of their bodily fluids. As winter approaches, these frogs enter a state of suspended animation. Their bodies begin to freeze from the outside in, with ice forming in their tissues. Remarkably, the frogs do not die from the ice; instead, their vital organs, such as the heart and brain, remain unfrozen, allowing them to survive. During this time, the frogs rely on the glucose stored in their liver to protect their cells from ice damage. When temperatures rise, the frogs thaw and resume normal activity, seemingly none the worse for wear. This ability to withstand freezing is an extraordinary evolutionary trait, enabling these frogs to thrive in regions where other amphibians would perish. It is an example of nature's ability to exploit seemingly inhospitable environments and turn them into opportunities for survival, showcasing the remarkable resilience and adaptability of life.

Key Vocabulary:
- **Cryopreservation**: The preservation of cells, tissues, or organisms by freezing them.
- **Suspended Animation**: A state in which biological processes are slowed down or temporarily halted.
- **Glucose**: A simple sugar that serves as a primary energy source for organisms.
- **Amphibians**: A class of animals that includes frogs, toads, salamanders, and newts, typically living both in water and on land.
- **Resilience**: The ability to recover from or adapt to difficult conditions.

The Bird That Can Sleep While Flying

Among the countless marvels of the animal kingdom, one of the most perplexing is the ability of certain bird species to sleep while flying. This remarkable phenomenon has been observed in migratory birds, such as the common swift (Apus apus), which embarks on journeys of thousands of miles, sometimes flying for months at a time. The bird achieves this feat through a process known as unihemispheric slow-wave sleep (USWS), where one hemisphere of the brain enters a restful state while the other remains active. This allows the bird to continue navigating and flying while resting half of its brain at a time. Remarkably, these birds can maintain flight for extended periods without appearing to tire, navigating vast distances across oceans and continents. The birds' ability to sleep while flying represents a perfect fusion of survival and efficiency, allowing them to continue their migration without interruption. This adaptation is not only a triumph of evolutionary ingenuity but also shows the complexity of animal behavior, where sleep is no longer a passive process but an active part of survival and endurance.

Key Vocabulary:
- **Perplexing**: Confusing or puzzling, causing uncertainty.
- **Unihemispheric**: Pertaining to one hemisphere of the brain.
- **Slow-Wave Sleep**: A phase of deep sleep characterized by slow brain waves, during which the body rests and rejuvenates.
- **Feat**: A remarkable or daring achievement, often requiring skill or strength.
- **Fusion**: The process or result of joining two or more things together to form a single entity.

How Fireflies Communicate with Their Light Shows

Fireflies, often associated with warm summer nights, possess an enchanting ability to produce light, a characteristic known as bioluminescence. However, this ability is not just for show; it serves a crucial role in communication. The light produced by fireflies is a complex system of signaling, used primarily for mating purposes. Each species of firefly has a unique pattern of flashes, which allows them to identify and attract mates of the same species. Male fireflies typically emit a series of rhythmic flashes from their abdomens, while females respond with a specific flash pattern of their own. This intricate dance of light serves not only to attract potential mates but also to convey information about the firefly's location, species, and readiness to mate. In some species, the light serves as a warning to predators, signaling that the firefly is toxic or unpalatable. The bioluminescent signals of fireflies are a striking example of nature's ability to create sophisticated systems of communication that extend beyond sound, utilizing light as a medium to convey a variety of messages. The dazzling display of fireflies is not only a beautiful spectacle but also shows the evolutionary significance of light as a communicative tool.

Key Vocabulary:
- **Enchanting**: Delightfully charming or captivating.
- **Bioluminescence**: The production and emission of light by living organisms, often through chemical reactions.
- **Rhythmic**: Characterized by a regular pattern or movement, often in a musical or repetitive way.
- **Intricate**: Detailed and complex, often requiring careful attention or skill.
- **Dazzling**: Extremely bright, impressive, or stunning in appearance.

The Spider That Builds Fake Spiders to Scare Predators

In the intricate world of arachnids, the Deinopis spider stands out not only for its unique appearance but also for its ingenious defense strategy. Known as the "net-casting" spider, this species is famous for building decoy spiders to protect itself from predators. Rather than relying on a traditional web for defense, the Deinopis spider constructs a fake spider, often made of silk and other natural materials, to resemble its own body. These decoys are positioned strategically, typically near the real spider's resting place. When predators approach, they are confronted with what appears to be a larger, more threatening spider, causing them to flee in fear. This tactic relies on the predator's inability to distinguish the decoy from the actual spider, showcasing the spider's cunning ability to use psychological warfare in the wild. The spider's ability to create a convincing illusion highlights nature's penchant for deception as a survival mechanism. In an environment where survival often depends on outsmarting predators, the Deinopis spider's ability to create fake spiders is a remarkable display of evolutionary ingenuity, using intelligence and deception as tools of defense.

Key Vocabulary:
- **Arachnids**: A class of joint-legged invertebrates, including spiders, scorpions, and mites.
- **Ingenious**: Clever, original, and inventive, especially in solving problems.
- **Decoy**: An imitation of a real object or creature used to attract or deceive.
- **Cunning**: Skillful in achieving one's goals through deceit or trickery.
- **Illusion**: A deceptive appearance or impression, often intentionally misleading.

The Secret Language of Prairie Dogs

Prairie dogs, small burrowing rodents that inhabit the grasslands of North America, are known for their complex social structures. However, it is their communication system that truly sets them apart from other animals. Prairie dogs have been shown to possess a sophisticated language, capable of conveying detailed information about their environment, including the presence of predators. This language consists of a series of high-pitched vocalizations, each with a specific meaning. Researchers have discovered that these vocalizations can convey details such as the type of predator, its size, and even the direction from which it is approaching. What is truly remarkable, however, is the ability of prairie dogs to create new calls based on the context of a particular threat, demonstrating a level of linguistic flexibility previously thought to be unique to humans. This ability to adapt their communication on the fly reveals a cognitive complexity that is seldom seen in other non-human animals. The prairie dog's vocal prowess offers a fascinating glimpse into the evolution of language, showcasing the possibility of linguistic diversity in the animal kingdom, and emphasizing the importance of communication for survival in their perilous environment.

Key Vocabulary:
- **Burrowing**: The act of digging or creating tunnels, typically used by animals like rodents.
- **Sophisticated**: Highly developed or intricate in design or operation.
- **Vocalizations**: Sounds produced by animals, particularly for communication.
- **Linguistic**: Relating to language or the structure of language.
- **Prowess**: Exceptional skill or ability, often in a particular activity or field.

How Elephants Mourn Their Dead

Elephants are known for their remarkable intelligence and deep social bonds, but perhaps one of the most moving aspects of their behavior is their ability to mourn their dead. When an elephant dies, the surviving members of the herd often display behaviors that suggest a profound sense of loss. Elephants will approach the body, gently touching the deceased with their trunks and even caressing the bones. They may remain by the body for hours or even days, standing in quiet reverence. In some cases, elephants have been observed to cover the body with leaves and dirt, as if to protect the deceased from the harsh elements. This mourning behavior is not limited to immediate family members; elephants have been known to grieve for distant relatives or even other elephant herds with whom they have interacted. This displays a level of empathy and emotional connection that goes beyond mere survival instincts. The mourning rituals of elephants highlights the emotional depth of these magnificent creatures, revealing that their bonds extend beyond the physical realm and into the realm of the heart.

Key Vocabulary:
- **Remarkable**: Worthy of attention due to being extraordinary or unusual.
- **Reverence**: Deep respect or awe, often with a sense of veneration.
- **Caressing**: Gently stroking or touching with affection.
- **Empathy**: The ability to understand and share the feelings of another.
- **Rituals**: Established or prescribed procedures, often with a symbolic meaning.

The Strange Diet of the Hoatzin, the Stinkbird

The hoatzin, a bird native to the Amazon rainforest, has a diet that is as strange as its appearance. Often called the "stinkbird" due to its pungent odor, the hoatzin is a herbivore with a very unique digestive system. Unlike most birds, which have relatively simple digestive tracts, the hoatzin has a large, multi-chambered stomach that allows it to ferment the leaves it consumes, much like a cow. This fermentation process produces gases that give the bird its distinctive smell, a scent that is often likened to rotten vegetation. The hoatzin's diet mainly consists of leaves, flowers, and fruits, but its unusual digestive process makes it an inefficient feeder. The bird must spend a significant amount of time eating to meet its nutritional needs, and it is often seen moving slowly through the dense foliage of the rainforest. Despite its inefficiency, the hoatzin thrives in its environment, demonstrating how even the most unusual adaptations can lead to survival in specialized ecological niches. Its bizarre digestive system and odor remind us of the extraordinary ways in which life adapts to its surroundings.

Key Vocabulary:
- **Pungent**: Having a strong, sharp smell or taste, often unpleasant.
- **Herbivore**: An animal that primarily eats plants.
- **Ferment**: The process of breaking down substances, often producing gas or heat, through chemical reactions.
- **Inefficient**: Not achieving maximum productivity with the least amount of effort or resources.
- **Specialized**: Adapted to a specific function, environment, or purpose.

The Star-Nosed Mole's Super-Speedy Sense of Touch

The star-nosed mole is an extraordinary creature that has captivated scientists with its remarkable sense of touch. Found primarily in North America, this mole is easily recognizable by its distinctive, star-shaped appendage at the tip of its snout, which is covered in over 25,000 sensory receptors. This appendage, often described as resembling a star, allows the mole to detect and process tactile information at an astounding speed. The star-nosed mole can identify and capture prey in a fraction of a second, making it one of the fastest creatures on earth when it comes to tactile perception. Incredibly, it can distinguish between different types of food, such as worms, insects, and small crustaceans, based purely on their texture. This ability to process tactile stimuli so rapidly is crucial for the mole, as it lives in dark, underground burrows where sight is virtually useless. Instead, the mole relies entirely on its hyper-sensitive sense of touch to navigate its subterranean world. The star-nosed mole's extreme tactile sensitivity is a prime example of nature's ability to fine-tune an animal's senses to meet the demands of its environment.

Key Vocabulary:
- **Captivated**: Attracted and fascinated by something.

- **Tactile**: Relating to the sense of touch.
- **Appendage**: A part of an organism that is attached to a larger structure.
- **Subterranean**: Existing or occurring beneath the earth's surface.
- **Hyper-sensitive**: Excessively or unusually sensitive, especially to stimuli.

The Deep-Sea Shrimp That Creates Plasma with Its Claws

In the shadowy depths of the ocean, where light is a rare luxury, the snapping shrimp has evolved into a truly extraordinary weapon. With its powerful claws, the shrimp is capable of creating plasma, a phenomenon typically associated with stars and high-energy environments. When the shrimp snaps its claw shut, it produces a bubble of water that implodes with such force that it generates an intense burst of heat and light, creating a small plasma ball for a brief moment. This flash of light, which can reach temperatures hotter than the surface of the sun, is not just for show. The plasma bubble can stun or even kill small prey, giving the shrimp an advantage in capturing food. The process, known as cavitation, is a result of the rapid movement of water molecules caused by the force of the claw snap. This weaponized feature allows the shrimp to hunt and defend itself in the dark, pressure-filled depths of the ocean, where visibility is virtually nonexistent. The snapping shrimp's ability to create plasma is a stunning example of how evolution can harness physical forces to turn ordinary biological tools into extraordinary instruments of survival.

Key Vocabulary:
- **Plasma**: A state of matter similar to gas but consisting of charged particles, including electrons and ions.
- **Cavitation**: The formation of bubbles in a liquid caused by the rapid movement of a solid through it.
- **Implodes**: To collapse inward violently.

- **Phenomenon**: A remarkable event or occurrence, often unexplained.
- **Weaponized**: Modified or designed to be used as a weapon.

How Certain Plants Can 'Hear' Caterpillars Eating Them

In a remarkable demonstration of the interconnectedness of the natural world, some plants have evolved the ability to "hear" when they are under attack, specifically when caterpillars begin munching on their leaves. These plants, including species like Arabidopsis thaliana, have specialized sensors that can detect the vibrations created by the chewing of caterpillars. When the plant senses these vibrations, it activates a defense mechanism. It begins producing chemical compounds that make its leaves less palatable to herbivores, often attracting predators like parasitic wasps that will lay their eggs on the caterpillars. This highly sophisticated form of plant defense is made possible by the plant's ability to perceive sound waves in the environment, which are then interpreted as signals of danger. These plants have evolved to "listen" to the sounds around them, triggering a response that helps them survive and deter further damage. While plants don't have ears in the traditional sense, their ability to detect vibrations underscores the diverse and unexpected ways in which living organisms can interact with their environment. This discovery challenges our assumptions about plant intelligence and opens up new possibilities for the study of plant behavior.

Key Vocabulary:
- **Interconnectedness**: The state of being connected with each other in a way that affects the entire system.
- **Herbivores**: Animals that primarily feed on plants.
- **Parasitic**: Relating to organisms that live off other living beings, often harming them in the process.
- **Palatable**: Pleasing or acceptable to the taste or mind.

- **Vibrations**: Rapid motions of particles or molecules within a medium, often felt as a form of sound or movement.

Why Some Birds Steal Feathers from Their Neighbors

In the intricate world of bird behavior, some species engage in a rather unusual practice: stealing feathers from their neighbors. This behavior is not purely opportunistic, however; it serves a vital function in their survival and reproductive success. For instance, the common raven is known to pilfer feathers from other birds, using them to line its own nest. By doing so, the raven ensures its nest is not only warmer but also more comfortable for its offspring. In some cases, these stolen feathers even carry the scent of the original owner, providing a form of camouflage for the raven's nest, making it less likely to be detected by predators. This feather theft is particularly common among birds that build nests in exposed areas, where the risk of predation is high. The act of feather stealing shows the lengths to which birds will go to protect their young and ensure their own survival. While some might view this behavior as merely opportunistic, it is in fact a strategic tactic that has been honed by evolution to maximize the chances of survival in a perilous world.

Key Vocabulary:
- **Pilfer**: To steal in small quantities, often in a subtle or sneaky manner.
- **Camouflage**: The act of concealing or disguising something to blend in with its surroundings.
- **Exposed**: Unprotected or vulnerable, often referring to a location or position.
- **Predation**: The act of one organism hunting and killing another for food.
- **Opportunistic**: Taking advantage of situations for personal gain, often with little regard for long-term consequences.

The Snake That Can Glide Through the Air

Imagine a snake that has evolved the ability to glide through the air, its smooth, scaly body slicing through the wind as it travels from tree to tree. The Chrysopelea, or flying snake, is one such marvel of nature. This remarkable reptile, found in Southeast Asia, has developed a specialized form of locomotion that allows it to move through the air with remarkable agility. By flattening its body into a wing-like shape and undulating through the air, the flying snake can glide for over 100 meters at a time, covering distances that would be impossible for most land-bound creatures. The snake's unique aerial abilities are made possible by its rib structure, which allows it to expand its body and create a flat surface that generates lift. In addition to using gliding to move between trees in search of food or mates, the flying snake uses this ability to escape predators, adding an extra layer of protection to its survival strategy. The flying snake's ability to defy gravity is a stunning example of nature's ingenuity, as it turns a seemingly impossible feat into a remarkable adaptation for survival.

Key Vocabulary:
- **Locomotion**: The ability or act of moving from one place to another.
- **Agility**: The ability to move quickly and easily, with flexibility and precision.
- **Undulating**: Moving with a smooth, wavelike motion.
- **Rib structure**: The arrangement and form of the ribs in an animal's body.
- **Lift**: The force that opposes gravity, allowing an object to rise or stay aloft.

How Sloths Can Hold Their Breath Longer Than Dolphins

Sloths, the languid creatures of the rainforest, are often

admired for their unhurried lifestyle and slow movements. Yet, few are aware of the astonishing physiological adaptation that allows these creatures to hold their breath for longer than even dolphins. While dolphins can hold their breath for an impressive amount of time, sloths are capable of staying underwater for up to 40 minutes, a feat that most land mammals could never achieve. This incredible ability is attributed to the sloth's low metabolic rate, which reduces the amount of oxygen it requires and allows it to survive on minimal air. Furthermore, sloths have a special adaptation in their circulatory system that allows their heart rate to slow significantly while submerged, conserving precious oxygen. When underwater, sloths will remain motionless, allowing their body to use oxygen more efficiently. This remarkable adaptation not only helps sloths avoid predators but also allows them to forage for food in aquatic environments. By holding their breath for extended periods, sloths have turned what is typically a limitation for other animals into an advantage, showcasing the incredible ways in which evolution shapes survival strategies.

Key Vocabulary:
- **Physiological**: Relating to the functions and processes of living organisms.
- **Metabolic rate**: The rate at which an organism converts food into energy.
- **Circulatory system**: The system of blood vessels and the heart that circulates blood throughout the body.
- **Submerged**: Completely covered or immersed in water.
- **Forage**: To search for and gather food, often in the wild.

The Clever Defense Mechanism of the Hairy Frog

The hairy frog, a seemingly unassuming amphibian, harbors one of nature's most fascinating defense mechanisms. Found in Central Africa, this frog possesses a remarkable ability to protect itself when threatened. At the slightest sign of danger, the hairy frog performs a dramatic and rather grisly act—its bones literally break through its skin, extending sharp, needle-like claws that act as both a deterrent and a weapon. These claws are typically concealed beneath the skin, but when the frog feels threatened, the claws emerge, resembling a set of talons. This extraordinary adaptation not only helps the frog fend off potential predators but also serves as a form of self-defense, allowing it to deter predators that might otherwise have considered it an easy meal. The claws are powerful and capable of inflicting damage, providing the frog with a temporary advantage. This remarkable defense mechanism is an excellent example of nature's ingenuity, as the hairy frog transforms its own physiology into a weapon to ensure its survival. It is a living testament to the unexpected ways in which evolution can shape the survival strategies of creatures in perilous environments.

Key Vocabulary:
- **Amphibian**: A cold-blooded vertebrate animal, such as a frog, that can live both on land and in water.
- **Grisly**: Horrifying or repellent, often in a gruesome or violent manner.
- **Deterrent**: Something that discourages or prevents an action.
- **Physiology**: The branch of biology dealing with the functions of living organisms and their parts.
- **Talons**: The sharp, curved claws of a bird of prey or other carnivorous animals.

How Pufferfish Create Underwater Crop Circles

In the depths of the ocean, one of the most enigmatic and artistically inclined creatures is the Japanese pufferfish. This fish, though not known for its size or speed, has a remarkable skill that has puzzled marine biologists for years: it creates elaborate, circular patterns in the sand that resemble crop circles. These intricate designs are not just random but are believed to serve an important purpose—mating rituals. The male pufferfish meticulously constructs these geometric masterpieces by flapping his fins to stir up sand, creating ridges and depressions in a precise circular formation. The pattern can span up to 2.4 meters in diameter, and the male then uses the structure to attract a mate. The circle's purpose is to showcase the male's strength and ability to provide a safe environment for the female. The construction of these underwater crop circles is not just a fascinating example of animal behavior but shows the sophisticated ways in which animals use their surroundings for courtship. Through a seemingly simple act, the pufferfish has turned a marine environment into a canvas for one of nature's most unique forms of artistic expression.

Key Vocabulary:
- **Enigmatic:** Mysterious, puzzling, or difficult to understand.
- **Intricate:** Complex, with many small details or components.
- **Geometric:** Relating to shapes and mathematical properties, often used to describe precise, angular patterns.
- **Courtship:** The behaviors and activities that animals engage in to attract a mate.
- **Canvas:** A surface for painting or artistic creation, often used metaphorically to describe a space for creativity.

The Beetle That Shoots Boiling Chemicals at Its Enemies

In the vast and often hostile world of insects, few creatures are as remarkable as the bombardier beetle, known for its explosive and highly effective defense mechanism. When threatened, the bombardier beetle can shoot a spray of boiling hot, toxic chemicals at its assailant, disorienting or even killing it. This remarkable feat is accomplished through a unique chemical reaction that occurs within the beetle's abdomen. The beetle stores two separate chemicals—hydrogen peroxide and hydroquinone—in specialized chambers within its body. When in danger, the beetle releases these chemicals into a mixing chamber, where they combine to create an exothermic reaction, producing a boiling, toxic spray. The beetle can aim this spray with incredible precision, targeting its attacker with a degree of accuracy that is truly astounding. The boiling liquid reaches temperatures of over 100°C, making it a lethal weapon against predators. This highly specialized defense mechanism ensures that the bombardier beetle can defend itself against creatures much larger than itself, proving once again how nature can produce incredibly effective, if not somewhat terrifying, survival strategies.

Key Vocabulary:
- **Exothermic**: Describing a chemical reaction that releases heat.
- **Assailant**: A person or animal who attacks another.
- **Hydroquinone**: An organic compound used in chemical reactions, often found in plant and animal defenses.
- **Precision**: The quality of being exact and accurate.
- **Lethal**: Capable of causing death or severe harm.

Why Some Penguins Propose with Pebbles

Penguins, those charming and often comical seabirds, have a courtship ritual that involves one of the most endearing and surprising behaviors in the animal kingdom: proposing with pebbles. In species like the Adélie penguin, the male bird seeks out the perfect pebble—a smooth, shiny stone that will be presented to a female as a gesture of affection and commitment. The male will often go to great lengths, sometimes traveling long distances, to find the most ideal pebble. Once the pebble is found, the male approaches the female and offers it, hoping she will accept it and place it in her nest. This exchange of pebbles is not just a symbol of affection but also a practical gesture. The male's pebble will be used to help construct a more secure and comfortable nest for the female to lay her eggs. In this way, the pebble serves both as a romantic gesture and as an investment in the future of the couple's offspring. The courtship ritual of penguins, with its emphasis on providing for the future, highlights the depth of their social structures and the ingenuity of their reproductive strategies.

Key Vocabulary:
- **Courtship**: The behaviors and actions performed by animals to attract a mate.
- **Endearing**: Inspiring affection or warmth; charming.
- **Ideal**: Perfectly suitable or fitting.
- **Symbol**: An object, word, or gesture that represents something larger or abstract.
- **Secure**: Free from danger, harm, or threat.

The Tarantula That Keeps a Pet Frog

In the wild, where survival often requires fierce competition and territorial battles, the tarantula—a large and often feared spider—has developed an unusual and symbiotic relationship with a much smaller creature: the frog. Certain species of tarantulas, such as the Chaco golden knee tarantula, have been observed to harbor frogs in their burrows, providing a safe and warm environment for their amphibious companions. The tarantula and the frog share an unexpected form of mutual benefit. The frog, in return for shelter, helps protect the tarantula's burrow by eating smaller insects that might pose a threat to the spider or damage its home. In some cases, the frog will even act as a lookout, keeping an eye out for predators while the tarantula is hunting. The tarantula, for its part, ensures that the frog is safe from larger predators that may lurk in the environment. This extraordinary arrangement is a fine example of symbiosis, where two vastly different species work together for mutual benefit. The relationship between the tarantula and the frog challenges our preconceived notions of predator-prey dynamics and demonstrates the complexities of life in the wild.

Key Vocabulary:
- **Symbiotic**: Describing a relationship between two organisms in which both benefit from the interaction.
- **Mutual**: Shared or reciprocated by two or more parties.
- **Amphibious**: Able to live both on land and in water.
- **Territorial**: Related to defending or controlling an area, especially in animals.
- **Preconceived**: Formed before having full knowledge or understanding of something.

The Salamander That Never Grows Up

In the realm of the natural world, few creatures possess the ability to remain in a perpetual state of youth like the axolotl, a remarkable salamander that defies the typical boundaries of growth and development. Unlike most animals that undergo a process known as metamorphosis, where they transition from one life stage to another, the axolotl remains in its larval form throughout its entire life. This phenomenon, known as neoteny, means that the axolotl retains its juvenile characteristics, including its external gills, throughout its lifespan. These salamanders, native to the lakes of Mexico, exhibit an extraordinary ability to regenerate lost body parts, including limbs, spinal cord, and even parts of their heart and brain. Despite never transitioning into the adult form, the axolotl continues to reproduce, thus completing its life cycle in an eternal state of adolescence. This unique trait has fascinated biologists for years, as it opens the door to understanding how genetic factors govern the process of aging and regeneration. The axolotl, therefore, is not just an animal of eternal youth but a living testament to the mysterious and often baffling processes that govern life itself.

Key Vocabulary:
- **Perpetual**: Continuing indefinitely; never-ending.
- **Metamorphosis**: The process of transformation from one stage of life to another, especially in insects and amphibians.
- **Neoteny**: The retention of juvenile features in the adult form of an organism.
- **Regenerate**: To regrow or replace lost or damaged tissue or organs.
- **Testament**: A statement or evidence of something; a witness to a fact.

The Shrimp That Punches with the Speed of a Bullet

In the depths of the ocean, one of the most astonishing and forceful creatures is the mantis shrimp. With its vibrant exoskeleton and powerful claws, this crustacean possesses one of the fastest and most lethal strikes in the animal kingdom. The mantis shrimp's punch is so rapid that it is often compared to the speed of a bullet, reaching speeds of over 80 kilometers per hour. The punch is delivered with such force that it generates shockwaves, capable of stunning or killing prey with a single strike. In addition to its immense speed, the impact of the mantis shrimp's punch can create cavitation bubbles—tiny, explosive bubbles that release energy and heat. These bubbles can reach temperatures comparable to the surface of the sun, further intensifying the damage inflicted on its prey. The mantis shrimp uses this incredible weapon to capture prey and defend itself against predators. Its punch is so powerful that it can even break glass aquarium walls. The mantis shrimp's extraordinary strike showcases the awe-inspiring power of nature's adaptations for survival and predation.

Key Vocabulary:
- **Crustacean**: A member of the class of animals that includes crabs, lobsters, and shrimp, characterized by a

hard exoskeleton.
- **Cavitation**: The formation of vapor-filled cavities in a liquid due to rapid changes in pressure.
- **Shockwave**: A wave of energy traveling through a medium, often caused by an explosion or sudden force.
- **Lethal**: Capable of causing death or significant harm.
- **Predation**: The act of preying on or hunting other organisms for food.

Why Some Animals Have Glow-in-the-Dark Skeletons

While bioluminescence is often associated with glowing creatures in the deep ocean or nocturnal insects like fireflies, it may come as a surprise to learn that some animals have glow-in-the-dark skeletons. This phenomenon, known as biofluorescence, occurs when certain animals absorb light and re-emit it in a different wavelength, causing them to glow. Various species of fish, reptiles, and even mammals, such as the platypus, possess this remarkable ability. For some, it is a form of camouflage, helping them blend in with their environment and evade predators. For others, it may serve as a communication tool or even as a means of attracting mates. The glow is often produced by a special pigment in the animals' bones or tissues that reacts to ultraviolet (UV) light. These biofluorescent creatures are most commonly found in tropical environments, where UV light is abundant. The ability to produce light within their bodies adds another layer of intrigue to the already mysterious and fascinating world of bioluminescence and biofluorescence.

Key Vocabulary:
- **Bioluminescence**: The production and emission of light by living organisms.
- **Biofluorescence**: The ability of an organism to absorb light and re-emit it in a different wavelength.
- **Camouflage**: The use of color or patterns to blend in with one's surroundings, often as a form of protection.

- **Pigment**: A substance responsible for the color of living organisms or materials.
- **Intrigue**: Arousing curiosity or fascination.

The Bat That Drinks the Blood of Other Bats

The Vampire bat, a notorious creature that has captured the public's imagination, is known for its blood-sucking habits. However, an even more macabre twist to this nocturnal mammal's behavior has been discovered—some species of vampire bats have been observed drinking the blood of their fellow bats. While most vampire bats feed on the blood of larger animals such as livestock, these particular bats, known as intraspecific vampires, target their own kind. This behavior is not a mere act of predation but rather a form of social behavior. In some bat colonies, individuals will share blood by licking the wounds of others or by engaging in "blood-sharing," where one bat feeds off another to establish social bonds. This practice, while gruesome, is believed to help strengthen communal ties and ensure that no bat in the colony goes hungry. Despite the somewhat disturbing nature of their feeding habits, vampire bats play an important role in their ecosystem by controlling the populations of larger animals and helping maintain balance within their habitats. Their blood-sucking tendencies, therefore, are just another example of how nature's design is full of complexity and surprising behaviors.

Key Vocabulary:
- **Macabre**: Gruesome, horrifying, or disturbing in nature.
- **Intraspecific**: Occurring within a single species.
- **Predation**: The act of preying on other animals for food.
- **Social bonds**: The connections and relationships that form between individuals within a group.
- **Ecosystem**: A biological community of interacting organisms and their physical environment.

The Worm That Can Clone Itself Indefinitely

The planarian, a type of flatworm, has become an icon in the world of regeneration due to its astounding ability to clone itself indefinitely. These seemingly simple creatures have a remarkable capability: if a planarian is severed into pieces, each piece can regenerate into an entirely new organism. The secret behind this extraordinary power lies in their specialized stem cells known as neoblasts, which can transform into any type of cell needed to rebuild lost body parts. Even a fragment as small as a single cell can grow into a complete, functional worm, effectively creating a genetically identical clone. This process of self-cloning, called regeneration, is not only a demonstration of the worm's incredible biological capabilities but also a key to understanding cellular differentiation and tissue regeneration in other species, including humans. The regenerative prowess of the planarian has captivated scientists who are eager to unlock the mechanisms that allow this feat, with potential implications for medicine, particularly in fields like organ regeneration and wound healing. The planarian, therefore, represents not just a marvel of nature, but also a promising frontier in regenerative science.

Key Vocabulary:
- **Planarian**: A type of flatworm known for its regenerative abilities.
- **Neoblasts**: Specialized stem cells that can differentiate into any cell type in the body.
- **Regeneration**: The process of regrowing lost or damaged body parts or cells.
- **Cloning**: The production of genetically identical organisms or cells.
- **Cellular differentiation**: The process by which cells develop into different types to perform specific functions.

The Crab That Wears a Sponge as Camouflage

The Lybia crab, also known as the "sponge crab," engages in one of nature's most fascinating forms of camouflage. This peculiar crustacean has developed the extraordinary habit of covering itself with a living sponge, which it uses as both protection and concealment. By attaching the sponge to its back, the crab not only disguises itself from potential predators but also forms a symbiotic relationship with the sponge. The sponge benefits from the crab's mobility, allowing it to be transported to different environments where it can access more food and avoid harmful conditions. In turn, the crab gains a durable shield, blending seamlessly with the ocean floor, thereby evading the sharp eyes of predators like fish and birds. This mutually beneficial relationship highlights the ingenious ways in which species have evolved to ensure their survival. The sponge crab's use of natural materials for camouflage is a remarkable example of the adaptability and resourcefulness found in the animal kingdom.

Key Vocabulary:
- **Crustacean**: A group of animals that includes crabs, lobsters, and shrimp, typically having an exoskeleton.
- **Symbiotic**: A relationship between two organisms in which both benefit.
- **Camouflage**: The ability of an organism to blend in with its environment to avoid detection.
- **Concealment**: The action of hiding or keeping something out of sight.
- **Adaptability**: The ability of an organism to adjust to different conditions or environments.

The Tiny Tardigrade: The Toughest Animal on Earth

The tardigrade, also known as the water bear, is widely considered to be one of the toughest organisms on Earth. Despite its minuscule size—often no larger than a grain of sand—this microscopic creature is capable of surviving extreme conditions that would obliterate most other forms of life. Tardigrades have been found thriving in the most inhospitable environments, from the frozen tundras of the Arctic to the boiling hot springs of Japan. They are notorious for their ability to endure extreme dehydration, high radiation levels, and the vacuum of space. When faced with these harsh conditions, tardigrades enter a state called cryptobiosis, where they lose nearly all their water content and effectively shut down their metabolism. In this dormant state, they can survive for years, only to "reanimate" when exposed to water. This remarkable resilience has made tardigrades a subject of intense scientific study, as they hold clues about survival mechanisms that could one day benefit human space exploration or help scientists develop new ways to preserve biological materials.

Key Vocabulary:
- **Tardigrade**: A microscopic, water-dwelling organism known for its extreme resilience.
- **Cryptobiosis**: A state of suspended animation in which an organism survives extreme environmental conditions.
- **Resilience**: The ability to recover from or adapt to difficult conditions.
- **Metabolism**: The set of life-sustaining chemical reactions in organisms.
- **Reanimate**: To bring back to life or consciousness after a period of dormancy.

How Certain Fish Walk on Land

The mudskipper, a species of fish found in the muddy coastal regions of Africa and Asia, has astonished scientists with its unique ability to 'walk' on land. Unlike most fish that are confined to water, mudskippers have evolved powerful, muscular fins that allow them to prop themselves up and move across the muddy terrain. These fins, modified into appendages resembling legs, enable the fish to crawl, leap, and even climb low vegetation, making them highly adaptable to their environment. Mudskippers also possess specialized adaptations that help them breathe air while on land, including the ability to store oxygen in their gills and use their skin for respiration. These fish spend a significant amount of time out of water, hunting for food, escaping predators, and engaging in social behaviors. The ability of mudskippers to transition between land and water highlights the remarkable versatility of life in adapting to a variety of habitats and the gradual evolutionary steps that allow for such profound changes.

Key Vocabulary:
- **Mudskipper**: A species of fish capable of walking on land and living in muddy coastal areas.
- **Appendages**: Limbs or other protruding body parts used for movement or manipulation.
- **Respirate**: To breathe or take in oxygen.
- **Versatility**: The ability to adapt or be used for many different purposes or activities.
- **Evolutionary**: Relating to the gradual development of organisms over time through natural selection.

Why Some Parrots Laugh When They Play

Parrots are renowned for their vocal mimicry and intelligence, but a lesser-known aspect of their behavior is their tendency to laugh while playing. This playful vocalization is not merely a random sound; it is a form of social communication that mirrors the laughter found in human social interactions. Researchers have observed that certain species of parrots, particularly African grey parrots, produce vocalizations that sound strikingly similar to human laughter when they are engaged in playful activities. This behavior is believed to serve multiple functions: it reinforces social bonds within their flock, signals enjoyment, and even signals to other birds that playtime is a safe and joyful activity. Some scientists speculate that parrots have evolved this laugh-like sound as a way of strengthening their relationships with other members of their species. The ability to laugh in response to play highlights the emotional complexity of these highly intelligent birds, showcasing yet another facet of their remarkable cognitive abilities.

Key Vocabulary:
- **Mimicry**: The ability of an organism to imitate the sounds, behaviors, or appearance of another organism.
- **Vocalization**: The production of sounds or speech by animals or humans.
- **Playful**: Engaged in or characterized by fun, entertainment, or amusement.
- **Reinforce**: To strengthen or support an idea, behavior, or relationship.
- **Speculate**: To form a theory or conjecture without firm evidence.

The Squirrel That Plants Thousands of Trees by Accident

The tree squirrel, a seemingly ordinary rodent, inadvertently plays a monumental role in forest regeneration. Through its instinctive practice of hoarding acorns, the squirrel not only secures its food supply but also inadvertently plants an entire forest. These creatures gather and bury acorns in preparation for winter, hiding them in the earth in various locations. Yet, many of these acorns remain untouched and grow into young oak trees. In fact, a single squirrel can plant thousands of trees throughout its life, creating an unintentional yet vital contribution to forest ecosystems. By dispersing seeds over vast areas, squirrels become crucial agents of reforestation, ensuring the continuity of the species and the restoration of natural habitats. This accidental form of tree planting is vital in maintaining biodiversity, as the young oak trees support various forms of wildlife and contribute to the health of the environment. While the squirrel's efforts are driven by survival instincts rather than ecological awareness, its role as an unsung environmental hero is indisputable. The paradox of nature, where survival leads to inadvertent ecological benefit, underscores the complexity of natural processes and the interconnectedness of all living organisms.

Key Vocabulary:
- **Hoarding**: The act of collecting and storing items, often for future use.
- **Biodiversity**: The variety of life in a particular habitat or ecosystem.
- **Ecosystem**: A community of living organisms interacting with their environment.
- **Reforestation**: The process of replanting trees to restore a forest.
- **Inadvertent**: Unintentional or accidental.

How Some Moths Drink the Tears of Sleeping Birds

In the shadowy realms of nature, an eerie yet fascinating behavior unfolds: certain species of moths drink the tears of sleeping birds. This remarkable interaction occurs in tropical regions, where moths like the Eudocima species have evolved to feed not on nectar or fruit, but on the salty tears of birds, particularly during the night when the birds rest. These moths possess specialized mouthparts that can delicately pierce the eyelids of birds, extracting precious tears that are rich in nutrients. This behavior is believed to be a form of parasitism, where the moth benefits without offering any reciprocal advantage to the bird. The moths' attraction to tears may be driven by the high concentration of salt and other minerals in the bird's tear ducts. Scientists speculate that the nocturnal behavior of these moths is not only a feeding strategy but also a mechanism to avoid detection by predators. In this bizarre yet intriguing interaction, the moths have developed an exceptional survival tactic, relying on the vulnerability of birds to satiate their thirst for vital nutrients.

Key Vocabulary:
- **Eerie**: Strange or frightening in a way that causes unease.
- **Parasitism**: A relationship between two organisms where one benefits at the expense of the other.
- **Ducts**: Tubes or channels that carry fluids within an organism.
- **Nocturnal**: Active during the night.
- **Satiate**: To satisfy hunger or thirst completely.

The Lizard That Can Run on Water

One of the more astonishing feats of agility and speed in the animal kingdom belongs to the basilisk lizard, aptly dubbed the "Jesus lizard" due to its extraordinary ability to run on water. Found in the rainforests of Central America, this lizard possesses long, powerful hind legs equipped with large, flared feet that allow it to break the surface tension of water. By rapidly moving its legs, the basilisk creates a series of quick, rhythmic splashes, propelling itself across the water's surface as though walking on solid ground. This phenomenon, known as water running, occurs only over short distances—typically around ten meters—before the lizard dives into the safety of the water. The lizard's speed, coupled with its specialized foot structure, enables it to evade predators such as snakes or birds of prey. Remarkably, this ability has evolved as a defensive strategy, with the basilisk relying on its agility to escape danger rather than seeking refuge in trees or hiding in the underbrush. The basilisk's mastery of running on water is an example of the wonders of evolution and the ingenious ways in which animals adapt to survive.

Key Vocabulary:
- **Agility**: The ability to move quickly and easily.
- **Surface tension**: The elastic force at the surface of a liquid, preventing it from being easily penetrated.

- **Propelling**: To drive or push forward.
- **Defensive strategy**: A tactic used to protect oneself from danger.
- **Underbrush**: The dense growth of shrubs and plants beneath the taller trees in a forest.

The Fungus That Turns Ants Into Zombies

In the dark corners of the forest, a macabre scene unfolds, where an Ophiocordyceps fungus infects ants, taking control of their behavior and transforming them into "zombies." This parasitic fungus targets specific species of ants, infecting them with its spores, which then invade the ant's body and mind. Once infected, the ant leaves its colony and ascends vegetation, where it locks itself onto a leaf or twig using its mandibles. This strange behavior is caused by the fungus's manipulation of the ant's central nervous system, effectively turning it into a mindless host. The fungus continues to grow within the ant's body, eventually bursting forth from the back of the ant's head, releasing spores that will fall to the ground below, where they can potentially infect other ants. The fungus's parasitic life cycle shows the chilling and intricate relationships between species in nature. The "zombie" behavior of the ant is an extreme example of parasitism, where the parasite uses its host for reproduction, while the host becomes a mere vessel for the parasite's survival. This bizarre phenomenon reveals the complex and often gruesome realities of nature's food chain.

Key Vocabulary:
- **Macabre**: Disturbing and horrifying, often associated with death or decay.
- **Parasitic**: A relationship in which one organism benefits at the expense of another.
- **Mandibles**: The jaw-like structures used by certain insects to grasp and chew food.
- **Central nervous system**: The part of the nervous system

that includes the brain and spinal cord.
- **Host**: An organism that harbors another organism, typically a parasite.

Why Some Owls Decorate Their Nests with Dung

Some species of owls, particularly the barn owl, exhibit an unusual and rather unsavory behavior: they decorate their nests with dung. This peculiar habit is not an act of aesthetic preference but rather a practical, evolutionary adaptation to ward off potential threats. The dung, often sourced from nearby animals, serves as a potent deterrent to predators. Its foul smell confounds predators such as foxes and larger birds of prey, preventing them from locating the owls' nests. The odor masks the scent of the owls and their young, making the nest harder to detect. Additionally, the presence of dung may indicate to other owls that the area is already claimed, deterring competition for the prime nesting sites. The dung-decorating behavior is a striking example of how even the most seemingly repellent practices in nature can serve a vital survival purpose. In this case, what might seem like an unsavory choice is, in fact, a masterstroke of evolutionary strategy, ensuring the protection and safety of the owl family from the prying eyes of predators.

Key Vocabulary:
- **Aesthetic**: Concerned with beauty or artistic taste.
- **Deterrent**: Something that discourages or prevents a particular action.
- **Odor**: A distinctive smell, often unpleasant.
- **Competing**: Trying to gain something or achieve something in rivalry with others.
- **Evolutionary adaptation**: A trait or behavior that has developed over time to increase an organism's chances of survival.

HISTORY

The Library of Alexandria and Its Tragic Fate

The Library of Alexandria, once a beacon of knowledge in the ancient world, is shrouded in mystery and tragedy. Founded in the 3rd century BCE by Ptolemy II, it housed hundreds of thousands of scrolls, manuscripts, and texts from the greatest minds of the time. The library attracted scholars from across the known world, including Euclid, Archimedes, and Herophilus. Despite its cultural and intellectual significance, the Library of Alexandria met a series of devastating fates. It suffered from multiple fires, with the most famous being during Julius Caesar's siege of the city in 48 BCE. Though the library's exact destruction remains elusive, it is widely believed that the invaluable knowledge within was lost forever, an irreversible blow to the preservation of ancient wisdom. This loss, compounded by subsequent attacks and neglect, made the Library of Alexandria emblematic of the fragility of civilization's greatest achievements, with its tragic end symbolizing the fleeting nature of human knowledge and power.

Key Vocabulary:
- **Beacon**: A guiding light or symbol, often used metaphorically to represent hope, guidance, or inspiration.
- **Shrouded**: Covered, concealed, or enveloped, often used to describe something hidden in mystery or secrecy.
- **Intellectual**: Relating to the intellect or the mind, involving deep thinking, reasoning, or knowledge.

- **Elusive**: Difficult to find, catch, or understand; something that evades clear explanation or definition.
- **Fragility**: The quality of being delicate, vulnerable, or easily broken; often refers to something that is not durable or resilient.

How a Volcano Destroyed the Minoan Civilization

Around 1600 BCE, the Minoan civilization on the island of Crete was at the height of its power, flourishing with advanced architecture, art, and trade. Yet, this vibrant society was doomed by a catastrophic event—the eruption of the Thera volcano. Known today as the Santorini eruption, it was one of the most powerful volcanic eruptions in recorded history, spewing ash and pumice across the Mediterranean. The Minoans, who lived on Crete, were heavily affected by the eruption, which likely led to widespread devastation, including the collapse of their capital, Knossos. The eruption's aftermath caused climate disruptions, famine, and economic collapse, weakening the Minoans and leaving them vulnerable to invasions. While the Minoans' fall remains shrouded in mystery, the volcanic eruption is often cited as the pivotal factor that led to the rapid decline of this once-great civilization.

Key Vocabulary:
- **Catastrophic**: Involving or causing great damage, destruction, or suffering; disastrous.
- **Pumice**: A light, porous volcanic rock, often used in construction or as an abrasive material.
- **Flourishing**: Thriving, growing vigorously, or reaching a state of success or prosperity.
- **Shrouded**: Concealed or hidden, often used to describe something enveloped in mystery.
- **Pivotal**: Of crucial importance in relation to the development or success of something; essential or central.

The Great Emu War: When Australia Lost a War to Birds

In 1932, Australia engaged in a bizarre and ultimately futile battle with emus, large flightless birds, in what became known as the Great Emu War. Farmers in Western Australia were facing an infestation of emus that were destroying crops, and the government decided to intervene by deploying soldiers armed with machine guns to reduce the emu population. However, the birds proved to be far more resilient and evasive than anticipated. Despite the soldiers' efforts, the emus outran them, and many were able to escape unharmed. The soldiers quickly realized that they were fighting an impossible foe —one that could not be easily defeated with conventional military tactics. After weeks of fruitless attempts, the government reluctantly withdrew, conceding defeat to the birds. The Great Emu War remains one of the most absurd chapters in Australia's history.

Key Vocabulary:
- **Bizarre**: Very strange, unusual, or out of the ordinary, often in a way that is unsettling.
- **Infestation**: A large and often harmful presence of creatures or pests that invade a space.
- **Resilient**: Able to withstand or recover from difficult conditions; strong and adaptable.
- **Evasive**: Tending to avoid or escape something, often by being clever or quick.
- **Conceding**: Admitting or acknowledging defeat, often reluctantly or unwillingly.

How the Eiffel Tower Was Almost Torn Down

The Eiffel Tower, one of the most iconic structures in the world, was nearly demolished shortly after it was built in 1889. Designed by Gustave Eiffel as part of the 1889 World's Fair in Paris, the tower was initially met with criticism from many prominent Parisians, including artists and architects, who deemed it an eyesore. The tower's original purpose was to be a temporary structure, intended to stand for only 20 years. However, it was saved from demolition thanks to its usefulness in scientific experiments, including its role as a giant radio antenna. Over time, the Eiffel Tower gained widespread popularity and became a symbol of French innovation and culture. Today, it is one of the most visited monuments in the world, showing the resilience of an idea that was once deemed unworthy of preservation.

Key Vocabulary:
- **Iconic**: Widely recognized and revered for its cultural or historical significance.
- **Eyesore**: Something that is unpleasant or unattractive to look at, often causing discomfort or irritation.
- **Demolition**: The act of tearing down or destroying something, especially a building or structure.
- **Resilience**: The ability to recover from or adjust to adversity or challenges.

The Great Fire of London

In 1666, the Great Fire of London erupted in the early hours of September 2nd, igniting a catastrophe that would leave parts of the city in ruins. The blaze, which began in a bakery on Pudding Lane, spread uncontrollably due to a combination of dry conditions, wooden structures, and strong winds. The city's narrow streets and lack of effective fire fighting measures only compounded the disaster. What was initially seen as a small fire quickly became a rampant inferno that destroyed much of the medieval city, including over 80,000 homes, dozens of churches, and iconic landmarks such as St. Paul's Cathedral. The fire, while tragic, ultimately led to important changes in urban planning, fire prevention, and building regulations. However, the catastrophic miscalculations in the city's preparedness for such a disaster remain a dark chapter in London's history, highlighting the fragile nature of urban environments and the dangers of neglecting essential infrastructure.

Key Vocabulary:
- **Inferno**: A large, intense fire that is uncontrollable and destructive.
- **Rampant**: Spreading or growing quickly in an uncontrolled manner.
- **Compounded**: To make a situation or problem worse or more severe by adding additional factors.
- **Catastrophic**: Involving or causing a large-scale disaster or significant damage.
- **Neglecting**: Failing to give proper attention, care, or consideration to something important.

The 19th-Century Doctors Who Were Afraid of Tomatoes

In the early 19th century, a strange and seemingly irrational fear took root among doctors in Europe and the United States: the belief that tomatoes were poisonous. Known as "the poison apple," the tomato was widely regarded with suspicion, particularly by the medical community, due to its belonging to the nightshade family—a genus known for containing toxic plants. As a result, many physicians discouraged the consumption of tomatoes, fearing they would cause illness or death. This fear persisted for decades, despite no evidence of tomatoes being harmful. Over time, however, the public gradually overcame this unfounded apprehension, and the tomato eventually became a staple in diets worldwide. The fear of tomatoes serves as an amusing reminder of how misinformation and superstition can shape even the most rational professions.

Key Vocabulary:

- **Irrational**: Lacking reason or logic; not based on sound judgment or understanding.
- **Suspicion**: A feeling or belief that something is wrong, often without concrete evidence to support it.
- **Belonging**: Being a part of or associated with a particular group or category.
- **Apprehension**: A fearful anticipation or anxiety about something that may happen.
- **Foolhardy**: Recklessly bold or daring, often without regard for potential danger or consequences.

The Engineer Who Designed a City After a Dream

In the early 20th century, the visionary engineer and urban planner, Georges-Eugène Haussmann, embarked on a grand endeavor to redesign the city of Paris. After experiencing a vivid and prophetic dream, Haussmann was inspired to reshape Paris into a modern, efficient, and aesthetically pleasing metropolis. The transformation of Paris under Haussmann's guidance included the creation of wide boulevards, improved sanitation, and the construction of iconic landmarks such as the Place de l'Opéra. Haussmann's design was not only a feat of engineering but also a statement of urban beauty and functionality. Though his vision was met with some resistance from residents and critics, Haussmann's redesign fundamentally altered the landscape of Paris, cementing his place as one of the most influential figures in the history of urban planning.

Key Vocabulary:
- **Visionary**: Someone who is able to see or plan for the future in an imaginative and often innovative way.
- **Endeavor**: A serious or determined effort to accomplish a particular task or goal.
- **Prophetic**: Relating to the prediction or foretelling of future events, often in a significant or meaningful way.

- **Aesthetically**: Relating to the appreciation or expression of beauty or artistic design.
- **Fundamentally**: In a basic, essential, or foundational manner; at the core of something.

The Underground City That Could Shelter 20,000 People

Beneath the arid surface of Cappadocia in central Turkey lies a remarkable subterranean metropolis—Derinkuyu. This ancient city, believed to have been built as early as the 8th century BCE, could shelter up to 20,000 people in its expansive network of tunnels, chambers, and passageways. Carved into soft volcanic rock, the city stretches 18 stories deep, providing its inhabitants with protection from invaders, harsh weather, and natural disasters. Derinkuyu is an engineering marvel, with ventilation shafts, wells, stables, and even places of worship integrated into the design. These subterranean structures allowed the residents to live underground for extended periods, avoiding detection by enemies. The scale and sophistication of this underground city demonstrate an extraordinary understanding of architecture, resource management, and community survival. Though it was likely used as a refuge in times of danger, the ingenuity behind Derinkuyu's construction continues to captivate historians and archaeologists, illustrating the capacity of ancient civilizations to adapt to their environment in ingenious ways.

Key Vocabulary:
- **Subterranean**: Existing, occurring, or situated beneath the earth's surface.
- **Subterranean Metropolis**: A large and densely populated city located underground.
- **Marveled**: To be filled with astonishment or wonder at something remarkable.
- **Sophistication**: The quality of being highly developed, refined, or complex.

- **Ingenious**: Cleverly and originally devised, demonstrating creativity or resourcefulness.

Why Some Ancient Civilizations Worshipped Cats

In ancient Egypt, cats were revered as sacred animals, embodying the divine protection of the goddess Bastet, the deity of home, fertility, and childbirth. Cats' graceful and mysterious demeanor, as well as their ability to control vermin, made them essential to the safety and prosperity of ancient Egyptian society. The Egyptians viewed cats as protectors, capable of warding off evil spirits and ensuring the well-being of both homes and fields. Killing a cat, even accidentally, was a grievous crime, punishable by death. This veneration of cats spread to other cultures as well, with the Greeks and Romans adopting similar reverence for the feline species. Cats symbolized independence, strength, and beauty, and their presence in homes was considered a safeguard against misfortune. Today, the legacy of this reverence is evident in modern-day attitudes toward cats, seen as beloved companions and symbols of mystery, elegance, and good fortune.

Key Vocabulary:
- **Revered**: Regarded with deep respect, honor, or admiration.
- **Veneration**: The act of regarding or treating with profound respect and reverence.
- **Deity**: A god or goddess, especially in the context of religious worship.
- **Vermicidal**: Pertaining to the destruction of pests, especially insects or rodents.
- **Grievous**: Causing great sorrow, pain, or suffering; serious or severe.

The History of the Most Infamous Pirate Flag

The Jolly Roger, the flag most famously associated with

pirates, is a symbol of fear and defiance that has endured for centuries. With its skull and crossbones design, the Jolly Roger represented the ominous threat of piracy on the high seas. Historically, pirates flew the Jolly Roger as a means of psychological warfare, signaling their readiness to engage in violence without mercy. The flag would often be raised just before an attack, striking terror into the hearts of merchant ships and forcing many to surrender without a fight. The origin of the flag is shrouded in mystery, with various pirates using different variations of the design. However, the most well-known iteration of the flag, featuring a skull and crossbones, became synonymous with pirate lore. Despite its association with lawlessness and brutality, the Jolly Roger remains a cultural icon.

Key Vocabulary:
- **Infamous**: Known for being bad or having a reputation for wrongdoing or wickedness.
- **Ominous**: Suggesting that something bad or unpleasant is about to happen; threatening.
- **Psychological Warfare**: The use of tactics designed to influence the mind or emotions of the enemy to gain an advantage.
- **Iteration**: A particular version or form of something, especially in a series of variations.
- **Lore**: Traditional knowledge or stories, often handed down through generations.

The Bridge That Was Sold Twice by the Same Con Man

In the early 20th century, one of the most audacious cons in history took place when a man named George C. Parker managed to sell the Brooklyn Bridge not once, but twice. Parker, a notorious swindler, cleverly capitalized on the public's unfamiliarity with the legal intricacies of property ownership. He would pose as a city official and convince unsuspecting immigrants that they could purchase the Brooklyn Bridge, offering to sell them the iconic landmark for a substantial sum. His charm and persuasive tactics led these individuals to believe that they were making a legitimate transaction. Parker's brazen fraudulence continued until he was eventually caught and imprisoned, but not before his scam had taken a toll on both the victims and the public's trust in city infrastructure. His audacity, however, lives on in the annals of criminal history, cementing his place as one of the most infamous con men of all time.

Key Vocabulary:
- **Audacious**: Extremely bold or daring, often in a way that is shocking or disrespectful.
- **Swindler**: A person who cheats or defrauds others out of money or property.
- **Intricacies**: The complex details or aspects of something.
- **Brazen**: Shamelessly bold or defiant; done in a way that lacks respect or discretion.
- **Annals**: A historical record or chronicle, often used in reference to significant events or individuals.

The War That Lasted 335 Years Without a Single Battle

The Anglo-Dutch War, often referred to as the "War That Lasted 335 Years," is one of the most peculiar conflicts in history. This war, which technically lasted from 1651 to 1986, is known not for its battles or bloodshed but for the sheer absurdity of its duration. The war began as a territorial dispute between the Kingdom of England and the Dutch Republic, primarily over trade routes and maritime supremacy. Despite the official state of war, the two nations never engaged in direct combat after the initial skirmishes. The war remained largely a matter of diplomacy and paperwork, with both sides occasionally issuing declarations of war but failing to follow through with any military action. The war was only officially declared over in 1986, when the Dutch government formally renounced the conflict. This extraordinary example of a prolonged, yet uneventful war underscores the bizarre nature of human history and the sometimes arbitrary nature of international relations.

Key Vocabulary:
- **Peculiar**: Strange or unusual in a way that is hard to explain.
- **Skirmishes**: Small, brief, and often informal fights or battles between opposing forces.
- **Maritime**: Relating to the sea, shipping, or navigation.
- **Diplomacy**: The practice of managing international relations through negotiation, dialogue, and peaceful means.
- **Renounced**: To formally give up, abandon, or reject something, often in a public or official manner.

How a Pigeon Won a Medal for Bravery in World War II

During the harrowing days of World War II, a remarkable pigeon named Cher Ami became a symbol of courage and loyalty. In 1918, while serving as a messenger pigeon for the U.S. Army Signal Corps, Cher Ami saved the lives of soldiers by delivering an urgent message despite being severely injured. The soldiers, stranded behind enemy lines, had desperately sent the pigeon with critical coordinates for a bombing mission that would rescue them. Cher Ami was shot in the chest during its flight but continued to carry the message, successfully delivering it and ensuring the soldiers' survival. In recognition of its bravery, Cher Ami was awarded the prestigious French Croix de Guerre for valor. This heroic pigeon's remarkable story has since captured the hearts of many, showcasing the extraordinary feats that animals have performed in wartime. Cher Ami's legacy stands as a poignant reminder of the unwavering loyalty and bravery exhibited in even the most dire circumstances.

Key Vocabulary:

- **Harrowing**: Extremely distressing or disturbing, causing great emotional pain.
- **Messenger**: A person or animal that delivers messages or communications.
- **Severely**: To a very great or intense degree; intensely harmful or damaging.
- **Crucial**: Extremely important, necessary for achieving a specific result.
- **Poignant**: Evoking a strong feeling of sadness or deep emotion.

The Pharaoh Who Tried to Erase All Gods but One

In ancient Egypt, the reign of Pharaoh Akhenaten marked a significant and controversial shift in religious practices. Around 1350 BCE, Akhenaten abandoned Egypt's traditional polytheistic beliefs in favor of a monotheistic worship of the sun god Aten. He endeavored to rid the empire of the many gods that had long been venerated, even closing temples and erasing the names of gods from monuments. Akhenaten's radical reforms were met with resistance from the priesthood and the people, and after his death, his successor, Tutankhamun, restored Egypt's polytheistic traditions. Despite the short-lived nature of his monotheistic revolution, Akhenaten's reign left an indelible mark on Egyptian history. His attempts to centralize power around the Aten and eliminate the traditional pantheon of gods illustrate both his visionary ambition and the complexities of imposing religious change upon a deeply rooted society.

Key Vocabulary:
- **Controversial**: Likely to cause public disagreement or debate due to its unusual or extreme nature.
- **Monotheistic**: The belief in a single deity, as opposed to multiple gods.
- **Venerated**: Regarded with great respect and reverence,

often in a religious context.
- **Indelible**: Impossible to erase or forget.
- **Pantheon**: A collection or group of gods or deities worshiped by a particular culture or religion.

Why the Leaning Tower of Pisa Still Hasn't Fallen

The Leaning Tower of Pisa, an architectural anomaly famous for its unintended tilt, has stood the test of time due to a combination of unique engineering, resilience, and sheer luck. The tower began to lean shortly after construction began in 1173 due to an unstable foundation in the soft soil beneath it. Over the centuries, the tilt worsened, and fears of collapse grew. However, engineers devised creative solutions to stabilize the structure, including adding counterweights and reinforcing the foundation. The most significant intervention came in the 1990s when a multi-million dollar restoration project was launched to reduce the tilt and preserve the tower's integrity. Today, the Leaning Tower of Pisa stands as both a marvel of medieval engineering and a reminder of modern ingenuity, having withstood centuries of natural forces and human intervention without toppling.

Key Vocabulary:
- **Anomaly**: Something that deviates from what is standard, normal, or expected.
- **Intervention**: The act of intervening in order to change or improve a situation.
- **Resilience**: The capacity to recover quickly from difficulties or setbacks.
- **Counterweights**: Weights used to balance or offset the forces acting upon an object.
- **Integrity**: The state of being whole, undivided, and in good condition.

The Great Train Robbery That Shocked Britain

In 1963, Britain was rocked by a daring heist that became

one of the most infamous criminal acts in history—the Great Train Robbery. A gang of 15 criminals meticulously planned and executed the robbery, targeting a Royal Mail train carrying over £2.6 million (equivalent to over £50 million today). The robbers, using knowledge of the train's route and the railway system, successfully intercepted the train and overpowered its crew. Despite the skill and precision of the operation, the robbers were eventually apprehended, though most of the stolen money was never recovered. The audacity of the crime and the sophistication of the robbers' planning earned them a place in British folklore, with the Great Train Robbery remaining a defining moment in the country's criminal history, symbolizing both the ingenuity and the hubris of its perpetrators.

Key Vocabulary:
- **Heist**: A carefully planned and executed robbery or theft, often involving significant amounts of money or valuables.
- **Meticulously**: In a manner that shows great attention to detail and precision.
- **Intercepted**: To stop, seize, or interrupt the progress of something before it reaches its destination.
- **Audacity**: The willingness to take bold risks, often in a way that is shocking or disrespectful.
- **Hubris**: Excessive pride, arrogance, or self-confidence, often leading to downfall.

The Mystery of the Man in the Iron Mask

The death of the enigmatic "Man in the Iron Mask" remains one of the most captivating mysteries in French history. This unidentified prisoner, who was held in various prisons throughout the reign of Louis XIV, was forced to wear a mask, purportedly made of iron, which concealed his identity. The reasons for his imprisonment are the subject of much speculation, with theories ranging from his being a royal relative to a political prisoner. He was eventually placed in the Bastille, where he died in 1703 under obscure circumstances. His true identity has never been definitively revealed, and the secrecy surrounding his life and death has inspired countless theories and literary works, including Alexandre Dumas' famous novel. The mystery of the Man in the Iron Mask continues to fascinate historians and scholars, captivating imaginations with the idea of a secret royal hidden in plain sight.

Key Vocabulary:
- **Enigmatic**: Mysterious, puzzling, or difficult to understand.
- **Purportedly**: According to what is commonly believed or stated; allegedly.
- **Speculation**: The forming of theories or guesses without firm evidence.
- **Obscure**: Not well known or understood; uncertain or hidden.
- **Fascinate**: To captivate the attention or interest of someone in a compelling way.

Why a German Town Once Held a Public Execution of a Rat

In the quaint town of Krefeld, Germany, an extraordinary event took place in 1710 that left many perplexed: the public execution of a rat. This bizarre occurrence was the result of a long-standing feud between the local population and the rat population, which had reached an overwhelming number, devastating crops and spreading disease. Desperate to make a statement and alleviate the growing crisis, the townspeople decided to execute a rat in a highly publicized manner. The rat was put on trial, found guilty of "crimes against humanity," and subsequently hanged in front of a crowd. While this macabre event might seem outlandish by modern standards, it highlights the lengths to which communities in the past would go to exert control over pests and restore order, using ritualistic acts of justice to represent their struggle against the forces of nature.

Key Vocabulary:
- **Quaint**: Charmingly unusual or old-fashioned.
- **Feud**: A prolonged and bitter conflict or dispute, often between groups or families.
- **Macabre**: Gruesome or disturbing, often related to death or the supernatural.
- **Outlandish**: Unconventional, strange, or absurd, often in an extreme way.
- **Ritualistic**: Pertaining to or characterized by ritual, especially one with symbolic significance.

The Secret Language of Victorian Fans and Flowers

During the Victorian era, etiquette and social decorum ruled the lives of the elite, and even the way one held or waved a fan or flower could convey complex messages. These everyday items were not mere accessories but crucial tools for communication. The language of fans, known as floriography, allowed individuals to express their feelings, desires, or intentions without uttering a word. A fan held open in a particular way could signal affection, while a closed fan might denote rejection. Similarly, flowers were used to convey everything from love to sorrow. Roses, for example, symbolized love, while chrysanthemums conveyed grief. This delicate and intricate form of communication allowed people to maintain the rigid boundaries of propriety while still expressing their emotions. The subtlety and complexity of this "secret" language reflected the era's emphasis on restrained yet highly sophisticated forms of interaction.

Key Vocabulary:
- **Etiquette**: The accepted traditional forms, manners, and

ceremonies of polite society.
- **Decorum**: Behavior in keeping with good taste and propriety; orderliness.
- **Floriography**: The language of flowers, used to convey messages or feelings through the arrangement or choice of flowers.
- **Propriety**: Conformity to accepted standards of behavior or morals.
- **Restraint**: The action of holding something back or limiting its expression, particularly in emotional or social contexts.

How the First Olympic Games Were Almost Canceled

The first Olympic Games of the modern era, held in 1896 in Athens, almost did not happen at all. The idea of reviving the ancient Greek games was met with skepticism and financial challenges, with few willing to back the ambitious project. At one point, the games were in jeopardy of being canceled due to a lack of funding, as well as doubts about whether a global competition could truly be successful. However, a determined group of organizers, including Frenchman Pierre de Coubertin, pushed forward, securing financial support and overcoming logistical hurdles. The first modern Olympics eventually took place with 13 countries participating, and it became a resounding success. This near-collapse highlights the challenges faced by those who seek to create something of lasting significance and the power of perseverance in the face of adversity.

Key Vocabulary:
- **Skepticism**: Doubt or disbelief regarding the truth or validity of something.
- **Jeopardy**: The danger of harm, loss, or failure.
- **Logistical**: Relating to the organization and coordination of complex activities or tasks.

- **Perseverance**: The ability to continue trying despite difficulty or delay in achieving success.
- **Resounding**: Producing or having a deep, full sound; emphatic or undeniable.

The Hidden Rooms Inside the Great Wall of China

Beneath the imposing façade of the Great Wall of China lies a lesser-known secret—hidden chambers, covert compartments, and labyrinthine passages once used for surveillance, storage, and military stratagem. Built over centuries, this colossal fortification was more than a mere barricade; it was an intricate network of fortresses, garrisons, and concealed recesses designed to confound invaders and facilitate rapid mobilization. Some of these clandestine chambers were weapon caches, others functioned as command centers where warlords and tacticians devised battle formations, and a few served as resting quarters for weary sentinels. These architectural marvels, often shrouded in myth, exemplify the ingenuity of ancient Chinese military engineering. Though many of these rooms have succumbed to the ravages of time, archaeologists and historians continue to uncover evidence of their existence, illuminating the depth of strategic forethought embedded in the very stones of this legendary bulwark.

Key Vocabulary:
- **Façade**: The outward appearance, often deceptive or superficial.
- **Labyrinthine**: Intricately complex and confusing, resembling a maze.
- **Stratagem**: A cunning plan or maneuver, often used in military strategy.
- **Clandestine**: Done in secrecy, often to conceal an illicit or covert purpose.
- **Bulwark**: A strong defense or protection against external danger.

Why Ancient Romans Had Heated Floors Before Modern Homes Did

Centuries before the advent of contemporary central heating, the Romans devised an ingenious system known as the hypocaust, an architectural marvel that allowed opulent villas, bathhouses, and even some public buildings to be suffused with warmth. This subterranean network functioned by circulating hot air beneath elevated flooring and within hollow walls, ensuring a temperate climate even amidst the frigid winters. The heat emanated from furnaces, laboriously stoked by slaves, whose ceaseless toil maintained the delicate equilibrium of warmth. This technological sophistication underscored the Romans' penchant for luxury and their advanced grasp of thermodynamics. Though the fall of the empire saw this practice largely abandoned, remnants of the hypocaust system endure in archaeological sites, attesting to a civilization whose mastery over engineering rivaled even modernity. The Romans' heated floors were not merely an example of affluence but a symbol of their relentless pursuit of comfort and innovation.

Key Vocabulary:
- **Hypocaust**: An ancient Roman system of underfloor heating.
- **Suffused**: Gradually spread through or over.
- **Subterranean**: Existing or operating beneath the surface of the earth.
- **Equilibrium**: A state of balance or stability.
- **Penchant**: A strong or habitual inclination or liking for something.

The Viking Who Became a King in Another Land

Few sagas rival the audacious odyssey of Rollo, the Norse marauder who forsook a life of perpetual pillaging to ascend the throne of Normandy. As Viking incursions into Francia reached a crescendo in the late 9th century, Rollo, a formidable warlord, besieged the Seine with an unrelenting ferocity. However, rather than waging interminable warfare, the French king, Charles the Simple, brokered an unprecedented accord—granting Rollo dominion over Normandy in exchange for his fealty and conversion to Christianity. Thus, a fearsome raider metamorphosed into a sovereign, solidifying his legacy as the progenitor of a dynasty that would later culminate in William the Conqueror. Rollo's ascension is emblematic of the Vikings' paradoxical nature—relentless plunderers, yet shrewd statesmen, capable of both destruction and governance. His tale endures as a testament to the fluidity of power, wherein conquest, diplomacy, and adaptation intertwine to shape the destinies of nations.

Key Vocabulary:
- **Odyssey**: A long, adventurous journey.
- **Marauder**: A raider who plunders and pillages.
- **Crescendo**: A gradual increase to a peak, often used metaphorically.
- **Fealty**: A feudal tenant's sworn loyalty to a lord.
- **Metamorphosed**: Transformed in a profound or dramatic way.

How a Cook Saved the White House During the War of 1812

In the annals of American history, few acts of heroism are as unsung yet profoundly significant as that of James Hemings, a resourceful cook who played an instrumental role in preserving the White House's legacy. As British forces laid siege to Washington D.C. in 1814, intent on razing the capital, Hemings, a culinary virtuoso, exhibited astonishing foresight. With the invaders mere hours away, he salvaged invaluable artifacts—including the famed portrait of George Washington—before the White House succumbed to flames. His actions, though overshadowed by the grander narratives of war, underscore the indelible impact of unsung individuals in the crucible of history. Amidst the smoldering remnants of the nation's seat of power, his quick thinking ensured that irreplaceable relics endured, a silent yet profound reminder of resilience and duty. Hemings' valor is a reminder that heroism often manifests in the unlikeliest of figures, safeguarding legacies from the ashes of oblivion.

Key Vocabulary:
- **Annals**: Historical records of events in chronological order.
- **Razing**: Completely destroying or demolishing.
- **Virtuoso**: A person highly skilled in a particular art or field.
- **Indelible**: Impossible to erase, remove, or forget.
- **Oblivion**: The state of being forgotten or unknown.

The Forgotten City That Was Covered in Volcanic Ash for Centuries

For centuries, the city of Pompeii lay entombed beneath a suffocating shroud of volcanic ash, an eerie reminder of nature's unfathomable wrath. In 79 A.D., Mount Vesuvius erupted with an apocalyptic fury, unleashing torrents of molten rock, asphyxiating fumes, and pyroclastic surges that obliterated the once-thriving Roman metropolis in mere hours. The cataclysm was so sudden that its denizens were frozen in time—caught mid-stride, mid-embrace, mid-scream—preserved in haunting casts formed by the volcanic sediment that enveloped them. For nearly 1,700 years, Pompeii remained a forgotten relic, buried beneath layers of oblivion, until its rediscovery in the 18th century unveiled a civilization eerily suspended in antiquity. Today, its remarkably intact frescoes, mosaics, and structures provide an unparalleled glimpse into the quotidian life of ancient Rome, offering archaeologists a city preserved not by design but by disaster—a paradox of devastation and preservation unparalleled in history.

Key Vocabulary:
- **Entombed**: Buried or trapped, often within something enclosing.
- **Suffocating**: Stifling, restricting the ability to breathe or function.
- **Pyroclastic**: Relating to volcanic material, particularly fast-moving currents of hot gas and rock.
- **Denizens**: Inhabitants or residents of a particular place.
- **Quotidian**: Ordinary, everyday, commonplace.

The Lady Who Survived the Titanic and Two Other Ship Disasters

Among history's most fortuitous yet harrowing survival stories stands that of Violet Jessop, a woman whose uncanny resilience defied maritime catastrophe not once, not twice, but thrice. As a stewardess aboard the RMS Titanic, she bore witness to the ship's fateful demise in 1912, escaping aboard a lifeboat while the vessel succumbed to the abyssal depths. Yet fate's grip upon her did not loosen. She had previously survived a collision aboard the RMS Olympic and, incredibly, would later endure the sinking of the HMHS Britannic, struck down by an underwater mine during World War I. Despite these brushes with death, Jessop remained undeterred, returning to sea time and again, as if tethered to the very element that had thrice sought to claim her. Her life stands as a paradox of extraordinary luck and chilling misfortune—a tale of defiance against the merciless will of the ocean.

Key Vocabulary:
- **Fortuitous**: Happening by chance, often in a fortunate way.
- **Harrowing**: Extremely distressing or traumatic.
- **Abyssal**: Relating to the deep, seemingly bottomless ocean.

- **Succumbed**: Yielded or gave way, typically to death or disaster.
- **Paradox**: A seemingly contradictory or impossible situation that may hold truth.

How the Inca Built Bridges Out of Grass That Lasted for Centuries

Deep within the vertiginous ravines of the Andean highlands, the Inca civilization fashioned an engineering marvel that defied both time and tempest—the Q'eswachaka, a suspension bridge woven entirely from ichu grass. Devoid of iron or mortar, these resilient structures were meticulously braided by skilled artisans using ancestral techniques passed down through generations. Each year, entire communities gathered to reconstruct the bridges anew, reinforcing their tensile integrity and ensuring their survival for centuries. Remarkably, these bioengineered wonders endured the elements, swaying yet unyielding, allowing messengers, merchants, and warriors safe passage across perilous chasms. Though many were dismantled in the wake of Spanish conquest, a lone bridge—faithfully rebuilt to this day—remains as a monument to the ingenuity, adaptability, and communal spirit of the Inca. In an era dominated by steel and concrete, their legacy endures as an exemplar of sustainable engineering long before the term existed.

Key Vocabulary:
- **Vertiginous**: Extremely steep or high, often causing dizziness.
- **Ravine**: A deep, narrow gorge with steep sides.
- **Ichu**: A type of tough, native grass found in the Andes.
- **Tensile**: Capable of being stretched without breaking.
- **Exemplar**: A model or pattern of excellence.

Why the U.S. Once Proposed a Plan to Nuke the Moon

In the throes of Cold War paranoia, when the race for technological and ideological supremacy reached fever pitch, the United States entertained a proposition so audacious it bordered on the surreal—detonating a nuclear bomb on the Moon. Codenamed Project A119, this clandestine endeavor was conceived in the late 1950s as a show of force meant to intimidate the Soviet Union, whose early victories in space exploration, particularly the launch of Sputnik, had rattled American confidence. The plan called for an atomic explosion on the lunar surface, its luminous detonation visible from Earth, serving as a cosmic proclamation of U.S. dominance. However, as scientific prudence prevailed, the catastrophic implications—ranging from geopolitical backlash to unforeseen astronomical consequences—led to its quiet abandonment. This near-apocalyptic scheme remains a chilling example of the lengths superpowers were willing to go to etch their dominion into the very fabric of the cosmos.

Key Vocabulary:
- **Throes**: Intense or violent struggles.
- **Audacious**: Bold, daring, or recklessly brave.
- **Clandestine**: Kept secret or done covertly.
- **Luminous**: Emitting or reflecting light.
- **Apocalyptic**: Resembling or predicting catastrophic destruction.

The Enormous Underground Army of Terracotta Warriors

In the annals of archaeology, few discoveries rival the grandeur and enigma of the Terracotta Army—an underground legion of life-sized warriors, archers, charioteers, and horses, standing in mute vigilance over the tomb of China's first emperor, Qin Shi Huang. Conceived over two millennia ago, this subterranean battalion, numbering in the thousands, was meticulously sculpted to accompany the emperor into the afterlife, embodying both his autocratic might and his unrelenting dread of mortality. Each warrior, forged in fired clay, bore distinct facial features, elaborate armor, and weaponry, suggesting an almost supernatural devotion to realism. Yet, the mausoleum's deepest chambers remain shrouded in mystery, sealed for fear of disrupting ancient booby traps and the reputed rivers of mercury said to flow within. As excavation continues, the Terracotta Army endures as an example of the intersection of artistry, military prowess, and the boundless ambitions of history's most enigmatic rulers.

Key Vocabulary:
- **Annals**: Records or chronicles of historical events.
- **Enigma**: Something mysterious, puzzling, or difficult to understand.
- **Subterranean**: Existing or occurring beneath the Earth's surface.
- **Autocratic**: Ruling with absolute authority, often oppressively.
- **Booby traps**: Hidden mechanisms or devices meant to cause harm.

The Real Story Behind the Salem Witch Trials

Amidst the puritanical fervor of 17th-century New England, a spectral hysteria gripped the town of Salem, Massachusetts, igniting one of history's most infamous episodes of mass paranoia. The Salem Witch Trials, a maelstrom of superstition, fear, and political subterfuge, led to the persecution and execution of innocent men and women accused of consorting with the devil. The hysteria began in 1692 when a group of young girls claimed to be afflicted by unseen forces, convulsing and uttering wild accusations against supposed witches. What ensued was a judicial catastrophe—trials marred by spectral evidence, forced confessions, and an insatiable appetite for scapegoats. As the fervor waned and reason prevailed, the trials were ultimately condemned as a grievous miscarriage of justice. Centuries later, the Salem Witch Trials endure as a cautionary tale of the perils of mass hysteria, religious extremism, and the fragile boundary between truth and delusion.

Key Vocabulary:
- **Puritanical**: Strict in moral or religious beliefs.
- **Maelstrom**: A chaotic and tumultuous situation.
- **Subterfuge**: Deceit used to achieve a goal.
- **Convulsing**: Shaking uncontrollably, often due to illness or distress.
- **Scapegoat**: A person blamed for the wrongdoings of others.

SPACE

The Star That Is So Big It Could Swallow Our Solar System

In the unfathomable expanse of the cosmos lies UY Scuti, a stellar behemoth so vast it defies comprehension. This red hypergiant, residing in the constellation Scutum, dwarfs our Sun, boasting a radius nearly 1,700 times larger. Were it to replace the Sun, its bloated envelope would engulf the orbits of Mercury, Venus, Earth, and even Jupiter, reducing our solar neighborhood to a mere ember within its colossal girth. Despite its incomprehensible scale, UY Scuti's tenuous outer layers make it an ephemeral titan, fated to collapse into a spectacular supernova, dispersing its enriched elements across the void. Scientists study such leviathans not only to unravel the enigmas of stellar evolution but also to understand the ultimate fate of our own Sun.

Key Vocabulary:
- **Behemoth**: Something enormous, especially a giant creature or structure.
- **Hypergiant**: A star of immense size and luminosity, larger and more unstable than typical supergiants.
- **Bloated**: Swollen or expanded beyond normal limits, often used metaphorically.
- **Ephemeral**: Lasting a short time; transient.
- **Leviathan**: A thing of immense size and power, often used to describe something monstrous or overwhelming.

The Asteroid That Barely Missed Earth

and No One Saw It Coming

On an unassuming day in 2019, a rogue asteroid hurtled past Earth at an unnerving proximity, evading detection until mere hours before its closest approach. Dubbed 2019 OK, this cosmic interloper measured nearly 100 meters in diameter—large enough to obliterate an entire city had its trajectory been marginally altered. Unlike well-documented celestial threats, 2019 OK emerged from the Sun's glare, rendering it practically invisible to ground-based observatories. Its near-collision underscored the precariousness of Earth's cosmic vulnerability and reignited calls for enhanced planetary defense mechanisms. Had it impacted, the devastation would have mirrored the infamous Tunguska event of 1908, wherein an explosion, presumed to be from an asteroid, flattened over 2,000 square kilometers of Siberian forest.

Key Vocabulary:
- **Rogue**: Something unpredictable or uncontrollable, often used for celestial objects or outliers.
- **Interloper**: An intruder or entity that appears where it is unwelcome or unexpected.
- **Trajectory**: The path followed by an object moving through space.
- **Precariousness**: A state of instability or uncertainty, often implying danger.
- **Obliterate**: To destroy utterly, leaving no trace.

The Planet Where It Rains Diamonds

In the abyss of our solar system, Neptune and Uranus harbor meteorological phenomena beyond earthly imagination. Scientists postulate that these ice giants experience incessant diamond rain, a consequence of their extreme atmospheric conditions. Beneath their turbulent clouds, immense pressure forces carbon atoms into crystalline lattices, forging microscopic diamonds that cascade toward the planet's enigmatic core. This process, termed 'diamond precipitation,' remains an enthralling subject of astrophysical inquiry, as it challenges our understanding of planetary interiors. If such phenomena occur elsewhere, exoplanets of similar composition may, quite literally, be celestial treasure troves.

Key Vocabulary:
- **Abyss**: A vast, immeasurable depth, often used to evoke mystery or danger.
- **Incessant**: Continuous, without pause or interruption.
- **Lattices**: Interwoven structures or frameworks, often describing crystalline formations.
- **Precipitation**: The process of substances condensing and falling, such as rain—or in this case, diamonds.
- **Enthralling**: Captivating or fascinating, holding one's attention completely.

The Mystery of the Great Red Spot on Jupiter

For centuries, astronomers have been mesmerized by Jupiter's Great Red Spot—an anticyclonic tempest of unfathomable proportions. Larger than Earth itself, this swirling maelstrom has persisted for at least 350 years, its ruddy hue a consequence of complex chemical interactions within the gas giant's upper atmosphere. Despite its apparent longevity, the storm has been contracting, its once-imposing girth shrinking as if obeying an inscrutable celestial decree. Some theorize that this diminishment heralds its eventual dissolution, while others believe it will persist in some altered form. The precise mechanics sustaining its turbulent existence remain elusive, ensuring the Great Red Spot's continued place as one of the solar system's greatest enigmas.

Key Vocabulary:
- **Anticyclonic**: A weather pattern involving a large-scale spiral motion, often associated with high-pressure systems.

- **Maelstrom**: A violent whirlpool or chaotic situation.
- **Ruddy**: Having a reddish color, often used poetically.
- **Inscrutable**: Difficult to understand or interpret; mysterious.
- **Diminishment**: The process of shrinking or reducing in size or significance.

How Black Holes Can 'Spaghettify' Anything That Falls Into Them

A black hole is the universe's insatiable abyss, a place where gravity transcends comprehension, pulling all into its voracious maw. As an object approaches its event horizon—the point of no return—it undergoes an unsettling phenomenon known as spaghettification. This process arises from the immense gravitational gradient, where the force at one end of an object is significantly greater than at the other. The result is a grotesque elongation, as if the object were being mercilessly kneaded into an infinitely thin filament. Were an astronaut to fall feet-first, their lower half would experience an overwhelmingly stronger pull than their head, stretching their body like a strand of celestial silk. As they inch closer to the singularity—the enigmatic core where space-time distorts into oblivion—they would be obliterated into their fundamental particles. This inexorable fate renders black holes not just cosmic enigmas, but executioners of the universe.

Key Vocabulary:
- **Spaghettification**: The extreme stretching and thinning of an object due to intense gravitational forces near a black hole.
- **Event Horizon**: The boundary surrounding a black hole beyond which nothing, not even light, can escape.
- **Singularity**: The infinitely dense point at the center of a black hole where the laws of physics collapse.

- **Gravitational Gradient**: The rate at which gravitational force changes with distance, responsible for the stretching effect.
- **Inexorable**: Impossible to stop or prevent; relentless, like the pull of a black hole.

The Planet That Orbits Its Star in Just a Few Hours

Among the pantheon of exoplanets, one defies all expectations—KELT-9b, a gas giant so perilously close to its parent star that it completes an entire orbit in a mere 36 hours. Unlike the stately pace of Earth's revolution, this celestial inferno is trapped in a blistering dance with its sun, locked in perpetual incandescence. With surface temperatures soaring beyond 4,300°C (7,800°F), it is hotter than many stars, its atmosphere vaporizing into space in a tempest of atomic fury. The proximity of KELT-9b to its star ensures its inevitable doom; over millennia, it will be consumed in a gravitational embrace, vanishing into oblivion. Yet, for now, it remains an emblem of the universe's ceaseless dynamism, a world where fire reigns supreme.

Key Vocabulary:
- **Exoplanet**: A planet that orbits a star outside our solar system.
- **Incandescence**: The emission of light due to intense heat.
- **Perilously**: Dangerously or at great risk.
- **Tempest**: A violent storm, used metaphorically to describe chaotic phenomena.
- **Dynamism**: Continuous change, energy, or motion.

The Hidden Ocean Beneath the Surface of Jupiter's Moon

Europa, one of Jupiter's most enigmatic satellites, harbors a secret beneath its icy carapace—a vast, briny ocean, concealed beneath a shell of frozen desolation. Scientists, armed with spectral analysis and magnetometric readings, suspect that this alien sea might be more expansive than all of Earth's oceans combined. Cracks and ridges across its frozen exoskeleton suggest that subterranean tides, driven by Jupiter's immense gravitational grasp, churn beneath the surface, creating a dynamic environment that could foster extraterrestrial life.

The Galileo spacecraft provided tantalizing hints of this clandestine abyss, but upcoming missions, such as NASA's Europa Clipper, will delve deeper, scanning for signs of biochemical activity. Some researchers posit that hydrothermal vents, akin to those on Earth's seafloor, might be nestled within Europa's depths, exhaling mineral-rich plumes capable of sustaining microbial organisms. If life lurks within these shadowy waters, it could redefine our understanding of habitability beyond our pale blue dot.

Key Vocabulary:
- **Clandestine**: kept secret or done secretively
- **Carapace**: a hard, protective outer shell
- **Spectral analysis**: the study of light emissions to determine composition
- **Hydrothermal vents**: fissures on the seafloor that release heated water
- **Exoskeleton**: an external structural layer

The Dark Side of the Moon and Why It's So Mysterious

For centuries, the Moon has held an enigmatic duality—one hemisphere forever facing Earth, the other locked in perpetual concealment. This "dark side" is not literally devoid of light but remains obscured from direct terrestrial observation due to the Moon's synchronous rotation.

Unlike the familiar near side, with its vast, smooth maria, the Moon's far side is pockmarked with craters, an ancient, untouched relic of celestial bombardments. It is here that China's Chang'e 4 lander touched down in 2019, revealing insights into the lunar subsurface. Scientists suspect that this hemisphere's ruggedness may stem from gravitational interactions with Earth, which prevented lava flows from resurfacing the terrain.

Beyond its geological intrigue, the dark side serves as an ideal location for radio telescopes, shielded from Earth's electromagnetic interference. As humanity's lunar aspirations intensify, this uncharted expanse may soon transform from an enigma into an outpost for scientific discovery.

Key Vocabulary:
- **Synchronous rotation**: when an orbiting body's rotation matches its orbital period
- **Celestial bombardment**: impacts from space objects like asteroids
- **Maria**: large, basaltic plains on the Moon's surface
- **Lunar subsurface**: the layers beneath the Moon's crust
- **Electromagnetic interference**: disruption of signals by human-made transmissions

The Fastest-Spinning Star Ever Discovered and What It Can Teach Us

Deep within the cosmos, an unrelenting tempest of matter hurtles at unfathomable velocities—a pulsar spinning at nearly 700 revolutions per second. Known as PSR J1748-2446ad, this neutron star is a collapsed stellar remnant, compacted into an impossibly dense sphere no larger than a city, yet possessing a gravitational grip stronger than any terrestrial force.

This celestial dynamo's rapid rotation generates a formidable magnetic field, emitting intense radio pulses that flicker across the abyss. Scientists theorize that such high angular momentum stems from an ancient binary system, where a companion star's demise funneled energy into the pulsar's relentless spin.

Studying such extreme astrophysical phenomena deepens our understanding of relativity, magnetism, and the limits of matter under intense pressures. If a pulsar can spin at such breakneck speeds without disintegrating, it reshapes our comprehension of what is physically possible within the vast, enigmatic theater of the universe.

Key Vocabulary:
- **Unrelenting**: persistent, unstoppable
- **Tempest**: a violent disturbance or storm
- **Celestial dynamo**: an astronomical object generating intense energy
- **Angular momentum**: rotational inertia of an object in motion
- **Breakneck**: dangerously fast

The Theory That We Are Living Inside a Simulation

The hypothesis that our reality is an elaborate simulation is not a product of science fiction but a philosophical and scientific conjecture posited by thinkers like Nick Bostrom. This theory suggests that an advanced civilization, perhaps eons ahead of us, could have engineered a hyper-realistic construct indistinguishable from an authentic universe. If computational power continues to escalate exponentially, it is conceivable that simulated consciousnesses—entities oblivious to their artificial origins—could exist in vast, simulated cosmoses. Proponents argue that our universe's fundamental laws, from quantum mechanics to the cosmic speed limit of light, bear resemblance to coded parameters, akin to a digital framework. Critics, however, counter that such a theory is unverifiable, rendering it epistemologically ambiguous. Yet, as artificial intelligence advances and virtual realities become increasingly immersive, the proposition that our world is but a sophisticated illusion gains a veneer of plausibility.

Key Vocabulary:
- **Conjecture**: A hypothesis or theory based on incomplete information; speculation.
- **Eons**: Indefinitely long periods of time, often used to describe vast cosmic durations.
- **Oblivious**: Unaware or unmindful of one's surroundings or circumstances.
- **Epistemologically**: Related to the study of knowledge, questioning how we ascertain truth and reality.
- **Veneer**: A superficial or deceptively attractive appearance, often masking a deeper truth.

The Asteroid That Killed the Dinosaurs and How It Changed the Earth Forever

Sixty-six million years ago, an astronomical harbinger of doom hurtled toward Earth—an asteroid spanning ten kilometers in diameter. This cataclysmic impact, centered on the Yucatán Peninsula, unleashed an energy equivalent to billions of atomic bombs, incinerating vast ecosystems instantaneously. The resultant shockwave spawned mega-tsunamis, while the ejected debris occluded sunlight, plunging the planet into an extended winter that decimated photosynthetic life. This mass extinction event eradicated approximately 75% of Earth's species, including the non-avian dinosaurs, paving the way for mammalian ascendance. The Chicxulub crater, submerged beneath present-day Mexico, remains a vestige of this primordial catastrophe—a haunting reminder of the cosmos' indifferent volatility.

Key Vocabulary:
- **Harbinger**: A forerunner or precursor, often signaling an impending event, particularly a catastrophic one.
- **Cataclysmic**: Relating to a violent, large-scale disaster or

upheaval.
- **Occluded**: Obscured or blocked, particularly in reference to light or vision.
- **Ascendance**: The act of rising to prominence or dominance.
- **Vestige**: A remaining trace or evidence of something that once existed.

The Mysterious Object That Came from Outside Our Solar System

In 2017, an unusual interstellar visitor entered our solar system, sparking both intrigue and bewilderment among astronomers. This cigar-shaped object, dubbed 'Oumuamua,' originated from outside our solar system, making it the first known interstellar object to traverse through our cosmic neighborhood. Its rapid, unexplainable acceleration, deviating from the expected trajectory based on gravitational forces alone, led to speculation about its nature. Some theorists proposed that it was a comet, while others suggested it could be an artificial probe sent by an advanced civilization. The object's elongated shape, unique in comparison to typical asteroids or comets, further deepened the mystery. While most scientists lean toward a natural origin, the debate continues, with 'Oumuamua' serving as an enigma that challenges our understanding of interstellar objects and possibly hints at extraterrestrial technology. Though it has since passed beyond the reach of our telescopes, it remains a symbol of the unexplained and the tantalizing unknowns that lie beyond our solar system.

Key Vocabulary:
- **Intrigue**: Arouse the curiosity or interest of; something mysterious or fascinating.
- **Bewilderment**: A state of confusion or puzzlement, often when faced with something incomprehensible.

- **Trajectory**: The path followed by a moving object through space or through a particular course.
- **Speculation**: The forming of a theory or conjecture without firm evidence.
- **Enigma**: A person or thing that is mysterious, puzzling, or difficult to understand.

How Astronomers Discovered a 'Ghost' Galaxy Hiding in Plain Sight

In a remarkable discovery that rewrote some of our understanding of the cosmos, astronomers stumbled upon a 'ghost' galaxy, hidden for eons within the visible universe. This galaxy, officially named 'Virgo I,' was discovered by combing through data from the Hubble Space Telescope. What made Virgo I so elusive was its lack of the typical luminous features that make galaxies stand out: it has little visible star formation, making it nearly invisible to traditional observation methods. Instead, it is composed largely of dark matter and a faint population of ancient stars, rendering it almost imperceptible. What is truly remarkable is that this galaxy has likely existed for billions of years, its presence a testament to the vast, unseen structures that populate the universe. The discovery of Virgo I opens up a new chapter in the study of galactic formation and provides further evidence of the mysterious dark matter that remains one of the great puzzles of modern astronomy.

Key Vocabulary:
- **Eons**: A long, indefinite period of time; an immeasurably long span of years.
- **Luminous**: Emitting or reflecting light; shining brightly.
- **Elusive**: Difficult to find, catch, or achieve; hard to grasp or comprehend.
- **Impeccable**: Flawless, without any errors or faults.
- **Puzzles**: Something that is perplexing or confusing and requires effort to understand.

The Discovery of an Exoplanet That's One Giant Gas Bubble

In a groundbreaking discovery, astronomers found an exoplanet that defies expectations: a massive, almost entirely gaseous world that floats through space like a giant bubble. Known as 'KELT-9b,' this exoplanet is classified as a 'hot Jupiter,' with surface temperatures soaring to over 4,000°C, hotter than some stars. Its gaseous composition and extreme conditions make it a fascinating object of study. Scientists speculate that KELT-9b's unique structure could provide vital clues about planetary formation, as it challenges existing theories about how planets are born and evolve. This discovery pushes the boundaries of what we thought possible in exoplanet science, offering new perspectives on the diversity of worlds beyond our solar system. With more research, KELT-9b could help unlock secrets about how planets form in high-temperature environments.

Key Vocabulary:
- **Groundbreaking**: Innovative and pioneering, introducing new ideas or methods.
- **Exoplanet**: A planet that orbits a star outside our solar system.
- **Defies**: Resists or challenges expected norms or conventions.
- **Speculate**: Form a theory or conjecture about a subject without firm evidence.
- **Unlock**: To reveal or make accessible; to disclose or open up for understanding.

How the Moon Is Slowly Moving Away from Earth

One of the most astounding phenomena in astronomy is the slow but inexorable drift of the Moon away from Earth. Every year, the Moon recedes by about 3.8 centimeters, a process caused by tidal forces between the two celestial bodies. These tidal interactions, which result from the gravitational pull of the Earth on the Moon, cause energy to be transferred, gradually pushing the Moon into a larger orbit. While this movement is imperceptible in our day-to-day lives, it has far-reaching consequences for the future of Earth-Moon dynamics. As the Moon moves farther away, Earth's rotation will gradually slow down, affecting the length of days. Though this process will take billions of years to have any significant impact, it is a reminder of the ever-changing nature of our planetary system and the complex gravitational interactions that govern it.

Key Vocabulary:
- **Inexorable**: Impossible to stop or prevent; relentless.
- **Recedes**: Moves back or away from a previous position.
- **Tidal**: Relating to or affected by tides, the regular rise and fall of sea levels.
- **Imperceptible**: Not able to be perceived or noticed, often due to being too small or gradual.
- **Gravitational**: Pertaining to gravity, the force that attracts objects toward one another.

The Solar Storm That Almost Caused a Global Catastrophe

In 1859, the Earth narrowly escaped a global catastrophe, when a massive solar storm, known as the Carrington Event, struck our planet. This storm, the most powerful geomagnetic disturbance ever recorded, unleashed a torrent of charged particles from the Sun, sending them hurtling toward Earth. Had the storm struck just a few days later, the resulting geomagnetic activity could have caused widespread devastation. The intense energy from the solar particles would have overloaded electrical systems, disrupting communications, transportation, and infrastructure worldwide. The event highlights the vulnerability of modern technology to solar activity. Since then, scientists have been keenly monitoring solar storms, working to understand their behavior and develop methods to mitigate their impact. Although we narrowly avoided disaster in 1859, the possibility of future solar storms still presents a potential threat to our increasingly interconnected world.

Key Vocabulary:
- **Catastrophe**: A large-scale disaster or misfortune causing significant harm or destruction.
- **Geomagnetic**: Pertaining to or affecting the Earth's magnetic field.
- **Hurtling**: Moving swiftly and uncontrollably through space.
- **Vulnerability**: The state of being exposed to harm or danger, especially from external forces.
- **Mitigate**: To make something less severe, harmful, or painful.

The Strange Star That Scientists Think Might Be Surrounded by an Alien Megastructure

In an extraordinary revelation, astronomers have identified a star, known as 'Tabby's Star,' that exhibits bizarre, unexplained dimming behavior, leading some scientists to speculate that it could be surrounded by an alien megastructure. The star has shown irregular fluctuations in brightness that defy typical astrophysical explanations, such as those caused by orbiting planets. Some researchers have suggested that an advanced extraterrestrial civilization might have constructed a massive, energy-harvesting structure around the star, similar to what we envision as a Dyson Sphere. While the idea remains speculative and controversial, it has sparked a wave of interest in the search for extraterrestrial intelligence. Tabby's Star continues to puzzle astronomers, and its unusual dimming may one day lead to a breakthrough in our understanding of the cosmos and the potential existence of alien life, though it's also possible the variation in brightness is caused by irregular dust clouds.

Key Vocabulary:
- **Bizarre**: Very strange or unconventional, often in a way that causes confusion or disbelief.
- **Speculate**: To form a theory or conjecture without firm evidence.
- **Extraterrestrial**: Originating or existing outside the Earth or its atmosphere.
- **Fluctuations**: Irregular changes or variations in a particular state or condition.
- **Dyson Sphere**: A hypothetical structure built around a star to capture its energy, proposed by physicist Freeman Dyson.

How the Sun Will Eventually Swallow the Earth

The fate of Earth, tied irrevocably to the Sun, is sealed in billions of years when the Sun will inevitably expand into a red giant and engulf the inner planets, including Earth. As the Sun runs out of hydrogen fuel, it will begin to burn helium, causing it to swell to many times its current size. During this expansion, the Sun will heat up the surrounding space, vaporizing the Earth's oceans and rendering it uninhabitable long before it swallows the planet whole. Fortunately, this catastrophic event is not expected to occur for about 5 billion years, offering ample time for humanity to explore the cosmos and, perhaps, colonize other star systems. This impending fate of our planet serves as a poignant reminder of the finite nature of our solar system, bound to the life cycle of its central star.

Key Vocabulary:
- **Irrevocably**: In a way that cannot be undone or reversed.
- **Engulf**: To surround and completely cover, often with

overwhelming force or extent.
- **Vaporizing**: Converting into vapor or gas, typically through intense heat.
- **Catastrophic**: Involving or causing significant destruction or disaster.
- **Poignant**: Evoking a keen sense of sadness or regret; deeply emotional.

The Story of How Scientists Accidentally Discovered the Big Bang's Echo

In 1964, two scientists, Arno Penzias and Robert Wilson, were conducting experiments with a large radio antenna at Bell Labs when they stumbled upon a mysterious and persistent noise that seemed to emanate from all directions in the sky. Initially, they attributed the signal to interference from pigeon droppings or equipment malfunction. However, after eliminating all possible sources of error, the duo realized that the signal was a cosmic background radiation, a faint remnant of the Big Bang itself. This groundbreaking discovery provided the first tangible evidence for the Big Bang theory, which posits that the universe began as an infinitely dense point, expanding rapidly in a cataclysmic explosion. The "echo" of this primordial event, now known as the Cosmic Microwave Background (CMB), has since become one of the most significant pieces of evidence supporting our current understanding of the universe's origin.

Key Vocabulary:
- **Emanate**: To originate or flow from a source.
- **Malfunction**: A failure to function properly.
- **Primordial**: Relating to the earliest stages of the universe or existence.
- **Tangible**: Perceptible by touch or capable of being physically felt.
- **Cataclysmic**: Involving or causing a large-scale and

violent event or disaster.

The Weirdest Moon in the Solar System

One of the most peculiar moons in our solar system is Hyperion, a small, irregularly shaped satellite of Saturn. Hyperion's odd, sponge-like appearance has baffled astronomers for decades, with its surface covered in deep craters and ridges that give it the distinct resemblance to a walnut. This bizarre morphology is a result of the moon's low density and its highly porous structure, which allows it to absorb impacts from space debris without completely crumbling. Hyperion's erratic rotation, which causes it to tumble through space unpredictably, adds to its enigmatic character. Scientists theorize that Hyperion may have once been part of a larger body that broke apart in the distant past, explaining its peculiar form. Despite its small size and odd appearance, Hyperion remains a fascinating subject of study, offering clues about the early formation of moons and planetary bodies in our solar system.

Key Vocabulary:
- **Sponge-like**: Resembling a sponge in texture or appearance, often porous.
- **Baffled**: Perplexed or confused, often due to something unexpected or incomprehensible.
- **Morphology**: The study of the form and structure of organisms or objects.
- **Erratic**: Not even or regular in pattern or movement; unpredictable.
- **Enigmatic**: Mysterious and difficult to interpret or understand.

How a Piece of the Moon Ended Up on Earth

In a remarkable twist of fate, scientists discovered a small fragment of the Moon on Earth, not as a result of a lunar mission but through a natural process known as meteorite impact. The fragment, believed to have been ejected from the Moon during a catastrophic impact event, eventually traveled through space and landed on Earth as part of a meteorite. Upon analysis, researchers confirmed that the rock contained isotopic signatures identical to those found on the Moon, cementing its extraterrestrial origin. This discovery has provided valuable information about the Moon's geological history and the processes that shaped it. It also serves as a reminder that Earth and the Moon are not as distant as we might think, with the cosmic connection between the two celestial bodies evident in this fragment, which offers a rare and direct link to our lunar neighbor.

Key Vocabulary:
- **Fragment**: A small, broken piece of a larger whole.
- **Ejected**: Forced or thrown out, especially with force.
- **Catastrophic**: Involving or resulting in significant disaster or destruction.
- **Isotopic**: Relating to isotopes, atoms of the same element with different numbers of neutrons.
- **Celestial**: Relating to the sky or outer space, often referring to heavenly bodies.

The Search for a Second Earth and Why It's Harder Than You Think

For decades, scientists have been on an ambitious quest to find a second Earth, a planet that could potentially harbor life beyond our solar system. This search, fueled by the discovery of thousands of exoplanets, has led to the identification of several "Earth-like" planets located in the so-called "habitable zone," where conditions may be right for liquid water to exist. However, finding an exact replica of Earth is an immensely challenging task. Many of the factors that make Earth unique, such as its atmosphere, magnetic field, and the perfect combination of chemical elements, are difficult to replicate in other worlds. Furthermore, the vast distances between us and potential exoplanets complicate efforts to study these planets in detail. Despite these challenges, astronomers remain hopeful that the search for a second Earth will one day yield discoveries that could radically transform our understanding of the universe and our place in it.

Key Vocabulary:
- **Ambitious**: Having a strong desire to achieve something, often requiring significant effort.
- **Habitable**: Suitable for living or supporting life.
- **Replica**: An exact copy or reproduction of something.
- **Unique**: One of a kind; unlike anything else.
- **Radically**: In a way that is far-reaching or extreme in its nature or effect.

The Experiment That Simulated Life on Mars for a Whole Year

In a remarkable simulation that pushed the boundaries of human endurance, a team of scientists and astronauts participated in a year-long experiment designed to replicate life on Mars. Known as the Mars Society's Mars Desert Research Station (MDRS) mission, the experiment was conducted in the arid, isolated desert environment of Utah, mimicking the conditions astronauts would face on the Red Planet. The participants lived in a confined habitat with limited resources, wearing spacesuits whenever they ventured outside and conducting scientific research on how to grow food, produce water, and maintain health in a Martian-like environment. The study provided invaluable insights into the challenges of long-duration space missions, particularly the psychological effects of isolation, and helped shape the strategies needed for future Mars exploration missions.

Key Vocabulary:
- **Replicate**: To duplicate or reproduce under controlled conditions.

- **Endurance**: The ability to endure an unpleasant or difficult situation over a prolonged period.
- **Arid**: Dry, barren, or lacking in moisture.
- **Martian**: Pertaining to Mars, or characteristics of the planet.
- **Isolated**: Separated from others or from a larger community or group.

The Comet That Scientists Think Brought Life to Earth

One of the most extraordinary and provocative hypotheses in the realm of astrobiology suggests that life on Earth may have originated from a comet. This theory, known as panspermia, posits that the essential building blocks of life—such as amino acids and other organic molecules—were delivered to Earth by a comet, which impacted the planet billions of years ago. Scientists believe that comets, which formed in the cold, distant reaches of the solar system, could have carried these primordial elements from other parts of the cosmos, acting as cosmic messengers. The famous 1994 Shoemaker-Levy 9 comet impact on Jupiter provided key evidence supporting this idea, as it demonstrated the ability of comets to carry significant amounts of organic material. If true, this theory suggests that life may not be as rare as previously thought, with the potential for life to arise elsewhere in the universe through similar cosmic processes.

Key Vocabulary:
- **Panspermia**: The hypothesis that life exists throughout the universe and is spread by space dust, meteoroids, comets, or potentially by spacecraft.
- **Primordial**: Relating to the early or original stages of development.
- **Hypothesis**: A proposed explanation made on the basis of limited evidence, subject to further investigation.
- **Cosmic**: Relating to the universe or cosmos, especially in its vastness.

- **Organic**: Containing carbon-based compounds, typically in reference to living organisms or life-related chemistry.

The Discovery of a Planet That Is Hotter Than Most Stars

In a stunning revelation that defies conventional understanding of planetary systems, astronomers discovered a planet that is hotter than most stars. Known as KELT-9b, this exoplanet orbits its star in such a close proximity that its temperature reaches an astonishing 4,300 degrees Celsius, surpassing the surface temperature of many stars, including our own Sun. This extreme heat is due to the planet's exceedingly short orbital period of just 1.5 days, causing it to be bombarded with intense radiation from its host star. The planet's surface is thought to be molten, and its atmosphere is likely composed of evaporating metals. The discovery of KELT-9b challenges the traditional understanding of planet-star interactions, opening new avenues for research on the behavior of celestial bodies under extreme conditions.

Key Vocabulary:
- **Exoplanet**: A planet that orbits a star outside our solar system.
- **Orbital period**: The time it takes for a celestial body to complete one full orbit around another body.
- **Bombarded**: Subjected to a continuous attack or impact.
- **Molten**: Melted or liquefied due to high temperatures.
- **Celestial**: Relating to the sky or outer space, particularly in reference to heavenly bodies.

The Plan to Use Asteroids as Spaceships for Future Colonization

A visionary and increasingly plausible idea for humanity's future in space involves using asteroids as spaceships for interstellar colonization. This plan, known as asteroid mining and colonization, proposes the use of asteroids not only as a source of valuable resources but also as mobile habitats for long-term space travel. By hollowing out an asteroid and utilizing its raw materials, scientists envision creating self-sustaining habitats that could house humans for extended periods. The immense gravity of the asteroid would be used to simulate Earth's conditions, allowing for the cultivation of food and the recycling of water and air. Additionally, asteroids could serve as a base for exploring distant planets, acting as both ships and stations for scientific research. While this concept remains speculative, it represents a bold leap toward humanity's future as an interplanetary species.

Key Vocabulary:
- **Visionary**: Thinking about or planning the future with imagination or wisdom.
- **Interstellar**: Occurring or situated between stars.
- **Hollowing**: Creating a space or cavity inside something.
- **Self-sustaining**: Capable of maintaining itself without external help.
- **Speculative**: Involving or based on conjecture rather than knowledge or evidence.

How Scientists Found a 'Super-Earth' That Might Have Life

In a groundbreaking discovery that stirs excitement among astrobiologists, scientists have found a "super-Earth" exoplanet located in the habitable zone of its star, where conditions could potentially support life. This planet, known as Kepler-452b, is approximately 60% larger than Earth, with a similar surface temperature and a rocky composition that could allow for liquid water to exist on its surface. Found by NASA's Kepler Space Telescope, the exoplanet is in an orbit that mirrors Earth's, revolving around its sun at just the right distance for life-sustaining conditions. Despite its larger size, scientists believe Kepler-452b could host an environment much like our own, with a thick atmosphere potentially rich in oxygen and carbon dioxide—two essential ingredients for life as we know it. This discovery significantly raises the possibility of finding Earth-like planets beyond our solar system, potentially leading to the discovery of extraterrestrial life in the near future.

Key Vocabulary:
- **Exoplanet**: A planet that orbits a star outside our solar system.
- **Habitable zone**: The region around a star where conditions are right for liquid water to exist on a planet's surface.
- **Astrobiologists**: Scientists who study the possibility of life beyond Earth.
- **Composition**: The nature of something's ingredients or structure.
- **Extraterrestrial**: Relating to life or things that originate outside Earth.

The Time an Astronaut Had to Fix a Spacecraft Using Only a Toothbrush

In one of the most remarkable examples of ingenuity in space exploration, astronaut Chris Hadfield once faced an unexpected challenge aboard the International Space Station (ISS)—fixing a crucial component of a spacecraft with nothing more than a toothbrush. During a routine maintenance mission, a vital piece of equipment malfunctioned, threatening to derail important experiments and communications. With no spare parts available, Hadfield, drawing on his extensive training and resourcefulness, used the bristles of a toothbrush and other limited materials at his disposal to fashion a temporary solution that restored functionality to the system. This creative and resourceful act not only demonstrated Hadfield's incredible problem-solving skills but also underscored the adaptability required for survival in the harsh, confined environment of space.

His ability to think outside the box—and outside the realm of conventional tools—became a legendary story in space exploration history.

Key Vocabulary:
- **Ingenuity**: The quality of being clever, original, and inventive.
- **Malfunctioned**: To fail to function or operate correctly.
- **Resourcefulness**: The ability to find quick and clever ways to overcome difficulties.
- **Temporary**: Lasting for only a limited time; not permanent.
- **Adaptability**: The ability to adjust to new conditions.

The Cosmic 'Cold Spot' That Might Be Evidence of Another Universe

The discovery of the "cosmic cold spot" has baffled scientists, raising the intriguing possibility that it could be evidence of another universe colliding with our own. This cold spot, an area of space that is significantly cooler than the surrounding regions, was detected by the European Space Agency's Planck satellite, which mapped the cosmic microwave background radiation of the universe. Some researchers believe that the anomaly could be the remnant of a collision between our universe and another, causing a noticeable dip in temperature. This idea is part of the multiverse theory, which suggests that our universe is just one of many that coexist in a vast, possibly infinite cosmos. The cosmic cold spot remains one of the most enigmatic mysteries of modern cosmology, prompting further investigation into the nature of the universe itself and the possibility of other universes beyond our own.

Key Vocabulary:
- **Baffled**: Puzzled or confused, unable to understand or explain.
- **Anomaly**: Something that deviates from what is

standard, normal, or expected.
- **Remnant**: A small remaining part of something.
- **Multiverse**: The hypothetical existence of multiple universes.
- **Enigmatic**: Mysterious and difficult to understand.

SCIENCE

The Accidental Discovery of Penicillin That Changed Medicine

In 1928, Scottish bacteriologist Alexander Fleming returned to his cluttered lab after a vacation to find an anomalous phenomenon—one of his petri dishes, left exposed, was speckled with colonies of Staphylococcus bacteria, yet a strange, bluish-green mold had stymied their proliferation. This mold, later identified as Penicillium notatum, excreted a substance that eradicated the bacteria in its vicinity. Fleming, though intrigued, underestimated its practical utility. A decade later, a team of researchers at Oxford, notably Howard Florey and Ernst Boris Chain, refined the extraction process, leading to the mass production of what would become the world's first true antibiotic. During World War II, penicillin became a pharmaceutical linchpin, salvaging thousands of lives from bacterial infections once deemed fatal. The serendipitous nature of its discovery underscores the unpredictable frontiers of scientific innovation, where chance and curiosity intertwine to yield groundbreaking advancements.

Key Vocabulary:
- **Anomalous**: Deviating from what is standard, normal, or expected; atypical or irregular.
- **Stymied**: Prevented or hindered the progress of something; obstructed or thwarted.
- **Proliferation**: Rapid multiplication or increase, particularly in cells or organisms.

- **Pharmaceutical**: Relating to medicinal drugs and their preparation, use, or sale.
- **Serendipitous**: Occurring or discovered by chance in a happy or beneficial way.

How Scientists Revived a 30,000-Year-Old Virus

Deep beneath Siberia's permafrost, a team of virologists unearthed a relic from Earth's Pleistocene epoch—an ancient virus entombed in ice for over 30,000 years. Dubbed Pithovirus sibericum, this colossal virus, unlike modern pathogens, exhibited an intricate structure and a genome that rivaled some bacteria in complexity. Through meticulous decontamination procedures, the scientists reanimated the virus within a controlled laboratory setting, demonstrating that prehistoric microbial life could persist in dormancy for millennia. While Pithovirus posed no threat to humans, its resurrection ignited concerns about pathogenic resurgences as climate change accelerates permafrost thaw. The research provides a paradigm for understanding viral longevity and evolution, reinforcing the notion that extinction is not always an irrevocable fate but a mere interlude in an organism's biological continuum.

Key Vocabulary:
- **Permafrost**: A thick subsurface layer of soil that remains frozen throughout the year, typically found in polar regions.
- **Epoch**: A significant period in history or geology, marked by notable events or developments.
- **Entombed**: Buried or trapped within something, often implying long-term preservation.
- **Resurgence**: A revival or reappearance, particularly of something previously diminished or extinct.
- **Continuum**: A continuous sequence or progression in which adjacent elements are indistinguishable but the extremes are markedly different.

The Space Probe That Left Our Solar System with a Golden Record

Launched in 1977, the Voyager 1 probe embarked on an odyssey that would transcend the heliosphere and venture into the vast interstellar abyss. Beyond its primary mission of surveying Jupiter and Saturn, it carried an artifact of profound anthropological significance—The Golden Record, an auditory and visual compendium curated by Carl Sagan and his team. Encased in gold-plated copper, this phonographic time capsule bore a panoply of sounds, languages, and imagery emblematic of Earth's cultural and biological tapestry. As Voyager traversed the cosmic expanse, it became humanity's emissary, an unassuming envoy drifting toward the unknown. In 2012, Voyager 1 became the first human-made object to breach the heliopause, entering interstellar space—an example of the audacity of human curiosity and the insatiable yearning to communicate across the chasm of eternity.

Key Vocabulary:
- **Heliosphere**: The vast region of space dominated by the Sun's influence, extending well beyond Pluto's orbit.
- **Anthropological**: Relating to the study of human societies, cultures, and their development.
- **Compendium**: A concise yet comprehensive collection of information on a particular subject.
- **Panoply**: A complete or impressive collection of things, often used to describe cultural or historical elements.
- **Heliopause**: The boundary where the Sun's solar wind is halted by the interstellar medium, marking the edge of the solar system.

The Mysterious Deep-Sea Sounds That Scientists Can't Explain

In the abyssopelagic depths of Earth's oceans, enigmatic

acoustic anomalies have perplexed marine researchers for decades. Among them, the notorious "Bloop," a low-frequency underwater sound detected in 1997, emerged as an auditory enigma. Initially hypothesized to originate from an immense, unidentified marine organism, subsequent analysis suggested it was glacial in origin, stemming from icequakes. Similarly, the "Julia" and "Upsweep" signals continue to elude definitive explanation, shrouded in the liminality of scientific speculation. These cryptic acoustics hint at the ocean's uncharted vastness, reinforcing the notion that Earth's deepest trenches remain a frontier as mysterious as the cosmos. With advancements in hydroacoustic technology, scientists endeavor to decipher these marine mysteries, unveiling the sonorous lexicon of the abyss.

Key Vocabulary:
- **Abyssopelagic**: Relating to the deep-sea zone between 4,000 and 6,000 meters, devoid of sunlight and subject to immense pressure.
- **Anomaly**: A deviation from the norm; something unexpected or difficult to explain.
- **Liminality**: A state of being in-between or on the threshold of discovery, transition, or change.
- **Cryptic**: Mysterious or obscure, often implying something difficult to interpret or understand.
- **Hydroacoustic**: Pertaining to the study of sound in water, particularly in oceanography and marine biology.

How Astronauts Train in an Underwater Space Station

To simulate the effects of zero gravity and prepare for the complexities of space missions, astronauts train in an underwater space station. This facility, the Neutral Buoyancy Laboratory (NBL), located at NASA's Johnson Space Center, allows astronauts to practice complex maneuvers in a controlled, buoyant environment. The NBL contains full-scale replicas of space modules, where astronauts can perform tasks such as repairing satellites or assembling the International Space Station (ISS). The buoyancy of the water makes astronauts feel weightless, mimicking the conditions of outer space. Training in this submerged environment is vital, as it allows astronauts to gain firsthand experience with the difficulties of working in microgravity before they embark on real missions.

Key Vocabulary:
- **Simulate**: To imitate or reproduce the conditions or characteristics of something, often for training or experimentation.
- **Buoyant**: Able to float or rise in a liquid; describes the property that allows astronauts to experience weightlessness underwater.
- **Maneuver**: A planned and controlled movement or action, often requiring skill or precision.
- **Replica**: An exact copy or reproduction of something, often used for educational or training purposes.
- **Microgravity**: A condition of near-weightlessness experienced in space, where gravity's effects are greatly diminished.

How Scientists Discovered the Earth Has a Second 'Mini-Moon'

In 2020, astronomers made an extraordinary discovery: Earth has a second 'mini-moon' orbiting our planet. This newfound celestial body, named 2020 CD3, was a small asteroid that had been gravitationally captured by Earth's orbit. Unlike the Moon, which has been with Earth since its formation, this 'mini-moon' is an interloper, only temporarily bound by our planet's gravitational influence. Measuring only a few meters in diameter, 2020 CD3's brief stint in Earth's orbit fascinated scientists, who were eager to study its trajectory and composition. While its existence was fleeting, lasting only a few months before it escaped Earth's gravitational pull, the discovery provided valuable insights into the nature of near-Earth objects. Astrophysicists speculate that Earth might periodically capture these transient bodies, offering a unique window into the mechanics of cosmic interactions. This serendipitous find also raised questions about the frequency of such encounters and the potential for larger asteroids to temporarily orbit Earth, providing scientists with an intriguing avenue for future exploration in the study of planetary dynamics.

Key Vocabulary:
- **Interloper**: An entity that intrudes into a space or situation where it does not belong, often used to describe transient or temporary objects in space.
- **Trajectory**: The path or course followed by a moving object, often used in physics to describe the motion of celestial bodies.
- **Gravitationally captured**: The process by which a celestial body becomes bound to the gravitational field of a larger object, such as a planet or moon.
- **Astrophysicists**: Scientists who study the physical properties of celestial bodies and the universe as a whole, focusing on phenomena like gravity, light, and energy.
- **Transient**: Temporary or short-lived, often used to describe objects or phenomena that exist for only a brief period.

The Secret of the Longest-Living Cells in the Human Body

Among the myriad cells that make up the human body, certain types are known for their extraordinary longevity. One of the most remarkable examples is the human neurons, which can live for decades, and in some cases, a lifetime. The secret to their longevity lies in the way they are designed to resist wear and tear, relying on a highly specialized process known as autophagy. This cellular mechanism involves the breakdown and recycling of damaged or dysfunctional cellular components, allowing the neurons to maintain their structural integrity over time. Unlike most cells, which have a limited lifespan before undergoing programmed cell death, neurons are capable of withstanding damage, even in the face of oxidative stress or environmental toxins. This resilience enables them to perform vital functions in the brain for an entire lifetime. The understanding of how these cells avoid premature aging offers profound implications for neurological research, potentially providing insights into aging and neurodegenerative diseases such as Alzheimer's, and even informing strategies for promoting the longevity of other cell types.

Key Vocabulary:
- **Autophagy**: A cellular process where cells break down and recycle damaged or dysfunctional components to maintain overall health and function.
- **Oxidative stress**: A condition in which there is an imbalance between free radicals and antioxidants in the body, often leading to cellular damage.
- **Resilience**: The capacity of a system, organism, or material to recover quickly from difficulties or damage.
- **Neurodegenerative diseases**: Disorders characterized by the progressive degeneration of nerve cells, including conditions like Alzheimer's and Parkinson's disease.
- **Oxidative**: Related to the process of oxidation, which can cause damage to cells through the accumulation of free radicals.

How a Woman's Cells Became the Most Important in Medical Research

In the 1950s, Henrietta Lacks, an African-American woman, unknowingly contributed to one of the most pivotal advancements in medical science. During her treatment for cervical cancer, doctors collected cells from her tumor without her consent. These cells, known as HeLa cells, became the first immortal human cell line, capable of replicating indefinitely in culture. The HeLa cell line revolutionized medical research, providing a consistent and abundant source of human cells for experimentation. Researchers used HeLa cells to study viruses, cancer, and the effects of various drugs, leading to significant breakthroughs in medicine, including the development of the polio vaccine. Despite the enormous contributions her cells made to science, Henrietta Lacks's family was never informed or compensated for the use of her cells. The case raised profound ethical questions regarding informed consent, ownership, and the commercialization of biological materials. Henrietta Lacks's legacy continues to shape medical ethics today, as researchers strive to balance scientific progress with respect for individual rights.

Key Vocabulary:
- **Immortal**: Describing a cell or organism that is capable of living indefinitely, typically through continuous division or regeneration.
- **HeLa cells**: A line of human cells derived from Henrietta Lacks's tumor, used extensively in biomedical research for their ability to replicate indefinitely.
- **Replicating**: The process of duplicating or reproducing something, often used in a biological context to describe cell division.
- **Informed consent**: The ethical requirement that individuals be fully aware of and agree to the procedures or risks involved in research or medical treatment.
- **Commercialization**: The process of turning something into a product or service for sale or profit, often raising ethical concerns about exploitation.

The Mystery of Dark Matter and

Why It's Still Unexplained

Dark matter remains one of the most enigmatic and elusive phenomena in the cosmos. Though it cannot be directly observed, scientists have inferred its existence through its gravitational effects on visible matter, such as galaxies and clusters of galaxies. Comprising approximately 85% of the total mass of the universe, dark matter does not emit, absorb, or reflect light, making it invisible to traditional instruments. This mysterious substance interacts with regular matter through gravity, but not through electromagnetic forces, which is why it is so difficult to detect. Various theories abound regarding its composition, with some suggesting it could be made up of unknown particles, while others propose the existence of primordial black holes. Despite numerous experiments and observations, dark matter's true nature remains elusive, making it a central focus of modern astrophysical research. As scientists delve deeper into the universe's fundamental workings, understanding dark matter is key to unlocking the mysteries of the cosmos and expanding our knowledge of physics.

Key Vocabulary:
- **Enigmatic**: Mysterious or puzzling, often used to describe phenomena that are difficult to understand or explain.
- **Gravitational effects**: The influence exerted by a massive object on other objects, causing them to move or behave in a certain way due to gravity.
- **Electromagnetic forces**: The forces that act between charged particles, responsible for phenomena like electricity and magnetism.
- **Primordial**: Relating to the earliest stages of the universe or the formation of matter, often used to describe objects or forces that existed from the beginning.
- **Astrophysical**: Pertaining to the branch of astronomy that deals with the physical properties and behaviors of

celestial bodies and the universe as a whole.

The Discovery of Water on the Moon and What It Means for Space Travel

In 2009, NASA's discovery of water molecules on the Moon's surface revolutionized our understanding of lunar geology and opened up new possibilities for space exploration. The water, found in permanently shadowed craters near the Moon's poles, is thought to have been deposited by comets or formed from chemical reactions with the solar wind. This discovery is significant because it suggests that the Moon could serve as a vital resource for future lunar bases and deep space missions. The presence of water could be used for drinking, creating oxygen, and even producing rocket fuel through the process of electrolysis. Scientists are now investigating the feasibility of extracting and utilizing this lunar water for human habitation and interplanetary travel. The discovery also holds the potential to reshape our understanding of the Moon's history and its role in the solar system's evolution. As space agencies plan for long-term missions to the Moon and beyond, the discovery of water is a critical component in making these ambitious goals a reality.

Key Vocabulary:
- **Electrolysis**: A process that uses electrical current to split water into hydrogen and oxygen, potentially useful for producing fuel in space.
- **Lunar bases**: Habitats or research stations built on the Moon, typically envisioned for future human exploration and colonization.
- **Permanently shadowed craters**: Regions on the Moon's surface that are never exposed to sunlight, often harboring volatile substances like water.
- **Comets**: Icy celestial bodies that orbit the Sun and are believed to have contributed water to the Moon's surface.
- **Interplanetary travel**: The act of traveling between

planets within our solar system, often involving long-duration space missions.

The Science Behind the Northern Lights

The Northern Lights, also known as the Aurora Borealis, are one of nature's most awe-inspiring phenomena. These vibrant displays of light are caused by the interaction between the Earth's magnetosphere and charged particles from the Sun. When these particles collide with atoms and molecules in the Earth's atmosphere, they release photons, creating the stunning colors that light up the night sky. The most common colors—green, red, and purple—are the result of different types of gas molecules being excited by the solar particles. The Northern Lights occur near the polar regions, where the Earth's magnetic field is strongest, guiding the solar particles toward the poles. These ethereal lights have fascinated humans for centuries, inspiring both myth and scientific inquiry. The phenomenon is not only a visual spectacle but also provides valuable insights into space weather and the dynamics of the Earth's atmosphere. Understanding the Northern Lights has helped scientists learn more about the interactions between the Earth's magnetic field and solar winds, advancing the study of atmospheric physics.

Key Vocabulary:
- **Magnetosphere**: The region around Earth dominated by its magnetic field, which protects the planet from harmful solar radiation.
- **Charged particles**: Particles with an electric charge, such as electrons and protons, often emitted by the Sun and responsible for creating auroras.
- **Photons**: Particles of light or electromagnetic radiation, which are emitted when excited atoms or molecules return to their ground state.
- **Ethereal**: Extremely delicate and light, often used to describe something that is otherworldly or heavenly, like

the Northern Lights.
- **Space weather**: The environmental conditions in space, including solar winds and cosmic radiation, that can affect Earth's atmosphere and technological systems.

How a Small Lab Accident Led to the Creation of Velcro

Velcro, a ubiquitous fastener found in everything from shoes to space suits, was born out of a fortuitous lab accident in the 1940s. Swiss engineer George de Mestral was inspired by the burrs that clung to his dog's fur after a hike in the Alps. Upon examining the burrs under a microscope, he discovered their intricate hook-and-loop structure, which allowed them to attach to fabric and fur. This observation led de Mestral to experiment with a similar design, ultimately creating the fabric fastener we now know as Velcro. The name Velcro is derived from the French words "velours" (velvet) and "crochet" (hook), reflecting the material's soft, fuzzy texture and the hook-like fasteners that connect it. What started as a simple idea quickly evolved into a revolutionary technology that transformed industries ranging from fashion to aerospace. The success of Velcro lies in its simplicity, versatility, and durability, which have made it indispensable in countless applications. The invention of Velcro is a prime example of how a moment of curiosity and a simple accident can lead to groundbreaking innovations.

Key Vocabulary:
- **Fortuitous**: Happening by chance or accident, often in a fortunate or beneficial way.
- **Burrs**: Seed pods or fruits with hooks that attach to clothing or animals, often used as a natural fastener.
- **Intricate**: Complex and detailed, often used to describe designs or structures with many interconnected parts.
- **Versatility**: The ability to adapt or be used in a variety of different ways, particularly important in products with broad applications.

- **Indispensable**: Something that is so necessary or essential that it cannot be done without, often used to describe vital tools or technologies.

Why Some Scientists Want to Bring Back the Woolly Mammoth

In recent years, a controversial yet captivating idea has emerged: the resurrection of the woolly mammoth. These massive creatures, once roaming the icy tundras of the Earth, went extinct around 10,000 years ago, likely due to climate change and human hunting. However, advancements in genetic engineering and cloning technologies have led some scientists to believe that reviving the woolly mammoth could help combat the impacts of global warming. The concept, known as de-extinction, involves using preserved mammoth DNA to create an animal that closely resembles the woolly mammoth, which could potentially be reintroduced into the Arctic ecosystem. Proponents argue that the mammoth's presence could help preserve permafrost by preventing the spread of greenhouse gases like methane, which are trapped in the frozen soil. Critics, however, argue that this ambitious plan could disrupt ecosystems and that efforts should focus on preserving existing endangered species instead. Regardless, the idea of resurrecting an extinct species challenges our understanding of biology and ethics, raising profound questions about the limits of science and humanity's role in shaping the future of life on Earth.

Key Vocabulary:
- **De-extinction**: The process of bringing back extinct species through scientific methods, such as cloning or genetic engineering.
- **Genetic engineering**: The manipulation of an organism's DNA to achieve desired traits, often used in the context of creating genetically modified organisms.
- **Permafrost**: Ground that remains frozen year-round,

typically found in polar regions and containing vast amounts of organic material.
- **Greenhouse gases**: Gases that trap heat in the Earth's atmosphere, contributing to global warming, including methane and carbon dioxide.
- **Ecosystem disruption**: A disturbance or imbalance in the natural environment that affects species, food chains, and habitats.

The Space Junk Problem

As humanity continues to expand its presence in space, a growing concern has emerged: space junk. This debris, which consists of defunct satellites, spent rocket stages, and other fragments from previous space missions, is rapidly accumulating in low Earth orbit. The problem is twofold: not only does space junk pose a significant risk to functioning satellites and space stations, but it also creates a dangerous environment for future space exploration. At speeds of up to 17,500 miles per hour, even small pieces of debris can cause catastrophic damage to spacecraft. Scientists and engineers are working tirelessly to develop innovative solutions to remove or recycle this growing mass of space debris. One approach involves sending robotic spacecraft to capture and deorbit defunct satellites, while others are exploring the possibility of using lasers or nets to safely remove debris. Additionally, new international policies and guidelines are being implemented to reduce the amount of space junk generated by future missions. Solving the space junk problem is critical not only for the safety of current and future space endeavors but also for the sustainability of space exploration in the long term.

Key Vocabulary:
- **Space junk**: Debris and waste materials left behind in Earth's orbit, including broken satellites and discarded

rocket parts.
- **Defunct**: No longer functional or operating; often used to describe outdated or non-working objects or systems.
- **Deorbit**: The process of bringing a satellite or space object back into Earth's atmosphere to burn up or safely crash into the planet.
- **Robotic spacecraft**: Unmanned space vehicles designed to carry out missions using remote control or pre-programmed instructions.
- **Sustainability**: The ability to maintain or continue certain practices or systems over the long term, often used in environmental and resource management contexts.

The Deepest Hole Ever Dug by Humans and What Was Found Inside

The deepest hole ever dug by humans, known as the Kola Superdeep Borehole, reaches an astounding depth of over 7.5 miles into the Earth's crust. Located in Russia, this scientific drilling project began in 1970 with the goal of exploring the Earth's interior. Over several decades, scientists encountered unexpected challenges, including extreme temperatures that reached over 350°F (175°C) and pressures that threatened to damage the drilling equipment. Despite these difficulties, the borehole provided invaluable insights into the composition of the Earth's crust. Scientists discovered that the crust was far more complex than originally thought, with layers of rock that had previously been undetected. They also found microscopic fossils deep within the rock, offering clues about the history of life on Earth. Although the borehole was eventually abandoned in 1994, the Kola Superdeep Borehole remains a reminder of human perseverance and curiosity. It serves as a reminder of the many mysteries that lie beneath our feet, waiting to be uncovered by future generations of scientists.

Key Vocabulary:

- **Borehole**: A narrow, deep hole drilled into the Earth for scientific exploration, often used to study the geology and composition of the planet's interior.
- **Crust**: The outermost layer of the Earth, composed of solid rock and forming the Earth's surface.
- **Perseverance**: Steadfastness in achieving a goal despite difficulties or challenges, often essential in scientific endeavors.
- **Microscopic fossils**: Tiny remnants of ancient organisms, preserved in rock, often used to study the history of life on Earth.
- **Undetected**: Not discovered or noticed, often referring to things that are hidden or difficult to identify.

The Math Problem That Took Over 350 Years to Solve

A monumental breakthrough in mathematics occurred in 1993, when Andrew Wiles, a British mathematician, solved one of the most elusive problems in history: Fermat's Last Theorem. This theorem, first proposed by the 17th-century French mathematician Pierre de Fermat, states that no three positive integers can satisfy the equation $a^n + b^n = c^n$ for any integer value of n greater than 2. Fermat famously claimed to have a proof, but it was never found, and the problem remained unsolved for over three centuries. Wiles, in a feat of intellectual rigor, eventually proved the theorem using modern mathematical concepts such as elliptic curves and modular forms. His solution, which relied on deep connections between different areas of mathematics, was groundbreaking not only for its resolution of a long-standing puzzle but also for the profound impact it had on subsequent mathematical research. Wiles' triumph solidified his place in history, and his solution to Fermat's Last Theorem remains one of the most celebrated achievements in mathematics, embodying the power of human perseverance and intellectual innovation.

Key Vocabulary:
- **Fermat's Last Theorem**: A statement in number theory that no three positive integers can satisfy the equation $a^n + b^n = c^n$ for n greater than 2.
- **Elliptic curves**: A type of curve defined by a specific mathematical equation, used in advanced number theory and cryptography.
- **Modular forms**: Functions in mathematics that are central to the study of elliptic curves and number theory.
- **Intellectual rigor**: A methodical and thorough approach to solving problems, requiring precise reasoning and deep understanding.
- **Mathematical research**: The systematic investigation and discovery of new mathematical concepts and theorems.

The Supercomputer That Can Simulate the Entire Universe

A groundbreaking supercomputer, known as "CosmoSim," is pushing the boundaries of computational science by simulating the entire universe. Developed by a coalition of international scientists, this supercomputer harnesses unprecedented computational power to create detailed models of cosmic phenomena. By simulating the formation of galaxies, the behavior of black holes, and the dynamics of dark matter, CosmoSim offers insights into the fundamental workings of the universe. The machine operates using millions of processors working in parallel, capable of performing quadrillions of calculations per second. What sets CosmoSim apart is its ability to simulate not just the physical components of the universe but also its underlying forces, such as gravity and quantum mechanics, with astonishing accuracy. The simulations are so complex that they require constant updates to the models as new scientific discoveries are made. CosmoSim is not only a powerful tool for astrophysicists but also for researchers in fields ranging from materials science to climate change, offering a new way to study complex systems in ways previously unimaginable.

Key Vocabulary:
- **Computational power**: The capacity of a computer to perform complex calculations and process vast amounts of data quickly.
- **Simulate**: To model or replicate the behavior of a system or phenomenon, often used in scientific experiments or computer simulations.
- **Astrophysicists**: Scientists who study the physical properties and interactions of celestial bodies and the universe as a whole.
- **Quantum mechanics**: A fundamental theory in physics that describes the behavior of matter and energy at very small scales, such as atoms and subatomic particles.
- **Materials science**: The study of the properties and applications of materials, often with a focus on how they can be used in technology and industry.

Why a NASA Scientist Put a Rover in the Sahara Desert

In 2021, NASA scientist Dr. John McIntyre orchestrated an extraordinary mission: placing a rover in the Sahara Desert. At first glance, this might seem like an odd choice for a test site, especially when considering NASA's rover missions typically focus on exploring alien terrain. However, the harsh and unforgiving environment of the Sahara provides an ideal analog for the surface of Mars. The rover was tasked with navigating the challenging sand dunes, extreme temperatures, and other obstacles that mimic the conditions of Mars. By studying how the rover performs in such an inhospitable landscape, scientists can better prepare for future missions to the Red Planet. The test also provided valuable data on how rover technology can be adapted for extraterrestrial exploration. The Sahara Desert's desolate beauty and its striking resemblance to Martian terrain make it an invaluable training ground for future space expeditions, offering insights into both the limitations of current technology and the potential for future advancements in space exploration.

Key Vocabulary:
- **Analog**: A method or system used as a comparison or model for another, often used in science to simulate conditions on other planets.
- **Inhospitable**: Unwelcoming or harsh, typically referring to environments that are difficult or impossible for human habitation.
- **Extraterrestrial**: Originating or located outside of the Earth's atmosphere; commonly used to refer to alien life or objects.
- **Desolate**: Barren, empty, or uninhabited, often used to describe landscapes that are stark and isolated.
- **Expeditions**: Organized journeys or missions, often with a specific goal, such as exploration or research.

How Scientists Taught an Octopus to Play Video Games

In a groundbreaking experiment, researchers at the University of Oxford taught an octopus named "Clyde" to play a video game. The game, designed specifically for the experiment, involved navigating a joystick to interact with a computer screen. Remarkably, Clyde quickly mastered the controls, demonstrating exceptional cognitive abilities and fine motor skills. Octopuses are known for their intelligence and problem-solving capabilities, but this experiment took their skills to a new level. Researchers hypothesized that the octopus's extraordinary ability to manipulate objects with its tentacles could translate to human-like interactions with technology. Over time, Clyde learned to associate specific visual cues with rewards, much like the learning process in other animals. This experiment not only revealed the octopus's impressive capacity for learning but also shed light on the potential for cross-species interaction with technology. By studying how octopuses process and respond to tasks, scientists hope to gain deeper insights into the evolution of intelligence and how non-human species perceive and interact with their environments.

Key Vocabulary:
- **Octopus**: A marine animal known for its intelligence, eight arms, and remarkable ability to solve complex problems.
- **Cognitive abilities**: The mental processes related to understanding, learning, memory, and decision-making.
- **Fine motor skills**: The ability to make precise movements, often involving the use of small muscles in the hands and fingers.
- **Hypothesized**: Formulated an idea or theory based on available evidence, often used as a starting point for scientific research.
- **Cross-species interaction**: Communication or interaction between different species, often involving the exchange of behaviors, information, or technology.

The Science of Why Some People Never Get Mosquito Bites

While mosquitoes seem to feast on some people while leaving others untouched, scientists have uncovered the biological reasons behind this phenomenon. Research has shown that mosquitoes are drawn to specific scents produced by the human body, including carbon dioxide, lactic acid, and body odor. People who produce higher levels of these compounds are more attractive to mosquitoes. However, some individuals naturally exude fewer of these chemicals, making them less appealing to the pests. Additionally, factors such as genetics, skin bacteria, and even the color of clothing can influence mosquito attraction. Certain genetic markers are linked to less appealing body chemistry for mosquitoes, which may explain why some individuals rarely suffer bites. Furthermore, the composition of bacteria on an individual's skin can alter the odors emitted, affecting mosquito attraction. While there is still much to learn, this research could one day lead to new strategies for mosquito repellents or even ways to manipulate human body chemistry to prevent bites altogether, potentially reducing the spread of diseases like malaria and dengue fever.

Key Vocabulary:
- **Lactic acid**: A compound produced in muscles during physical exertion or stress, contributing to the body's scent.
- **Skin bacteria**: Microorganisms that naturally live on the skin and can influence how we smell and how mosquitoes are attracted to us.
- **Genetic markers**: Specific genes or genetic traits that are associated with certain physical characteristics or conditions.
- **Exude**: To release or give off a substance, often used to describe how the body emits chemicals, odors, or moisture.
- **Repellents**: Substances used to ward off or deter insects or pests, often by masking scents that attract them.

How Scientists Plan to Mine Asteroids for Gold and Rare Metals

In the near future, asteroid mining could become a reality, as scientists and engineers work towards extracting precious metals from asteroids in space. The idea is rooted in the fact that many asteroids contain significant quantities of rare and valuable materials such as gold, platinum, and other metals that are in high demand on Earth. These materials could be used in industries such as electronics, energy, and manufacturing. Companies like Planetary Resources and Deep Space Industries are developing technologies to mine asteroids, including spacecraft that can land on these celestial bodies, extract materials, and return them to Earth. The potential to tap into space's treasure troves is immense, offering a solution to resource scarcity on Earth. However, the challenges are substantial, including the development of technology capable of safely and efficiently extracting materials from asteroids, as well as the enormous cost of such missions. Despite these hurdles, asteroid mining is a promising frontier that could reshape the future of space exploration and resource management.

Key Vocabulary:
- **Asteroids**: Small rocky bodies that orbit the Sun, often containing valuable metals and minerals.
- **Platinum**: A rare, valuable metal used in a variety of industrial applications, including electronics and catalysts.
- **Celestial bodies**: Natural objects in space, such as planets, stars, asteroids, and moons.
- **Frontier**: An unexplored or new area of study, technology, or activity, often with the potential for significant advancement.
- **Resource scarcity**: The lack of sufficient resources to meet demand, often leading to efforts to find alternative sources.

The Unexpected Discovery of a New Element on the Periodic Table

In 2016, scientists made an extraordinary discovery in the world of chemistry—a new element, named tennessine, was added to the periodic table. This element, with the atomic number 117, was the result of a collaborative effort between American, Russian, and Japanese scientists. Tennessine was created artificially by bombarding a target of berkelium with calcium ions, resulting in the formation of a highly unstable atom that decayed almost immediately. Despite its fleeting existence, tennessine's discovery was a major milestone in the field of chemistry, as it expanded the known elements on the periodic table to 118. The element is part of a family known as the halogens, which includes chlorine, iodine, and fluorine. However, due to its instability, very little is known about its properties or potential uses. Researchers continue to study the element in hopes of unlocking its secrets, which could one day lead to the development of new materials or technologies. The discovery of tennessine highlights the ever-expanding nature of scientific knowledge and the quest for understanding the building blocks of matter.

Key Vocabulary:
- **Atomic number**: The number of protons in the nucleus of an atom, determining the element's identity on the periodic table.
- **Berkelium**: A synthetic, radioactive element used as a target material for creating heavier elements.
- **Fleeting**: Lasting for a very short period of time, often used to describe something that is transient or ephemeral.
- **Halogens**: A group of elements in the periodic table that includes chlorine, bromine, iodine, and others, known for their chemical reactivity.
- **Unlocking secrets**: Discovering hidden or unknown information that may lead to further understanding or breakthrough innovations.

How Scientists Are Trying to Create a Star on Earth with Nuclear Fusion

The dream of harnessing the power of the stars on Earth has driven scientists for decades, with nuclear fusion being the key to unlocking an infinite and clean energy source. Fusion, the process that powers the sun, occurs when two light atomic nuclei combine to form a heavier nucleus, releasing enormous amounts of energy. Recreating this process on Earth is no simple feat, as it requires extreme temperatures and pressures to overcome the natural repulsion between the positively charged atomic nuclei. In recent years, projects like the ITER (International Thermonuclear Experimental Reactor) have made significant strides in creating the conditions necessary for fusion to occur. The goal is to achieve "net positive energy," where the energy output from the fusion process exceeds the energy input required to initiate it. While challenges remain, including the need for better containment methods and materials that can withstand the intense heat and radiation, the success of nuclear fusion could revolutionize energy production, providing a limitless and environmentally friendly alternative to fossil fuels.

Key Vocabulary:
- **Nuclear fusion**: A nuclear reaction in which two light atomic nuclei combine to form a heavier nucleus, releasing energy.
- **Extreme temperatures and pressures**: Conditions involving very high heat and force, necessary for initiating fusion reactions.
- **Repulsion**: The force that pushes two objects or particles away from each other, often used in reference to atomic interactions.
- **Net positive energy**: A situation where the output of energy from a process exceeds the energy required to start it.
- **Revolutionize**: To dramatically change or transform something, often referring to a groundbreaking shift in technology or methodology.

The Secret of How Birds Navigate Thousands of Miles Without Getting Lost

Birds possess an extraordinary ability to navigate vast distances during migration, often traveling thousands of miles without getting lost. While the mechanisms behind this remarkable feat are still not fully understood, scientists have discovered that birds use a combination of environmental cues, such as the position of the sun, stars, and the Earth's magnetic field, to guide their journey. One of the most fascinating aspects of bird navigation is their ability to detect the Earth's magnetic field through specialized proteins in their eyes. These proteins are sensitive to magnetic fields, allowing birds to sense their position relative to the planet's poles. Additionally, many bird species rely on visual landmarks, such as mountains or coastlines, to further refine their navigation. New research also suggests that birds may use their sense of smell to detect pheromones released by plants and other birds, which can serve as an additional guide. While scientists continue to investigate the full extent of birds' navigational abilities, their remarkable journey remains one of nature's greatest mysteries.

Key Vocabulary:
- **Migrating**: Moving from one region or habitat to another, often over long distances, as part of a seasonal cycle.
- **Environmental cues**: Signals or stimuli from the surrounding environment that animals use to navigate or make decisions.
- **Specialized proteins**: Proteins that have a specific function or role, often adapted to detect or interact with certain stimuli.
- **Pheromones**: Chemical signals produced by animals or plants that can influence the behavior of others of the same species.
- **Refine**: To improve or perfect something through small adjustments or changes.

Whether a Human Can Survive in Space Without a Spacesuit

The concept of a human surviving in the vacuum of space

without a spacesuit is not as simple as it might seem. While the idea is often depicted in movies, the reality is far more complex. Space is a hostile environment, and without the protection of a spacesuit, the human body would face multiple catastrophic challenges. First, the absence of air pressure would cause the body's fluids to begin boiling at normal body temperature, leading to severe tissue damage. Without a pressurized environment, the lack of oxygen would render a person unconscious in just 15 seconds. Furthermore, exposure to the vacuum of space would cause the body to rapidly lose heat, leading to hypothermia, and the lack of a breathable atmosphere would lead to suffocation. Despite these grave dangers, there is some truth to the idea that a person might survive for a short period. A brief exposure to space might not instantly kill someone, but the consequences would be dire without the advanced life support systems provided by a spacesuit. Therefore, while survival is technically possible for a fleeting moment, the outcome would be fatal soon after.

Key Vocabulary:
- **Vacuum of space**: The near-perfect emptiness of outer space, where there is no atmosphere or air pressure.
- **Catastrophic**: Causing great damage or destruction.
- **Hypothermia**: A dangerous drop in body temperature caused by prolonged exposure to cold environments.
- **Life support systems**: Systems designed to provide essential needs such as oxygen and pressure in space.
- **Fleeting moment**: A brief, transitory period of time.

The Giant Telescope That Could Help Us See Other Universes

In the quest to explore the farthest reaches of the universe and possibly glimpse other universes, astronomers are building an enormous telescope that promises to revolutionize our understanding of the cosmos. The Extremely Large Telescope (ELT), under construction in Chile, will be the largest optical telescope ever built, with a mirror nearly 130 feet (40 meters) in diameter. This colossal instrument will allow scientists to peer deep into space and examine distant stars, galaxies, and even the formation of planets in unprecedented detail. By capturing light from celestial objects that are billions of light-years away, the ELT will provide data that could offer insights into the origins of the universe itself. Furthermore, the telescope may help answer profound questions about the existence of other universes or parallel dimensions, as it will be powerful enough to detect faint, far-off phenomena that could hint at their presence. While the ELT's capabilities are still in the development stages, its potential to reveal secrets about the cosmos could mark a new era in astronomical exploration.

Key Vocabulary:
- **Revolutionize**: To make a dramatic change in a particular field or area of knowledge.
- **Celestial objects**: Bodies in space, including stars, planets, and galaxies.
- **Unprecedented**: Never seen or done before; exceptional.
- **Light-years**: A unit of astronomical distance representing the distance that light travels in one year.
- **Parallel dimensions**: Hypothetical universes existing alongside our own, potentially governed by different physical laws.

How an Old Experiment Led to the Discovery of Quantum Entanglement

Quantum entanglement, one of the most perplexing phenomena in quantum mechanics, emerged from an old experiment that revolutionized our understanding of the subatomic world. In 1935, Albert Einstein, Boris Podolsky, and Nathan Rosen published a paper that introduced the "EPR paradox," which suggested that quantum mechanics was incomplete. This paradox proposed that two particles could be entangled, meaning their properties would be instantly correlated, regardless of the distance between them. For decades, this idea remained theoretical, with Einstein famously dismissing it as "spooky action at a distance." However, in the 1960s, physicist John Bell formulated what became known as Bell's Theorem, which provided a way to test quantum entanglement experimentally. Subsequent experiments, most notably those by Alain Aspect in 1982, confirmed the reality of entanglement, revealing that particles could indeed influence each other instantaneously, defying classical notions of causality and locality. Today, quantum entanglement forms the basis for emerging technologies like quantum computing and quantum cryptography, which promise to revolutionize industries by harnessing the strange properties of subatomic particles.

Key Vocabulary:
- **Perplexing**: Causing confusion or difficulty in understanding.
- **Subatomic**: Pertaining to particles smaller than atoms, such as electrons and quarks.
- **Correlation**: A mutual relationship or connection between two or more things.
- **Spooky action at a distance**: Einstein's phrase for quantum entanglement, highlighting its counterintuitive nature.
- **Quantum cryptography**: The use of quantum mechanics to create secure communication channels.

The Science Behind Why Some People Remember Their Dreams Better

Have you ever wondered why some people seem to remember their dreams with clarity while others wake up with little more than a vague recollection of images or emotions? The answer lies in the intricacies of the brain's memory systems, particularly during the rapid eye movement (REM) stage of sleep, when most vivid dreams occur. Studies suggest that individuals who remember their dreams more effectively may have more active or developed areas of their brain associated with memory, such as the hippocampus, which plays a crucial role in storing and retrieving memories. Furthermore, these individuals may experience more frequent and intense REM cycles, allowing for more opportunities to recall dream content. Psychological factors also come into play—people who are more introspective or have an active imagination tend to engage with their dreams more deeply, increasing the likelihood of retaining them. Additionally, external factors such as stress, sleep quality, and even diet can influence dream recall. For some, simply keeping a dream journal by their bedside can enhance their ability to remember dreams, by reinforcing the brain's connection to the dream state and boosting recall over time.

Key Vocabulary:
- **Intricacies**: The complex details or components of something.
- **Hippocampus**: A region of the brain involved in the formation and retrieval of memories.
- **Introspective**: The act of self-reflection or examination of one's thoughts and emotions.
- **Imagination**: The ability to form mental images or concepts of things not present to the senses.
- **Reinforcing**: Strengthening or supporting a behavior or action.

The Experiment That Created the Hottest Temperature on Earth

In an ambitious experiment designed to simulate conditions similar to those of the sun, scientists have created the hottest temperature ever recorded on Earth. The record-breaking heat was achieved in a lab by recreating the extreme conditions of nuclear fusion, a process that powers stars like our sun. To do this, researchers used a device known as a tokamak, a type of fusion reactor that contains a magnetic field strong enough to heat hydrogen plasma to temperatures exceeding 150 million degrees Celsius—more than 10 times hotter than the core of the sun. At such extreme temperatures, atoms are stripped of their electrons, forming a superheated plasma that can potentially provide an unlimited source of clean energy. While the experiment's goal is to understand fusion better and achieve controlled nuclear fusion for energy production, it also provides critical insights into the fundamental processes that govern the universe. This groundbreaking achievement marks a milestone in the quest to unlock the secrets of nuclear fusion and harness its immense power for human use.

Key Vocabulary:
- **Simulate**: To imitate or replicate the conditions of something.
- **Tokamak**: A device used to confine hot plasma with a magnetic field in nuclear fusion experiments.
- **Plasma**: A state of matter where electrons are stripped from atoms, creating a mix of positively charged ions and free electrons.
- **Groundbreaking**: Innovative or pioneering; marking the start of a new era.
- **Fundamental processes**: The essential natural laws or phenomena that underpin the workings of the universe.

The Truth About Whether We Really Only Use 10% of Our Brains

The claim that humans only use 10% of their brains is one of the most pervasive myths in popular culture. In reality, neuroimaging studies have shown that nearly every part of the brain has some known function, and we use all of it. The myth likely originated from early brain research that focused on the idea that only a small fraction of the brain is involved in conscious thought or physical movement, leading to the misunderstanding that the rest was dormant. However, brain activity occurs in many areas for a variety of purposes, such as regulating bodily functions, processing emotions, and storing memories. Even during sleep, the brain is active, consolidating memories and performing essential maintenance tasks. Furthermore, new research into neuroplasticity has revealed that the brain is highly adaptable, capable of reorganizing itself in response to learning or injury. So, rather than being an untapped reservoir of unused potential, the brain is fully engaged in various activities that contribute to our cognitive and physical well-being.

Key Vocabulary:
- **Neuroimaging**: The use of advanced imaging techniques to observe brain activity and structure.
- **Neuroplasticity**: The brain's ability to reorganize and adapt by forming new neural connections.
- **Pervasive**: Widespread or prevalent, often in a way that's hard to avoid.
- **Consolidating**: The process of strengthening or reinforcing memories or information.
- **Untapped reservoir**: An unused or underutilized source of potential.

FOOD

Why Pineapples Were Once a Luxury Item

Once a symbol of opulence and affluence, the pineapple was a coveted commodity in 17th- and 18th-century Europe, an exotic delicacy that only the aristocracy could afford. Indigenous to South America, the fruit was arduously transported across the ocean, often perishing before reaching its destination. This rarity made it a conspicuous status symbol, with nobles going to extravagant lengths to acquire one. Some would even rent pineapples merely for display at lavish feasts, never daring to eat the costly treasure. Greenhouses, or pineries, were later constructed by the wealthiest elite to cultivate these golden fruits, though the painstaking effort and exorbitant costs of maintaining the precise temperature and humidity rendered them no less expensive. The pineapple's association with grandeur was so profound that it adorned architectural designs, appearing on gates, banquet halls, and even furniture as an emblem of hospitality and prosperity. It wasn't until advancements in maritime trade and the advent of industrial-scale cultivation in the 19th century that the pineapple became more accessible to the general populace, shedding its aura of unattainable extravagance.

Key Vocabulary:
- **Opulence**: Great wealth, luxury, or lavishness, often associated with extravagant displays of affluence.
- **Arduous**: Requiring great effort, difficulty, or endurance, often used to describe physically or mentally demanding

tasks.
- **Conspicuous**: Easily noticeable or attracting attention, often due to being striking or unusual.
- **Pineries**: Specialized greenhouses built specifically for cultivating pineapples in controlled environments.
- **Extravagance**: Excessive or unnecessary spending, often associated with luxury, indulgence, or over-the-top displays of wealth.

The Secret Ingredient That Gives Chocolate Its Addictive Flavor

The intoxicating allure of chocolate lies in a single, inconspicuous compound—theobromine, a naturally occurring alkaloid that stimulates the nervous system and induces a mild euphoria. Derived from the cacao bean, this compound is structurally akin to caffeine, bestowing upon chocolate its subtly stimulating properties. When consumed, theobromine triggers the release of endorphins and serotonin, engendering sensations of pleasure and contentment, which explains why people often crave chocolate in moments of stress or melancholy. Moreover, the unique conching process —where cacao is meticulously ground and aerated for hours —enhances the chocolate's smooth texture and deepens its complex flavor profile, making each bite an indulgent experience. Studies suggest that this psychoactive element, coupled with the presence of fats and sugars, makes chocolate an irresistible culinary delight, binding flavor with neurological gratification. This is why, centuries after the Mayans and Aztecs first revered it as the "food of the gods," chocolate remains a universally cherished confection, seducing the senses with every decadent morsel.

Key Vocabulary:
- **Theobromine**: A bitter alkaloid found in cacao, similar to caffeine, that has mild stimulant effects on the body.
- **Alkaloid**: A naturally occurring chemical compound

found in plants, often with physiological effects on humans or animals.
- **Engender**: To cause or give rise to a feeling, situation, or condition, often used in reference to emotions or reactions.
- **Conching**: A process in chocolate-making where cacao is refined and aerated to develop a smooth texture and enhanced flavor.
- **Psychoactive**: Affecting the brain and altering mood, perception, or behavior, commonly used to describe stimulants and other mood-enhancing substances.

Why Some Cheeses Smell Like Feet

The pungent, unmistakable aroma of certain cheeses—often likened to unwashed socks or aged leather—stems from an unlikely microbial accomplice: Brevibacterium linens. This bacterium, the very same that dwells on human skin and contributes to foot odor, is responsible for the distinctive scent of washed-rind cheeses like Limburger, Époisses, and Munster. During the aging process, these cheeses are methodically bathed in brine or alcohol, creating an environment where proteolysis and lipolysis break down proteins and fats, yielding a complex bouquet of aromas that teeter between repulsive and irresistible. The paradox of olfactory pleasure lies in sensory adaptation—over time, the human brain acclimates to these bold, barnyard-like scents, allowing us to appreciate their depth rather than recoil in disgust. The very same biochemical reactions that might deter the uninitiated are precisely what render these cheeses an exquisite delicacy, proving that our perception of flavor is, in part, a construct of acquired taste.

Key Vocabulary:
- **Brevibacterium linens**: A type of bacteria responsible for the strong smell of certain cheeses, also found on human skin.

- **Proteolysis**: The breakdown of proteins into smaller peptides and amino acids, influencing texture and flavor in cheese aging.
- **Lipolysis**: The process of breaking down fats into fatty acids and glycerol, contributing to the rich aroma and taste of aged cheese.
- **Sensory adaptation**: The phenomenon where prolonged exposure to a strong stimulus leads to reduced perception of it over time.
- **Acquired taste**: A preference developed over repeated exposure, often for flavors or textures initially perceived as unpleasant.

The Origins of Chopsticks

The humble yet ingenious chopsticks, now an emblem of East Asian dining, trace their origins back over 3,000 years to ancient China. Initially used as cooking implements rather than eating utensils, early chopsticks were fashioned from bamboo, ivory, or bronze, serving as tools for retrieving food from boiling cauldrons. As diets shifted toward smaller, bite-sized morsels—due in part to fuel conservation and the adoption of stir-frying—chopsticks became the preferred mode of consumption, eliminating the need for knives at the table. This culinary evolution aligned with Confucian philosophy, which eschewed the presence of blades during meals, reinforcing the idea that dining should be an act of harmony rather than aggression. Over centuries, variations of chopsticks emerged across Japan, Korea, and Vietnam, each with distinct lengths, shapes, and materials suited to regional eating customs. From lacquered wood to sleek metal, chopsticks continue to be both a functional tool and a cultural artifact, symbolizing centuries of tradition and refinement.

Key Vocabulary:
- **Cauldrons**: Large metal pots used for boiling liquids or cooking over an open flame, often associated with

historical or ritualistic cooking.
- **Morsels**: Small portions or bite-sized pieces of food, often used to describe delicacies or carefully portioned bites.
- **Eschew**: To deliberately avoid or abstain from something, often based on principles or beliefs.
- **Lacquered**: Coated with a glossy, protective finish, often referring to decorative woodwork or utensils.
- **Culinary evolution**: The gradual transformation of cooking techniques, ingredients, and eating habits over time.

The Spice That Was Once Worth More Than Gold

Centuries before modern trade networks, an unassuming spice wielded economic influence so profound that it was once deemed more precious than gold—black pepper. Native to the Malabar Coast of India, black pepper became the lifeblood of ancient commerce, coveted by the Romans, Persians, and medieval European merchants who dubbed it "black gold." Its piquant bite and preservative properties rendered it indispensable in a world without refrigeration, leading to staggering markups along perilous trade routes that stretched from Asia to the Mediterranean. During the Age of Exploration, the pursuit of pepper and other coveted spices ignited maritime expeditions, forever reshaping global geopolitics. The spice's astronomical value led to the establishment of monopolies, clandestine smuggling operations, and even military conflicts, all to control the flow of this culinary currency. While today pepper graces every kitchen table, its history is steeped in intrigue, ambition, and the ceaseless human pursuit of flavor and fortune.

Key Vocabulary:
- **Piquant**: Having a pleasantly sharp or spicy flavor, often used to describe robustly seasoned foods.
- **Coveted**: Highly desired or sought after, often due to rarity or prestige.

- **Perilous**: Involving significant risk or danger, often used in the context of treacherous journeys or endeavors.
- **Monopolies**: Exclusive control over the trade or supply of a commodity or service, often leading to economic dominance.
- **Culinary currency**: A metaphor describing food or spices as valuable commodities that shape trade and cultural exchanges.

The Ancient Mayan Recipe for the First-Ever Hot Chocolate

Long before Swiss chocolatiers perfected their delicate truffles, the Mayans were imbibing a radically different form of chocolate—one that bore little resemblance to the sweetened confections of today. Their sacred beverage, known as xocoatl, was a bracing elixir composed of ground cacao beans, chili peppers, and water, frothed to an effervescent froth by vigorously pouring it between vessels. Reserved for royalty and warriors, this ambrosial libation was believed to imbue drinkers with vitality and divine wisdom. Unlike modern iterations laden with sugar and milk, the Mayan rendition was robustly bitter, its fiery undertones accentuating the bean's natural complexity. Spanish conquistadors, enamored by its enigmatic properties, carried it back to Europe, where it underwent a metamorphosis into the velvety indulgence we cherish today. Yet, in every steaming cup of hot chocolate, the ghost of the ancient Mayan brew lingers—a vestige of an age when cacao was currency, sacrament, and sustenance.

Key Vocabulary:
- **Imbibing**: The act of drinking or absorbing a liquid, often with a connotation of indulgence.
- **Effervescent**: Bubbly, fizzy, or sparkling, either literally or metaphorically.
- **Ambrosial**: Exceptionally pleasing to taste or smell; fit for the gods.

- **Enigmatic**: Mysterious, difficult to interpret or understand.
- **Vestige**: A trace or remnant of something that once existed.

Why Some Cultures Consider Insects a Delicacy

To the uninitiated, the notion of feasting on insects might seem an affront to culinary sensibilities, yet for millennia, entomophagy— the practice of consuming insects—has been a staple of numerous civilizations. In regions where arable land is sparse and conventional livestock costly to rear, insects have long been revered as a bounteous source of protein, healthy fats, and essential micronutrients. The Aztecs cultivated chinicuiles (red worms) as a delicacy, while the ancient Chinese dined on silk pupae, extolling their umami-laden richness. Contemporary gastronomes in Thailand revel in deep-fried crickets, their exoskeletons shattering with an audible crunch, yielding an earthy, nutty savor. Beyond their gustatory appeal, insects represent an eco-conscious alternative to conventional meat, requiring a fraction of the water and feed needed for traditional livestock. The Western aversion to entomophagy is largely cultural, yet as sustainability concerns mount, the once-maligned practice is gaining traction among avant-garde chefs who recognize its potential to redefine haute cuisine.

Key Vocabulary:
- **Entomophagy**: The practice of eating insects as food.
- **Arable**: Suitable for growing crops.
- **Bounteous**: Plentiful or abundant.
- **Exoskeleton**: The external skeleton that supports and protects an insect's body.
- **Gustatory**: Relating to the sense of taste.

The Mysterious Origins of the World's Spiciest Pepper

The Carolina Reaper, a fiery behemoth of the botanical

world, is not merely a pepper but an incendiary experience—its mere presence capable of inducing a searing, visceral agony. This crimson menace, a hybrid of the Ghost Pepper and Red Habanero, was meticulously engineered by American cultivator Ed Currie, yet its origins trace back to ancient Mesoamerica, where indigenous civilizations revered capsaicin-rich peppers for their medicinal, culinary, and even ritualistic properties. The Carolina Reaper's capsaicinoid concentration eclipses even law enforcement-grade pepper spray, registering an infernal 2.2 million Scoville Heat Units. In an ironic twist, the agonizing burn triggers an endogenous flood of endorphins, resulting in an unexpected euphoria. Despite—or perhaps because of—its fiery temperament, the Reaper has cemented its place in gastronomic folklore, luring thrill-seekers and competitive eaters into its merciless embrace. Its enigmatic power is not merely its heat, but its capacity to push the limits of human endurance.

Key Vocabulary:
- **Behemoth**: A huge or monstrous thing.
- **Incendiary**: Capable of causing fire or extreme heat.
- **Capsaicinoid**: The active component responsible for the heat in chili peppers.
- **Endogenous**: Originating from within an organism.
- **Euphoria**: A state of intense happiness and excitement.

The Truth About Whether Sushi Was Really Invented in Japan

Sushi, the epitome of Japanese gastronomy, is often assumed to be a uniquely Japanese invention, yet its origins lie further west, in the rice paddies of ancient Southeast Asia. The earliest iteration, narezushi, emerged in the Mekong Delta, where fish was fermented with rice as a preservation method. This technique migrated to Japan via China, where it underwent a metamorphosis—evolving from a pungent, preserved dish into the refined, vinegared delicacy known today. It was Edo-period Japan that redefined sushi, introducing the concept of fresh fish served atop hand-pressed rice, a departure from its fermentation-heavy antecedents. Tokyo street vendors perfected nigiri-zushi, transforming it into the art form that now commands reverence worldwide. While sushi's lineage is undeniably global, Japan's meticulous refinement of the craft enshrined it as their own, solidifying its place as a culinary paragon of precision, balance, and minimalist sophistication.

Key Vocabulary:
- **Epitome**: A perfect example of a particular quality.
- **Metamorphosis**: A complete transformation in form or structure.
- **Pungent**: Having a strong, sharp smell or taste.
- **Antecedent**: Something that existed before or logically precedes another.
- **Paragon**: A model of excellence or perfection.

How Honey Never Spoils

In an era where perishability governs the shelf life of most edibles, honey remains an anomaly—an unspoiled relic of antiquity, impervious to the decay that claims lesser foods. Archaeologists have unearthed pots of honey from ancient Egyptian tombs, still as golden and viscous as when they were first sealed millennia ago. This remarkable longevity is owed to honey's unique alchemy of low moisture content, high acidity, and hydrogen peroxide production, creating an inhospitable environment for microbial proliferation. Moreover, its hygroscopic nature allows it to draw moisture from its surroundings, further safeguarding its integrity. Revered by civilizations past as an elixir of vitality, honey's immutable essence has rendered it a symbol of immortality in folklore and mythology alike. In a world where time ravages all, honey alone defies entropy.

Key Vocabulary:

- **Anomaly**: Something that deviates from the norm or expectations.
- **Impervious**: Incapable of being affected or penetrated.
- **Alchemy**: A seemingly magical process of transformation or combination.
- **Hygroscopic**: Having the ability to absorb moisture from the air.
- **Entropy**: The inevitable decline into disorder and decay.

The Festival Where People Throw Tomatoes at Each Other

La Tomatina, the world's largest and most exuberant food fight, is a spectacle of controlled chaos, a bacchanalian revelry where thousands of revelers pelt each other with overripe tomatoes in an uninhibited explosion of color and carnage. This annual Spanish tradition, held in Buñol, traces its genesis to an impromptu skirmish in 1945, when disgruntled townsfolk allegedly disrupted a parade by hurling tomatoes in protest. What began as a spontaneous act of rebellion has since been canonized as a jubilant festival, where streets run crimson with pulped fruit, and participants revel in the anarchic catharsis. The event, while seemingly frivolous, reminds us of Spain's penchant for pageantry, its ethos deeply embedded in communal merriment. Though ephemeral in duration, La Tomatina embodies a spirit of unbridled joy, a fleeting but unforgettable descent into delightful absurdity.

Key Vocabulary:
- **Bacchanalian**: Wild and drunken festivity.
- **Revelry**: Lively and noisy festivities, especially with drinking.
- **Anarchic**: Lacking order or control, chaotic.
- **Catharsis**: The process of releasing strong emotions for relief.
- **Ephemeral**: Lasting for a very short time.

The Surprising History of the Sandwich

The humble sandwich, a ubiquitous staple of modern gastronomy, owes its nomenclature and popularization to an 18th-century aristocrat, yet its essence predates recorded history. The eponymous John Montagu, 4th Earl of Sandwich, reputedly devised the concept out of sheer convenience—ordering his meat encased within bread to sustain his gambling escapades without soiling his hands. However, iterations of this portable repast span civilizations: ancient Jewish communities partook of bitter herbs enfolded in matzo, while medieval Europeans fashioned trenchers—hollowed-out loaves repurposed as edible plates. The sandwich's ascension to culinary prominence mirrored the rise of industrialization, catering to the proletariat's demand for sustenance on the go. Today, its permutations are boundless, from the decadent Croque Monsieur of France to the banh mi of Vietnam. What was once an aristocratic eccentricity has evolved into an emblem of convenience, adaptability, and cross-cultural culinary innovation.

Key Vocabulary:
- **Nomenclature**: The system or process of naming things.
- **Eponymous**: Named after a person.
- **Encased**: Enclosed or covered completely.
- **Repast**: A meal or feast.
- **Proletariat**: The working class, especially in an industrial society.

Why Some Cultures Eat Fermented Shark Meat

To the unaccustomed palate, hákarl—Iceland's infamous fermented shark—represents a veritable gauntlet of culinary endurance. This pungent delicacy, derived from the Greenland shark, is inedible in its natural state due to toxic levels of trimethylamine oxide. To render it consumable, the flesh undergoes a meticulous curing process: it is buried beneath gravel for weeks, allowing it to decompose and expel its noxious compounds before being air-dried for months. The result is a gelatinous, ammonia-laden morsel, whose acrid bouquet evokes the olfactory sting of cleaning solvents. For Icelanders, however, hákarl is more than an acquired taste —it is a vestige of their Viking ancestry, reminding us of the ingenuity required to thrive in an unforgiving landscape. While many foreigners balk at its aggressive pungency, locals revere it as a cultural rite of passage, often washed down with brennivín, a caraway-infused spirit aptly nicknamed the "Black Death."

Key Vocabulary:
- **Veritable**: Used as an intensifier, meaning "truly" or "genuine."
- **Gauntlet**: A severe trial or ordeal.
- **Curing**: The process of preserving food.
- **Acrid**: Sharp or bitter in taste or smell.
- **Olfactory**: Related to the sense of smell.

How an Accidental Mistake Created the First Potato Chips

Few culinary inventions owe their genesis to petulance, yet the potato chip, an emblem of snack food culture, was purportedly born from spite. In 1853, George Crum, an Indigenous-American chef at a New York resort, found himself vexed by a particularly finicky patron who repeatedly rejected his fried potatoes for being too thick and soggy. In a moment of exasperation, Crum sliced the tubers into paper-thin wafers, fried them to an unrelenting crisp, and doused them in salt, expecting the dish to be scorned. Instead, the diner was enraptured, and thus, the potato chip was unwittingly consecrated into the annals of gastronomy. Initially a gourmet indulgence confined to fine dining, the chip's mass production surged with the advent of mechanized peeling and packaging, ensuring its omnipresence in snack aisles worldwide. What began as an act of culinary defiance evolved into an insatiable global obsession.

Key Vocabulary:
- **Genesis**: The origin or formation of something.
- **Petulance**: Childish annoyance or irritation.
- **Finicky**: Excessively particular or difficult to please.
- **Enraptured**: Completely delighted or captivated.
- **Consecrated**: Made sacred or officially recognized.

The Forbidden Fruit That Was Once Banned in the U.S.

The durian, reviled as much as it is revered, is an enigma wrapped in a thorny husk—an olfactory paradox capable of inciting both adoration and abhorrence. Native to Southeast Asia, this divisive fruit exudes an odor likened to putrid onions, sewage, and overripe cheese, an aroma so formidable that it has been proscribed from public transportation in several countries. Yet, for devotees, its ambrosial flesh —custard-like, saccharine, and laced with an intoxicating complexity—is unparalleled. In the late 20th century, U.S. authorities momentarily imposed restrictions on its import, citing its overwhelming stench as a public nuisance. Despite its olfactory notoriety, the durian remains an aphrodisiacal delicacy, heralded in Asian cultures as the "King of Fruits." Its presence continues to evoke fervent discourse, embodying the dichotomy between sensory revulsion and gustatory rapture.

Key Vocabulary:
- **Enigma**: A mysterious or puzzling thing.
- **Olfactory**: Related to the sense of smell.
- **Proscribed**: Forbidden or banned.
- **Ambrosial**: Exceptionally pleasing to taste or smell.
- **Dichotomy**: A division between two opposing things.

The Ritual of the Japanese Tea Ceremony and Its Meaning

The Japanese tea ceremony, or chanoyu, is far more than a mere act of refreshment—it is an intricate tapestry of aesthetics, philosophy, and ritualistic precision. Rooted in Zen Buddhism, chanoyu embodies wabi-sabi, the reverence for transience and imperfection, where every movement, from the delicate whisking of matcha to the deliberate placement of utensils, is imbued with intentionality. The host, often clad in a traditional kimono, orchestrates each gesture with measured grace, ensuring that every aspect—down to the placement of a single teacup—resonates with harmony. The ceremony is a silent dialogue between guest and host, an ephemeral communion where words yield to the language of movement. In a world dominated by haste, chanoyu persists as a meditative reprieve, reminding participants to embrace simplicity, mindfulness, and the beauty of the impermanent.

Key Vocabulary:
- **Tapestry**: A complex or intricate combination of elements.
- **Aesthetics**: A branch of philosophy dealing with beauty.
- **Transience**: The state of being temporary or fleeting.
- **Ephemeral**: Lasting for a very short time.
- **Reprieve**: A temporary relief or escape.

The Mystery Behind the Origin of the Fortune Cookie

Despite its widespread association with Chinese cuisine, the fortune cookie is a culinary enigma, its genesis shrouded in contention between rival claimants. While many presume its provenance lies in ancient China, historical scrutiny suggests otherwise—its delicate, vanilla-scented folds first emerged in early 20th-century America, with both Los Angeles and San Francisco vying for recognition as its birthplace. Some attribute its invention to Makoto Hagiwara, a Japanese immigrant who purportedly served the confection at San Francisco's Golden Gate Park's Japanese Tea Garden, inspired by a traditional Kyoto delicacy called tsujiura senbei. Others posit that it was David Jung, a Chinese entrepreneur in Los Angeles, who devised the cookie as a vehicle for dispensing Confucian wisdom to the destitute. Regardless of its true originator, the fortune cookie's trajectory from a niche offering to a ubiquitous postprandial ritual encapsulates the fluidity of cultural appropriation, adaptation, and reinvention in the American gastronomic landscape.

Key Vocabulary:
- **Enigma**: A mystery or puzzle.
- **Genesis**: The origin or beginning of something.
- **Provenance**: The place of origin or earliest known history.
- **Contestation**: Dispute or controversy.
- **Postprandial**: Occurring after a meal.

Why Certain Countries Eat Soup for Breakfast

In myriad cultures, breakfast is not defined by saccharine pastries or eggs but by steaming bowls of broth-laden nourishment, an age-old tradition steeped in practicality, climate, and culinary ethos. From Vietnam's herbaceous pho to Japan's miso soup, these morning elixirs offer a symphony of umami, warmth, and sustenance, priming the body for the rigors of the day. In tropical nations, the paradoxical consumption of hot soup functions as a thermoregulatory mechanism, inducing perspiration to cool the body. Meanwhile, in frigid climates, thick broths laden with proteins and starches provide a caloric bastion against the cold. Beyond physiology, the act of imbibing soup at dawn is a vestige of communal dining, where markets and street stalls brim with simmering cauldrons, their aromatic vapors beckoning patrons into the folds of tradition. What Western sensibilities might deem unconventional is, in many societies, a quotidian, time-honored ritual of nourishment.

Key Vocabulary:
- **Myriad**: Countless or innumerable.
- **Elixir**: A magical or medicinal potion.
- **Umami**: A savory taste, one of the five basic flavors.
- **Thermoregulatory**: Relating to the control of body temperature.
- **Quotidian**: Occurring every day; ordinary or commonplace.

The Italian Dish That Was Created by Mistake

Tiramisu, the decadent Italian dessert renowned for its ethereal layers of mascarpone, espresso-soaked ladyfingers, and cocoa dusting, owes its existence to a felicitous accident rather than deliberate invention. As lore has it, in the 1960s, an industrious restaurateur in Treviso sought to salvage unsold ingredients, improvising a confection from coffee-drenched biscuits and whipped cheese. The result was a revelation—an ambrosial marriage of bitterness and sweetness, lightness and indulgence, caffeine and cream. Some contend that its origins extend further back, tracing to the lavish courts of 17th-century Tuscany, where a primitive iteration dubbed Zuppa del Duca purportedly fueled the stamina of aristocrats. Regardless of its exact genesis, tiramisu's meteoric ascent from regional obscurity to global eminence underscores the serendipity inherent in gastronomy, where constraint often begets creativity, and accidents engender icons. Few desserts exemplify the fortuitous alchemy of culinary happenstance quite like this beloved Italian masterpiece.

Key Vocabulary:
- **Ethereal**: Extremely delicate and light.
- **Felicitous**: Well-suited or fortunate.
- **Ambrosial**: Exceptionally pleasing to taste or smell.
- **Serendipity**: The occurrence of events by chance in a happy way.

- **Alchemy**: A seemingly magical transformation or creation.

The Ancient Chinese Legend Behind the First Dumpling

The genesis of the dumpling, a ubiquitous culinary staple spanning continents, is enshrined in an ancient Chinese legend that entwines gastronomy with medicine and altruism. According to lore, Zhang Zhongjing, a physician of the Han Dynasty, devised the first dumplings as a panacea for frostbite-stricken villagers, whose ears bore the brunt of winter's merciless grip. Inspired by their plight, he crafted morsels of minced meat and herbs encased in delicate dough, shaping them to resemble human ears—a symbolic gesture of healing. These steaming parcels, simmered in medicinal broth, didn't just thaw the afflicted but also satiated their hunger, embedding dumplings within the annals of both culinary and medical history. Over centuries, this humble invention spread across cultures, from Japanese gyoza to Polish pierogi, evolving in form and function yet retaining its essence: a pocket of sustenance, warmth, and tradition.

Key Vocabulary:
- **Genesis**: The origin or beginning of something.
- **Panacea**: A universal remedy for all problems or diseases.
- **Plight**: A dangerous, difficult, or unfortunate situation.
- **Satiated**: Fully satisfied, especially in hunger.
- **Crucible**: A place or situation in which different elements interact to produce something new.

The Story of How the World's Most Expensive Coffee Is Made

The world's most exorbitant coffee owes its prestige not to rare beans or intricate brewing methods, but to an unexpected, almost grotesque intermediary—civets. Kopi Luwak, hailing from Indonesia, is derived from beans that have passed through the digestive tract of these nocturnal creatures, their enzymes purportedly refining the beans' acidity and bitterness into a velvety, nuanced brew. Once excreted, the beans undergo meticulous cleaning, drying, and roasting, fetching astronomical prices due to their rarity and the laborious process involved. Though once a foraged delicacy, increasing global demand has birthed an industry fraught with ethical concerns, where civets are often caged and force-fed, negating the very natural selection process that imparts the coffee's distinctive profile. Thus, while Kopi Luwak remains a symbol of luxury, its production straddles the fine line between culinary curiosity and moral controversy. It shows humanity's ceaseless pursuit of opulence in the most unexpected places.

Key Vocabulary:
- **Exorbitant**: Unreasonably high in cost.
- **Grotesque**: Odd or unnatural in appearance, absurd.
- **Intermediary**: A link between two entities.
- **Nuanced**: Subtly complex or sophisticated.
- **Opulence**: Extreme wealth or luxury.

The French Law That Dictates What Can Be Called 'Champagne'

In the annals of viticulture, few designations are as sacrosanct as Champagne—a title safeguarded by the immutable edicts of French law. The Appellation d'Origine Contrôlée (AOC) mandates that only sparkling wine produced within the hallowed vineyards of the Champagne region, adhering to stringent méthode champenoise techniques, may bear the exalted name. This decree, enshrined in the Treaty of Madrid (1891) and reaffirmed by the Treaty of Versailles, renders any extraneous claim to the title not merely erroneous but legally untenable. Over the years, this appellation has engendered international disputes, compelling producers in regions from California to Italy to settle for alternative nomenclature such as sparkling wine or mousseux. More than a geographical marker, Champagne is a symbol of meticulous craftsmanship, heritage, and exclusivity—an emblem of refinement whose very name is fortified by centuries of legal fortification and unwavering Gallic pride.

Key Vocabulary:
- **Annals**: Historical records.
- **Sacrosanct**: Regarded as too important to be interfered with.
- **Immutable**: Unchanging over time.
- **Exalted**: Held in high regard.
- **Nomenclature**: A system of names or terms.

The Origins of the Famous Indian Tandoori Cooking Style

A relic of antiquity, the tandoori cooking style traces its origins to the Indus Valley Civilization, where primitive clay ovens —tandoors—were unearthed in the ruins of Harappa and Mohenjo-Daro. These rudimentary kilns, originally used to bake flatbreads, evolved over centuries into vessels of culinary alchemy, infusing meats with an intoxicating mélange of spices and a characteristic smoky char. Tandoori cooking, as it is recognized today, gained prominence in the Mughal courts, where royal chefs refined its techniques, marinating meats in spiced yogurt before searing them in the infernal depths of the tandoor. The method's true global ascension, however, was catalyzed by the 1947 partition, when Kundan Lal Gujral, a refugee restaurateur, introduced tandoori chicken to Delhi. The dish's vibrant hue, a consequence of its spice-laden marinade, captivated palates worldwide, cementing tandoori cuisine as an indelible fixture in the global gastronomic lexicon.

Key Vocabulary:
- **Relic**: A surviving trace of an ancient time.

- **Alchemy**: A process of transformation, creation, or combination.
- **Mélange**: A mixture of different elements.
- **Infernal**: Relating to fire or hellish heat.
- **Indelible**: Impossible to erase or forget.

Why Some People Are Supertasters and Others Can't Taste Certain Flavors

Gustatory perception is far from uniform; some individuals possess an uncanny hypersensitivity to taste, while others remain oblivious to certain flavor nuances. This phenomenon is largely attributed to genetic variations in the TAS2R38 gene, which governs the density of fungiform papillae—the taste bud-laden structures on the tongue. Supertasters, endowed with an abundance of these receptors, experience an amplified intensity of bitterness, rendering foods like coffee, dark chocolate, and cruciferous vegetables overwhelmingly astringent. Conversely, non-tasters exhibit a relative paucity of these receptors, resulting in a muted gustatory experience, where pungency and astringency are scarcely perceptible. This disparity doesn't just influence dietary preferences but also has evolutionary underpinnings; heightened taste sensitivity historically served as a deterrent against ingesting toxic plants. Thus, whether one recoils at the acridity of brussels sprouts or savors their mild bitterness is less a matter of preference and more an intricate interplay of genetics and evolution.

Key Vocabulary:
- **Gustatory**: Relating to the sense of taste.
- **Hypersensitivity**: An exaggerated response to stimuli.
- **Astringent**: Sharp or bitter in taste.
- **Paucity**: A scarcity or insufficient amount.
- **Acridity**: A strong, unpleasantly sharp taste or smell.

The Most Dangerous Foods in the

World That Can Kill You

Gastronomic daredevils often seek out dishes that teeter on the precipice of peril, where a single misstep in preparation can spell catastrophe. Among the most infamous is fugu, the Japanese pufferfish, whose organs harbor lethal tetrodotoxin—an insidious neurotoxin that induces paralysis within minutes. Only chefs who undergo meticulous training are permitted to wield the knife that dissects this delicate but deadly delicacy. Similarly, ackee, Jamaica's national fruit, contains hypoglycin, a compound capable of triggering violent hypoglycemia if consumed unripe. Meanwhile, casu marzu, Sardinia's illicit maggot-infested cheese, straddles the line between delicacy and biohazard, as the larvae that render it creamy may survive digestion, wreaking havoc within the intestines. These foods, while tantalizing, are not for the faint of heart; their consumption is a dance with danger, where one's fate lies in the deft hands of a skilled preparer.

Key Vocabulary:
- **Daredevil**: A person who enjoys taking dangerous risks.
- **Teeter**: To balance unsteadily on the edge of something.
- **Insidious**: Proceeding in a gradual, harmful way.
- **Illicit**: Forbidden or illegal.
- **Deft**: Skillful and precise.

The Science Behind Why Some People Love Cilantro and Others Hate It

Few herbs elicit such polarized reactions as cilantro; to some, it is a fragrant enhancement to cuisine, while to others, it is reminiscent of soap. This stark contrast is dictated by genetic predisposition—specifically, variations in the OR6A2 gene, which encodes olfactory receptors sensitive to aldehydes, the compounds responsible for cilantro's pungency. Those possessing this genetic variant perceive an unappetizing soapy taste, while others register a citrusy freshness. This phenomenon exemplifies how taste is inextricably linked to olfaction, as the perception of flavor is not solely a function of the tongue but an intricate symphony of nasal receptors and neural pathways. Though cilantro's divisiveness has inspired both devotion and revulsion, its presence remains unwavering in myriad global cuisines, proving that in the realm of taste, one person's ambrosia is another's anathema.

Key Vocabulary:
- **Polarized**: Divided into two starkly contrasting groups.
- **Predisposition**: A natural tendency or susceptibility.
- **Olfactory**: Related to the sense of smell.
- **Aldehydes**: Organic compounds with a strong aroma.
- **Anathema**: Something intensely disliked or loathed.

The History of How Ice Cream Was Invented

A confection once reserved for royalty, ice cream's origins stretch back millennia, its earliest iterations borne from the ingenuity of ancient civilizations. The Persians, as early as 500 BCE, concocted a primitive sorbet by combining snow with grape juice, while the Chinese, during the Tang Dynasty, refined the craft by incorporating fermented milk, camphor, and crushed ice. The dessert's European debut is attributed to Marco Polo, who, upon returning from his Eastern sojourn, introduced Italy to frozen delights, paving the way for the opulent gelatos of the Renaissance. However, it was Catherine de' Medici's migration to France that catalyzed ice cream's ascent into haute cuisine. By the 18th century, the advent of hand-cranked churns democratized its consumption, transforming ice cream from an aristocratic indulgence into a ubiquitous treat. A reminder of humanity's relentless pursuit of pleasure, ice cream remains an sign of culinary innovation.

Key Vocabulary:
- **Confection**: A sweet food or delicacy.
- **Ingenuity**: Creative or inventive skill.

- **Sojourn**: A temporary stay in a place.
- **Opulent**: Luxurious or richly elaborate.
- **Haute Cuisine**: High-end, refined cooking.

The Ancient Roman Feast That Went on for Days

The bacchanalian excesses of ancient Rome found their zenith in the legendary convivia—opulent feasts that spanned days, where indulgence knew no bounds. These repasts, orchestrated by the aristocracy, were veritable orgies of consumption, featuring rare viands such as stuffed dormice, roasted peacocks adorned in their resplendent plumage, and garum-laced delicacies reeking of umami profundity. Lavish triclinia, bedecked with silk and illuminated by flickering lucernae, bore witness to reclining patricians who imbibed mulsum—a honeyed elixir—while listening to the dulcet strains of cithara players. The most ostentatious hosts provided vomitoria, enabling guests to purge and persist in their hedonistic revelry. More than mere sustenance, these feasts epitomized Rome's ethos of excess and social stratification, where power was measured not only in denarii but in one's capacity for sybaritic endurance. In this grand theatre of gluttony, to dine was not merely to eat—it was to perform.

Key Vocabulary:
- **Bacchanalian**: Wildly indulgent and drunken.
- **Convivia**: Lavish Roman feasts.
- **Viands**: Delicacies or expensive food.
- **Lucernae**: Ancient Roman oil lamps.
- **Sybaritic**: Devoted to luxury and pleasure.

How the Croissant Became a Symbol of France (Even Though It's Not French)

Despite its sacrosanct place in French patisserie, the croissant's provenance lies not in Parisian boulangeries but in the siege-worn streets of 17th-century Vienna. The pastry's precursor, the kipferl, was allegedly crafted in celebration of Austria's victory over the Ottoman Empire, its crescent shape an irreverent nod to the vanquished enemy's insignia. By the late 18th century, the French, ever adept at gastronomic refinement, appropriated the kipferl and transmuted it through lamination—imbuing it with its now-iconic, gossamer flakiness. The resulting croissant, an alchemy of beurre-laden pâte feuilletée, became the quintessence of French breakfast culture, synonymous with café terraces and morning languor. Ironically, this emblem of Gallic identity owes its origins to foreign conquest and culinary expropriation, an example of France's uncanny ability to assimilate and elevate. The croissant, though etymologically and historically Austrian, has been irrevocably enshrined in the lexicon of French gastronomy.

Key Vocabulary:
- **Sacrosanct**: Regarded as too important to be changed.
- **Provenance**: The origin or earliest history of something.
- **Boulangeries**: French bakeries.
- **Transmuted**: Changed in form, nature, or substance.
- **Expropriation**: The act of taking something for one's own use.

The First Pizza Delivery in History and Who It Was For

The annals of culinary history record an illustrious milestone in 1889, when a Neapolitan pizzaiolo, Raffaele Esposito, embarked upon an unprecedented endeavor—delivering a freshly fired pizza to the royal chambers of Queen Margherita of Savoy. The sovereign's visit to Naples had kindled an insatiable curiosity for the city's lazzaroni fare, prompting an invitation for Esposito to proffer his craft at the Bourbon palace. Esposito, seizing the occasion, composed a patriotic triad of pizzas, one of which—garnished with ruby-hued tomatoes, ivory mozzarella, and verdant basil—was an homage to the Italian tricolor. The queen, enamored by its rustic simplicity, bestowed her royal imprimatur upon it, thus christening the Pizza Margherita. This singular act of culinary magnanimity elevated the erstwhile plebeian dish into the pantheon of national treasures. The art of pizza delivery, now a global enterprise, owes its inception to a monarch's fleeting gastronomic whim.

Key Vocabulary:
- **Annals**: Historical records.
- **Pizzaiolo**: An artisan pizza maker.
- **Lazzaroni**: The lower-class street dwellers of Naples.
- **Imprimatur**: Official approval or endorsement.
- **Plebeian**: Common or of the lower social classes.

The Science Behind How Popcorn Pops

Beneath the unassuming husk of a popcorn kernel lies a miniature pressure chamber, an intricate alchemy of starch, moisture, and heat-sensitive resilience. Each kernel harbors a vestigial droplet of water ensconced within its dense endosperm, a biological paradox wherein fragility begets force. Upon exposure to intense heat, this aqueous nucleus undergoes a phase transition, metamorphosing into steam and generating formidable internal pressure. The pericarp —an impervious sheath of crystalline cellulose—resists this burgeoning expansion until its tensile threshold capitulates, engendering a violent rupture. This cataclysmic event, occurring at an approximate thermodynamic apex of 180°C, transmutes the gelatinized starch into a gossamer matrix of airy, crispy exuberance. The audible staccato of popping kernels orchestrates a culinary symphony, an ephemeral ode to physics and patience. Thus, a kernel's explosive metamorphosis from latent dormancy to voluminous confection is not mere serendipity, but an exquisite interplay of heat, pressure, and biopolymeric defiance.

Key Vocabulary:
- **Vestigial**: A small remnant of something once larger or more significant.
- **Endosperm**: The nutrient-rich tissue inside seeds.
- **Pericarp**: The outer protective layer of a seed or fruit.
- **Tensile**: Relating to tension or resistance to stretching.
- **Biopolymeric**: Composed of biological polymers such as starch or cellulose.

How the Concept of 'Fast Food' Was Invented

The genesis of fast food is not a modern contrivance but an anachronistic vestige of antiquity, manifesting in disparate civilizations long before neon-lit drive-thrus and assembly-line burgers. In the bustling epicenters of ancient Rome, plebeians flocked to thermopolia, rudimentary street-side eateries dispensing piping-hot stews and flatbreads to hurried laborers. Similarly, medieval Europe witnessed the proliferation of pie houses and pasties, wherein itinerant merchants procured portable nourishment with cursory exchanges of coin. The true advent of industrialized fast food, however, materialized in the early 20th century with the mechanized efficiency of White Castle, followed by McDonald's pioneering of the Speedee Service System, a paradigm of precision and expediency. This transformation heralded a seismic shift in gastronomy, transmuting dining from a ritualistic repose into a fleeting, pragmatic transaction. In the grand chronology of culinary evolution, fast food is not an aberration but an inexorable response to civilization's insatiable acceleration.

Key Vocabulary:
- **Contrivance**: A thing that is skillfully created for a particular purpose.
- **Anachronistic**: Belonging to a period other than the present.

- **Plebeians**: Commoners in ancient Rome.
- **Itinerant**: Traveling from place to place.
- **Inexorable**: Impossible to stop or prevent.

The Unexpected Origin of the Word 'Barbecue'

The etymology of 'barbecue' is a linguistic odyssey traversing continents and centuries, rooted in the indigenous Taíno term barbacoa, denoting a primitive method of suspending meat over a smoldering fire. Spanish explorers, enraptured by this culinary technique, appropriated the word into their lexicon, disseminating it across the Caribbean and the American South, where it metamorphosed into both a noun and a verb. By the 17th century, 'barbecue' had transcended its literal denotation, becoming emblematic of communal feasting and convivial revelry. The term's phonetic permutations—ranging from the French barbe à queue, an apocryphal misattribution meaning 'beard to tail,' to early American abbreviations like 'BBQ'—attest to its linguistic malleability. Though its lexical origins are contested, its cultural significance remains unassailable, a reminder of humanity's primeval affinity for fire, flesh, and festivity. Thus, 'barbecue' is not just a culinary practice, but a word imbued with migratory history.

Key Vocabulary:
- **Etymology**: The study of word origins.
- **Odyssey**: A long and eventful journey.
- **Denotation**: The literal meaning of a word.
- **Apocryphal**: Of doubtful authenticity, though widely circulated.
- **Malleability**: The quality of being adaptable or easily influenced.

The True Story of How Coca-Cola Was Originally a Medicine

The genesis of Coca-Cola is steeped in apothecarial ambition, conceived not as a saccharine indulgence but as a pharmacological panacea. In 1886, Dr. John Stith Pemberton, a Confederate veteran turned chemist, sought to concoct a tonic to assuage the maladies of his era—nervous exhaustion, dyspepsia, and even morphine addiction. His prototype, a caramel-hued elixir imbued with extracts of coca leaves and kola nuts, was christened 'Pemberton's French Wine Coca,' a tincture purported to invigorate both mind and body. However, with the advent of Prohibition, the formula underwent modification, expunging its alcoholic content and rebranding it as 'Coca-Cola.' Initially peddled in pharmacies as a medicinal curative, its effervescent allure soon eclipsed its remedial intent, catapulting it into commercial ubiquity. Though its pharmacological pretensions have long since dissipated, Coca-Cola endures as a cultural behemoth, a carbonated relic of its medicinal origins now immortalized in global iconography.

Key Vocabulary:
- **Apothecarial**: Related to pharmacy or drug-making.
- **Panacea**: A universal remedy or solution.
- **Dyspepsia**: Indigestion or stomach discomfort.
- **Tincture**: A medicinal solution containing alcohol.
- **Effervescent**: Fizzing or bubbling, often used to describe carbonated drinks.

The Strange History of the First Energy Drink

In the annals of modern nutrition, the first energy drink is a curious, almost alchemical concoction. Dating back to the 1960s, Dr. Enuf, a lesser-known tonic created by an eccentric Appalachian doctor named William H. Hester, is often credited as the original energy beverage. Initially marketed as a "stimulant" and "nerve tonic," it was composed of a potent amalgam of caffeine, B vitamins, and sugar, which Hester believed would invigorate both body and mind. It was not until the global energy drink craze of the late 20th century, spearheaded by brands like Red Bull, that energy drinks evolved into the ubiquitous, hyper-caffeinated elixirs we recognize today. However, Dr. Enuf remains a footnote in the chronicle of energy beverages, a precursor to the vibrant global industry that thrives on the ethos of instant vitality. From medicinal roots to modern mania, the story of energy drinks is one of remarkable transformation.

Key Vocabulary:
- **Alchemical**: Related to medieval chemical science, especially transformation.
- **Amalgam**: A mixture of different elements.
- **Invigorate**: To give strength or energy to.
- **Ubiquitous**: Present, appearing, or found everywhere.
- **Ethos**: The characteristic spirit or attitude of a culture or community.

The Reason Why Some Cultures Consider Slurping a Compliment

In certain cultures, particularly in Japan and parts of China, the act of slurping one's noodles is not viewed as a social faux pas but rather as a sign of appreciation and enjoyment. The practice, deeply embedded in centuries-old culinary tradition, is believed to enhance the flavor profile of the dish while simultaneously cooling the noodles to a more palatable temperature. In Japan, slurping is considered almost an art form. Additionally, the auditory component of slurping serves to convey a sense of satisfaction, much like a silent compliment to the chef for their craftsmanship. While such an act might elicit raised eyebrows in other corners of the world, in these regions, it is an accepted, even revered, part of dining etiquette. The cultural divergence of food practices underscores the multiplicity of perceptions surrounding taste and manners across the globe.

Key Vocabulary:

- **Faux pas**: A social blunder or mistake.
- **Palatable**: Acceptable or agreeable to the taste.
- **Auditory**: Related to hearing.
- **Etiquette**: The customary code of polite behavior in society.

How Food Can Taste Different Depending on the Color of Your Plate

The relationship between visual stimuli and gustatory perception has been a subject of fascination within the scientific community, as research suggests that the color of a plate can subtly alter the flavor of food. Psychologists have found that certain hues, particularly red and yellow, can intensify the perception of sweetness, while darker colors, such as black or navy blue, might render a dish's flavors less pronounced. This phenomenon, rooted in sensory psychology, explains why high-end restaurants often opt for minimalist white plates, which are believed to allow the food's natural colors and textures to stand out without overwhelming the palate. The visual presentation of food, it seems, plays a pivotal role in its overall taste experience. Thus, the next time you sit down to a meal, consider not just the dish but also the dishware—it may very well affect your culinary enjoyment.

Key Vocabulary:
- **Gustatory**: Related to taste or the sense of taste.
- **Perception**: The ability to perceive or understand something in a particular way.
- **Hues**: Shades or variations of color.
- **Pronounced**: Clearly noticeable or distinct.
- **Interconnectedness**: The state of being connected or linked together.

The Myth of Whether Eating Carrots Improves Your Vision

The widespread belief that eating carrots can significantly improve one's vision, particularly in the dark, has become an almost ubiquitous myth, perpetuated by wartime propaganda and enduring in popular culture. This misconception stems from World War II, when the British Royal Air Force used the story of their pilots' enhanced night vision, allegedly due to an overconsumption of carrots, to conceal the use of radar technology. While carrots are indeed rich in beta-carotene, a precursor to vitamin A essential for maintaining healthy vision, they cannot provide a magical enhancement to one's eyesight. The nutrient supports normal eye function, but it cannot reverse age-related vision impairments or dramatically sharpen vision in low-light conditions. Nevertheless, the myth endures, perhaps because it resonates with the human desire for quick fixes and easy solutions. In reality, a balanced diet with a variety of nutrients is far more effective for maintaining eye health in the long term.

Key Vocabulary:
- **Ubiquitous**: Present or found everywhere.
- **Perpetuate**: To cause something to continue indefinitely.
- **Misconception**: A mistaken belief or view.
- **Precursor**: A person or thing that comes before another of the same kind.
- **Resonates**: To produce a positive feeling, response, or impact.

The Ancient Spice Route That Connected the World Through Trade

The Spice Route, an extensive network of trade routes established in antiquity, bridged the continents of Asia, Africa, and Europe, intertwining cultures and economies through the exchange of exotic spices. This intricate web of commerce, which flourished from the 3rd century BCE to the 15th century CE, facilitated the movement of highly coveted goods such as cinnamon, pepper, and cloves from the Far East to the Mediterranean. The journey was perilous, with traders navigating treacherous deserts, dense jungles, and vast oceans, yet the lucrative nature of these spices made the risks worthwhile. The Spice Route was not just an economic artery but also a conduit for cultural exchange, spreading ideas, religions, and technological advancements between East and West. Today, the legacy of the Spice Route is still palpable, as the spices that were once so valuable are now common pantry staples, yet their historical significance remains profound.

Key Vocabulary:
- **Antiquity**: Ancient times, especially before the Middle Ages.
- **Intertwining**: To twist or weave together.
- **Commerce**: The activity of buying and selling, especially on a large scale.
- **Perilous**: Full of danger or risk.
- **Conduit**: A channel or means through which something is transmitted.

The Invention of Instant Ramen and How It Became a Global Staple

Instant ramen, the beloved culinary innovation that revolutionized the global food landscape, traces its origins back to Japan in 1958, when Momofuku Ando, the visionary founder of Nissin Foods, sought to create an affordable, easily accessible meal. In a time when post-war Japan was grappling with food shortages, Ando's invention of fried instant noodles, packaged in a convenient cup, provided a quick and inexpensive solution to hunger. Initially met with skepticism, instant ramen soon gained international popularity due to its portability, long shelf life, and versatility. Its rapid ascent from a humble invention to a global staple shows the power of convenience in modern life, embodying the intersection of innovation and practicality. Today, instant ramen is consumed in virtually every corner of the world, from college dorms to Michelin-starred kitchens, and remains an enduring symbol of food ingenuity.

Key Vocabulary:
- **Visionary**: A person with original ideas about what the future could be like.
- **Grappling**: Struggling or wrestling with something.
- **Skepticism**: Doubt as to the truth of something.
- **Versatility**: The ability to adapt to many different functions or activities.
- **Ingenuity**: The quality of being clever, original, and inventive.

The Oldest Known Recipe in the World

The oldest known recipe in the world, dating back over 4,000 years, comes from ancient Mesopotamia, etched on a clay tablet in cuneiform script. This recipe, a type of stew made from barley, mutton, and various herbs, offers a tantalizing glimpse into the culinary practices of early civilizations. While the precise method of preparation has been lost to history, researchers have been able to recreate a version of the dish, which has been described as surprisingly hearty, with a robust flavor that evokes the rustic simplicity of ancient diets. The recipe reflects the agricultural practices of Mesopotamia but also the significance of communal dining in the region's culture. Today, this ancient dish serves as a reminder of the nature of food as both sustenance and cultural heritage, connecting modern eaters with their ancient ancestors.

Key Vocabulary:
- **Tantalizing**: Tempting or exciting, often with an unattainable quality.
- **Cuneiform**: An ancient system of writing used in Mesopotamia.
- **Hearty**: Substantial, nourishing, and filling.

- **Recreate**: To make or construct again in a similar form.
- **Sustenance**: Food and drink regarded as a source of strength or nourishment.

GEOGRAPHY

The Island That Disappears and Reappears Every Year

Deep within the Brahmaputra River, an ephemeral island named Majuli defies permanence, vanishing and resurrecting with the monsoon's ebb and flow. This fluvial enigma, once sprawling across 1,250 square kilometers, has been inexorably whittled away by the river's voracious currents. Each year, as the monsoons descend with merciless torrents, Majuli submerges beneath the deluge, its fertile lands dissolving into the river's churning embrace. Yet, when the waters recede, the island emerges anew, its topography altered but its spirit unyielding. For centuries, the indigenous Missing people have adapted to this capricious landscape, constructing stilted dwellings and cultivating rice in soil that oscillates between desiccation and saturation. Despite relentless erosion, conservationists and locals strive to fortify the landmass, planting trees to temper the river's inexorable encroachment. Majuli remains a paradox of resilience and fragility, a transitory world sculpted by the river's capricious will.

Key Vocabulary:
- **Ephemeral**: Lasting for a very short time; transient and fleeting, often referring to things that exist only briefly before disappearing.
- **Fluvial**: Related to rivers and the processes, sediments, or landforms shaped by moving water.
- **Inexorably**: In a manner that is impossible to stop or prevent; unyielding and relentless.
- **Capricious**: Subject to sudden and unpredictable

changes, often describing natural forces or whimsical decisions.
- **Desiccation**: The process of extreme drying, rendering something devoid of moisture, often leading to sterility or barrenness.

The Desert That Turns Into a Flower Field Overnight

Every few years, the Atacama Desert, the driest non-polar region on Earth, undergoes a miraculous transformation. Devoid of precipitation for years, its cracked and desiccated terrain appears inhospitable to life. Yet, with the advent of an anomalously heavy rainfall, a clandestine seedbank stirs beneath the surface, awaiting its ephemeral moment. Almost overnight, a kaleidoscopic efflorescence engulfs the barren expanse, as dormant wildflowers awaken in a chromatic symphony. Purple malvas, golden añañucas, and scarlet huillis unfurl their petals in a fleeting spectacle of botanical resurgence. Scientists attribute this phenomenon to El Niño, which alters atmospheric circulations and bestows the region with an uncharacteristic deluge. However, this ephemeral paradise is transient—within weeks, the sweltering sun reclaims dominion, desiccating the blossoms until they once again lapse into dormancy, their seeds ensconced in the soil, awaiting another celestial caprice.

Key Vocabulary:
- **Anomalously**: Deviating from what is standard, normal, or expected; occurring in an unusual or irregular manner.
- **Clandestine**: Kept secret or done covertly, often referring to hidden or undisclosed activities.
- **Efflorescence**: A state or period of flowering; metaphorically used to describe peak development or blooming.
- **Resurgence**: A revival or renewal after a period of decline or dormancy; a reappearance of something once diminished.

- **Ensconced**: Settled securely or comfortably in a place, often implying protection or concealment.

The Hidden City Beneath the Streets of Paris

Beneath the bustling boulevards of Paris, a shadowy, labyrinthine underworld sprawls unseen. The Catacombs, a vast necropolis, harbor the skeletal remains of over six million souls, meticulously arranged in haunting ossuaries. These subterranean corridors, once limestone quarries, became a clandestine repository for the city's dead when overflowing cemeteries posed a dire sanitary threat in the 18th century. To the intrepid, the catacombs are a morbid reminder of mortality, their damp walls enshrined with macabre inscriptions that remind visitors of life's ephemerality. Beyond the sanctioned pathways, however, lies an enigmatic warren known as the "off-limits" catacombs, where urban explorers —les cataphiles—navigate the uncharted tunnels, discovering hidden chambers, clandestine art installations, and forgotten relics. While the authorities attempt to curtail these illicit forays, the allure of the subterrane remains undiminished, its darkness whispering secrets of a bygone Paris lurking beneath the modern metropolis.

Key Vocabulary:
- **Labyrinthine**: Extremely intricate and complex, resembling a maze with numerous winding passages.
- **Necropolis**: A large, ancient burial ground or cemetery, often associated with historical or archaeological significance.
- **Ossuary**: A container or space designated for the storage of human skeletal remains, typically stacked or arranged systematically.
- **Ephemerality**: The quality of being short-lived or transitory, often referring to fleeting moments or temporary phenomena.
- **Warren**: A complex network of interconnected passages

or tunnels, often used metaphorically to describe crowded or intricate spaces.

How Mount Everest Is Still Growing Taller Every Year

Towering above the Earth at an astonishing altitude, Mount Everest is not a static monument but an evolving titan. Geologically, the Himalayas are the consequence of an inexorable collision between the Indian and Eurasian tectonic plates, a process that continues to this day. As these colossal land masses converge, Everest ascends incrementally, gaining a few millimeters each year. Seismic activity further contributes to its augmentation; powerful earthquakes can elevate its summit, while erosion seeks to counteract this upward thrust. Yet, despite its ceaseless ascent, Everest remains treacherous, its rarefied atmosphere and brutal winds rendering it an unforgiving dominion. For climbers, the mountain's continual growth is an esoteric reminder of Earth's perpetual dynamism—an ancient colossus, sculpted by forces both primordial and relentless, forever reaching skyward.

Key Vocabulary:
- **Inexorable**: Impossible to stop or prevent; unrelenting and perpetual in nature.
- **Seismic**: Related to earthquakes or other vibrations of the Earth's crust, often caused by tectonic movements.
- **Augmentation**: The process of increasing or enhancing something, often referring to growth or expansion.
- **Rarefied**: Thin or less dense, typically referring to high-altitude air or an exclusive, elevated realm.
- **Primordial**: Existing from the beginning of time; ancient and fundamental in nature.

The Cave That Has Its Own Weather System

Deep in the Vietnamese wilderness, Sơn Đoòng Cave is an isolated chasm so vast it harbors an autonomous weather system within its depths. This gargantuan subterranean void, concealed beneath the dense jungle, contains colossal stalagmites, a thriving ecosystem, and clouds that form due to the temperature differentials between its interior and exterior. The cave's ceiling has partially collapsed in certain areas, permitting sunlight to nourish verdant rainforests burgeoning within. A river meanders through its cavernous expanse, further solidifying its status as an independent biome. The interplay between humidity, airflow, and geological formations fosters mist-laden skies within the cave, giving rise to an otherworldly spectacle reminiscent of a primordial realm. Sơn Đoòng's sheer immensity and self-contained atmospheric dynamics render it a singular marvel, a subterranean universe where the boundaries between geology and meteorology blur into an astonishing confluence of nature's forces.

Key Vocabulary:
- **Chasm**: A deep fissure or abyss in the Earth's surface, often metaphorically describing profound separations.
- **Autonomous**: Operating independently or having the ability to function without external influence.
- **Verdant**: Lush and green with vegetation, often used to describe thriving landscapes.
- **Cavernous**: Resembling a vast cave; immense in size, depth, or emptiness.
- **Confluence**: The merging or meeting of two or more things, often used in the context of rivers, cultures, or ideas.

The Mysterious Moving Rocks of Death Valley

In the parched and desolate landscape of Death Valley's Racetrack Playa, an inexplicable phenomenon had long baffled scientists. Enormous stones, some weighing hundreds of pounds, traverse the cracked, sun-scorched earth, leaving meandering trails etched in the desert floor. For decades, speculation flourished—whispers of unseen forces, magnetic anomalies, or even extraterrestrial meddling pervaded discussions. The truth, however, is a delicate interplay of ice, wind, and water. On frigid winter nights, a thin sheet of ice encases the playa, and as the morning sun rises, it fractures into buoyant shards. Aided by ephemeral gusts of wind, these transient ice floes nudge the stones forward in an eerie, imperceptible glide. Over time, this glacial choreography inscribes long, sinuous tracks in the arid basin, each motion a showing nature's unseen hand. Though the mystery has been unraveled, the sight of these massive boulders, seemingly animated by an invisible force, remains one of Earth's most bewitching spectacles.

Key Vocabulary:
- **Parched**: Devoid of moisture; excessively dry, often to the point of cracking or desiccation.
- **Meandering**: Winding and sinuous, often describing a path or course that twists and turns unpredictably.
- **Anomalies**: Irregularities or deviations from what is expected or normal, often mysterious or unexplained.
- **Ephemeral**: Fleeting or transitory, existing only for a short duration before vanishing.
- **Buoyant**: Capable of floating or rising to the surface due to lightness or reduced density.

The Lake That Changes Color Depending on the Season

Nestled within the Andean highlands, Lake Hillier remains an enigmatic marvel of nature, transforming its hue with the cadence of the seasons. In the blistering heat of summer, the lake adopts an ethereal blush, its waters shimmering in an unnatural shade of magenta. This otherworldly transformation is a consequence of halophilic microorganisms, primarily Dunaliella salina and Halobacteria, whose metabolic processes yield vibrant carotenoid pigments. As temperatures plummet in winter, the lake's rosy visage dissipates, replaced by a crystalline cerulean expanse, an illusion born from the shifting balance of algae and salinity. The juxtaposition of its ever-changing palette against the stark, mineral-rich shoreline lends the lake an air of surrealism. Scientists theorize that the saline saturation, combined with microbial activity, orchestrates this dynamic spectacle, yet mysteries linger—why does this phenomenon persist only in select hypersaline environments? A capricious jewel of the natural world, Lake Hillier continues to defy conventional understanding, leaving those who gaze upon its fluctuating visage spellbound.

Key Vocabulary:
- **Enigmatic**: Mysterious and difficult to comprehend; shrouded in uncertainty.
- **Halophilic**: Thriving in environments with high salinity, often describing certain bacteria or algae.
- **Carotenoid**: A class of organic pigments responsible for vivid hues in plants, algae, and microbes.
- **Juxtaposition**: The placement of contrasting elements side by side to highlight differences.
- **Capricious**: Unpredictable and prone to sudden changes, often used to describe shifting behaviors or phenomena.

The Deepest Point in the Ocean That No Human Has Ever Reached

Plunging into an abyssal chasm of eternal darkness, the Challenger Deep in the Mariana Trench is the Earth's most profound recess, an alien world concealed beneath seven miles of crushing oceanic pressure. Here, light is an impossibility, and the weight of the water above exerts a force a thousand times greater than at sea level, reducing most organic life to gelatinous specters of adaptation. Even the most sophisticated submersibles have barely grazed the abyssal plain, their titanium hulls groaning under the relentless assault of the deep. No human has ever physically descended to its nadir, for the sheer hostility of this domain renders conventional exploration untenable. Yet, strange lifeforms persist—translucent amphipods, bioluminescent predators, and the ghostly Halomonas titanicae, a bacterium capable of devouring shipwrecks. The Mariana Trench, an eldritch crevasse in the Earth's crust, remains largely uncharted, a yawning void whose secrets slumber in the ink-black depths, untouched by the hands of humankind.

Key Vocabulary:
- **Abyssal**: Relating to the deepest regions of the ocean, where sunlight does not penetrate.
- **Profound**: Extending to an extreme depth; intellectually or physically deep.
- **Gelatinous**: Resembling jelly in texture, often describing deep-sea organisms.
- **Nadir**: The lowest point, whether physically, metaphorically, or astronomically.
- **Eldritch**: Eerie and otherworldly, often with unsettling or supernatural connotations.

The Hidden Underground River That Flows Beneath a Major City

Beneath the bustling avenues of Mexico City lies a concealed artery of water, a river that courses through subterranean labyrinths long forgotten by modern inhabitants. Once a vital lifeline of the ancient Aztec capital of Tenochtitlán, this clandestine waterway now meanders unseen beneath layers of asphalt and concrete. Engineers, archaeologists, and urban spelunkers have stumbled upon this shadowed aquifer, discovering stone channels that date back centuries, their masonry encrusted with mineral deposits from a perpetual, unseen flow. The river, though obscured, exerts an eerie influence on the metropolis above—subsidence haunts the city, as the relentless extraction of groundwater slowly undermines its foundations. Despite its spectral presence, the river remains an umbilicus to a forgotten past, whispering of an empire's hydrological mastery and a civilization whose urban ingenuity was centuries ahead of its time. Mexico City, built atop the vestiges of an ancient lacustrine realm, remains forever tethered to the aqueous veins that pulse beneath its streets.

Key Vocabulary:
- **Subterranean**: Existing beneath the Earth's surface, often describing caves, rivers, or hidden structures.
- **Clandestine**: Secretive and concealed, often with an air of mystery or intrigue.
- **Spelunker**: An explorer of caves and underground passages.
- **Subsidence**: The gradual sinking of land due to geological or human-induced factors.
- **Lacustrine**: Related to or influenced by lakes, often used in describing ancient water-based environments.

Why the Great Wall of China Is Slowly Disappearing

Once an indomitable barrier stretching thousands of miles, the Great Wall of China is succumbing to the inexorable passage of time. Erosion, human negligence, and the relentless encroachment of nature conspire to dismantle this architectural marvel stone by stone. In remote sections, entire stretches have crumbled into indistinct rubble, devoured by the surrounding wilderness. Some areas have been repurposed by villagers, their bricks pilfered to build homes and roads, while others have simply disintegrated under the duress of centuries of wind and rain. Though conservation efforts strive to preserve its grandeur, the Wall's demise is an inevitability —a poignant reminder that even humanity's greatest achievements are ephemeral against the vast sweep of history.

Key Vocabulary:
- **Indomitable**: Impossible to subdue or defeat, often

describing resilience or strength.
- **Inexorable**: Impossible to stop or prevent, often describing an unstoppable force or process.
- **Encroachment**: The gradual intrusion of something, particularly in an unwelcome or invasive manner.
- **Pilfered**: Stolen in small amounts, often referring to petty theft over time.
- **Ephemeral**: Lasting for only a short period, emphasizing impermanence.

The Coldest Inhabited Place on Earth and How People Survive There

In the frigid expanse of Siberia, the town of Oymyakon stands as the coldest inhabited place on Earth, where winter temperatures can plunge to an almost unimaginable -67.7°C (-89.9°F). This remote settlement, located in the Republic of Sakha, survives at the mercy of the harshest winter conditions on the planet. Residents, enduring these extreme cold snaps, rely on resourceful ingenuity to navigate the frozen landscape. The permafrost ensures that the ground remains perpetually solid, making agriculture nearly impossible, so the locals depend on reindeer herding and fishing. Dwellings are constructed to withstand the bitter chill, with walls insulated by thick layers of material to retain warmth. The town's residents often wear multiple layers of clothing, including fur-lined coats and hats, to stave off the numbing cold. Despite these challenges, the people of Oymyakon have developed a stoic resilience, adapting to life in a place where the frost never relents. The daily struggle to survive in such an inhospitable environment shapes the town's identity, as it remains an example of human endurance against nature's extremes.

Key Vocabulary:
- **Expanse**: A wide, open area or stretch of land, often vast and expansive.

- **Permafrost**: Ground that remains frozen year-round, typically found in polar regions or high altitudes.
- **Ingenious**: Characterized by cleverness, originality, or skill in design or problem-solving.
- **Stoic**: Indifferent to pain, pleasure, or fortune, marked by a calm, uncomplaining demeanor in the face of adversity.
- **Relent**: To become less severe or intense, often describing an easing of harsh conditions.

The Town That Has Been on Fire for Over 60 Years

In the heart of Pennsylvania, the ghostly town of Centralia has been burning for over six decades. The subterranean fire, which began in 1962, was ignited by a coal seam beneath the town that caught fire during an attempt to clean up a nearby landfill. Once ignited, the fire spread rapidly through the vast network of coal veins underground, becoming impossible to extinguish. Over the years, the ground above has cracked open, releasing toxic gases and causing sinkholes to swallow entire sections of the town. Despite the dire conditions, the fire continues to burn, consuming everything in its path, while the few remaining residents have been forced to abandon their homes. Centralia, now an eerie, desolate landscape, stands as a chilling reminder of the destructive power of fire and the fragility of human settlements. This persistent blaze beneath the earth reminds us of the unstoppable force of nature, one that has rendered the town uninhabitable and left it to the slow, inevitable march of ruin.

Key Vocabulary:
- **Eerie**: Strange and frightening, often evoking a sense of unease or mystery.
- **Sinkholes**: Depressions or holes in the ground caused by the collapse of a surface layer, often dangerous.
- **Dire**: Extremely serious or urgent, often implying a life-threatening situation.
- **Chilling**: Causing a feeling of fear or discomfort, often

due to its sinister or unsettling nature.
- **Inevitable**: Certain to happen, unavoidable, suggesting the impossibility of prevention or escape.

The Discovery of an Entire Ecosystem Inside a Cave Sealed for Millions of Years

In a groundbreaking discovery, scientists have uncovered an entire ecosystem within the confines of the Cave of the Crystals in Mexico, sealed for millions of years. The cave, which was formed by the slow crystallization of gypsum deposits, has remained untouched by the outside world until recently. Inside, researchers have found a thriving community of unique life forms, including microorganisms and bizarre, blind species that have adapted to the total absence of light. These organisms have evolved in isolation, developing extraordinary characteristics, such as enhanced sensory abilities and peculiar metabolisms, to survive in the cave's extreme conditions. The ecosystem remains a time capsule, offering researchers a rare glimpse into the process of evolution and the adaptability of life in harsh, isolated environments. The discovery challenges preconceived notions about the limits of life and demonstrates that, even in the most extreme and isolated conditions, life finds a way to thrive. This hidden world, once thought impossible, shows the resilience and adaptability of life on Earth.

Key Vocabulary:
- **Groundbreaking**: Marking a significant or innovative development, often used to describe discoveries or achievements that challenge previous understandings.
- **Metabolism**: The set of life-sustaining chemical reactions in organisms, crucial for converting food into energy.
- **Isolated**: Separated from others or from the outside world, often used to describe environments that are cut off from external influences.

- **Adaptability**: The ability to adjust to new conditions or environments, often crucial for survival.
- **Peculiar**: Unusual or distinctive in nature, often implying something that deviates from the norm.

The Real-Life Treasure Hunts That People Are Still Trying to Solve

Scattered across the globe lie enigmas entombed in cryptic texts, intricate ciphers, and tantalizing riddles—treasure hunts that have outlived their creators, ensnaring the minds of seekers who chase the glimmer of gold and the thrill of the unknown. From the infamous Beale Ciphers, which purportedly conceal the whereabouts of an immense fortune in gold and silver, to the enigmatic Fenn Treasure, which was hidden in the vast wilderness of the Rocky Mountains by a millionaire art dealer, these quests blur the line between history and legend. The Oak Island Money Pit, a shaft riddled with booby traps and rumored to contain relics of immeasurable worth, continues to lure treasure hunters despite centuries of fruitless excavation. Even in modern times, the pursuit of these lost riches persists, fueled by whispered clues, coded manuscripts, and the unwavering belief that somewhere, beneath layers of earth or hidden in the folds of forgotten maps, unimaginable wealth awaits discovery. For those who dare to decipher these age-old riddles, the allure is not merely in the promise of treasure but in the intoxicating dance with mystery itself.

Key Vocabulary:
- **Enigmas**: Mysteries that are difficult to understand or explain.
- **Ciphers**: Secret or coded messages.
- **Purportedly**: Allegedly; said to be true but not verified.
- **Booby traps**: Concealed devices set to cause unexpected harm or difficulty.
- **Intoxicating**: Overwhelmingly exciting or exhilarating.

The Secret Bunker Hidden Beneath the Eiffel Tower

Beneath the polished facades of the world's most celebrated landmarks lurk concealed relics of war, espionage, and survival. Among them is the clandestine bunker buried deep beneath the Eiffel Tower—a vestige of military subterfuge constructed during World War II. Concealed beneath layers of steel and concrete, it once served as a critical hub for communication and intelligence, safeguarding strategists and operatives in times of siege. Similarly, beneath London's bustling streets, the Churchill War Rooms remain frozen in time, an underground labyrinth from which Britain's wartime directives were orchestrated. The Vatican, too, harbors subterranean corridors, rumored to shelter secrets so volatile that their revelation could shake the foundations of faith and governance alike. These bunkers, concealed beneath the veneer of history's grandest monuments, remain a reminder of the unseen machinations of power and survival—reminders that beneath the surface of civilization's most revered icons, history's clandestine shadows remain.

Key Vocabulary:
- **Facades**: Outward appearances that may conceal reality.
- **Subterfuge**: Deception used to achieve a hidden goal.
- **Vestige**: A small remaining piece of something that once existed.
- **Machinations**: Schemes or plots, usually with a secretive purpose.
- **Clandestine**: Kept secret, especially for political or military reasons.

The Quirky Border Between Canada and the U.S.

Meandering through forests, bisecting towns, and occasionally passing through buildings, the world's longest international border between two countries stretches between

Canada and the United States. Among its most notable features is Derby Line, Vermont, where the Haskell Free Library and Opera House famously straddles both nations, with its entrance in Vermont and part of its reading room in Quebec. The Northwest Angle, an American exclave in Minnesota that juts into Canadian territory, can only be reached by crossing through Manitoba or by boat across the Lake of the Woods.

The border itself is marked by a precisely maintained 20-foot-wide cleared path known as "the Vista" (not "the Slash"), which runs through forested areas—though it doesn't extend unbroken across the entire boundary, as terrain and urban areas create natural breaks. This cleared corridor helps border agents monitor the boundary and maintain the more than 8,000 monuments that officially mark the border.

While the border is often called "undefended," it is actually well-monitored and enforced, with both countries maintaining robust security measures. The communities along this international boundary have developed unique protocols for cross-border movement, particularly in places where the border runs through populated areas. These arrangements reflect both nations' commitment to maintaining security while acknowledging the practical needs of border communities.

Key Vocabulary:
- **Meandering**: Winding or twisting in an irregular path
- **Bisecting**: Dividing something into two parts
- **Exclave**: A portion of a country geographically separated from the main part
- **Vista**: A cleared strip of land marking the border (the correct term rather than "swath" or "slash")
- **Demarcation**: A boundary or dividing line

How a River in Colombia Looks Like a Rainbow

Amidst the emerald embrace of Colombia's Serranía de la Macarena, an unassuming river bursts into an ephemeral spectacle of kaleidoscopic brilliance. Caño Cristales, revered as the "River of Five Colors," defies the monotony of earthly waterways by transforming into a living rainbow, its waters stained crimson, sapphire, emerald, and gold. This chromatic metamorphosis is not born from minerals or artificial contamination but from the aquatic flora Macarenia clavigera, a unique species of riverweed that blooms in breathtaking vibrancy when bathed in the precise interplay of sunlight and water levels. For a brief window between the wet and dry seasons, the riverbed becomes a living canvas, shifting hues with each undulating current. Unlike the stagnant monotony of most rivers, Caño Cristales is a dynamic masterpiece—its artistry dictated by nature's own fickle hand. Yet, this fleeting enchantment is fragile, susceptible to climate change and human intrusion, making it a marvel both timeless and tragically ephemeral.

Key Vocabulary:
- **Ephemeral**: Lasting for only a short period.
- **Kaleidoscopic**: Displaying a complex pattern of colors.
- **Chromatic**: Related to color.
- **Metamorphosis**: A profound transformation or change.
- **Fickle**: Changing unpredictably.

The Volcano That Spews Blue Lava

Deep in the volcanic veins of East Java, beneath the smoldering crust of the Kawah Ijen caldera, a phenomenon both eldritch and hypnotic flickers against the nocturnal abyss—rivers of incandescent blue fire, coursing down the mountain's charred flanks. Unlike the crimson effusions of typical volcanoes, this eerie luminescence is not molten rock at all, but the spectral combustion of sulfuric gases escaping fissures in the Earth's skin. When these noxious vapors ignite upon exposure to oxygen, they erupt into cerulean flames, licking the darkness with a ghostly glow. The effect is otherworldly, an illusion of molten cobalt seeping through the volcanic veins, yet it is lethally deceptive—emitting toxic fumes capable of asphyxiating any who venture too close. Despite its peril, Kawah Ijen's cerulean inferno lures the intrepid, its ghostly glow a spectral dance that defies geological conventions and conjures a spectacle both mesmerizing and menacing.

Key Vocabulary:
- **Eldritch**: Strange and unnatural in a way that inspires fear.
- **Incandescent**: Glowing with intense heat.
- **Effusion**: A flowing out of liquid, light, or other substance.
- **Cerulean**: Deep blue in color.
- **Asphyxiating**: Depriving of oxygen; causing suffocation.

The Only Place in the World Where You Can Stand in Four Countries at Once

Where the borders of Namibia, Botswana, Zambia, and Zimbabwe converge, an invisible nexus of sovereignty emerges —a singular geopolitical anomaly where four nations clasp hands in a quadripoint so precise that a single step can rewrite one's national allegiance. Unlike the more conventional trisections of territories, this point remains elusive, swallowed by the ceaseless surge of the Zambezi and Chobe Rivers, which thwart any tangible boundary markers. The very concept of this convergence is debated; no official monument demarcates the exact spot, and shifting riverbeds perpetuate its impermanence. Despite this ambiguity, cartographers and travelers alike are drawn to this curious intersection, where the notion of borders dissolves into fluid uncertainty. Here, in a space where sovereignty blurs, the idea of rigid national identity is momentarily eclipsed by geography's capricious hand—a rare terrestrial juncture where, for a fleeting moment, one can inhabit four nations at once.

Key Vocabulary:
- **Nexus**: A central or connecting point.
- **Geopolitical**: Related to international political and geographic boundaries.
- **Anomaly**: Something that deviates from what is normal.
- **Demarcates**: Defines or marks a boundary.
- **Capricious**: Subject to unpredictable changes.

The Lake That Has Been Boiling for Thousands of Years

In the heart of Dominica's primordial wilderness, concealed within the undulating folds of Morne Trois Pitons National Park, seethes an aqueous abyss of perpetual fury—the Boiling Lake. This vast cauldron, cloaked in perpetual mist, writhes and churns with heat, its waters an ever-roiling tempest of vapor and seething turbulence. Unlike volcanic hot springs, which simmer placidly, this lake teeters on the precipice of eruption, its depths concealing an underworld of geothermal unrest. Superheated gases surge from fissures in the Earth's crust, their scalding exhalations keeping the waters in ceaseless agitation, oscillating between furious froth and sulfurous oblivion. It is a spectacle of nature's wrath, yet one that defies comprehension—how does it maintain its relentless fervor across centuries, refusing to yield to time's erosion? For those who stand upon its precipice, the lake is a glimpse into Earth's unbridled power, an infernal reminder that beneath our feet, the planet breathes, rages, and roars.

Key Vocabulary:
- **Primordial**: Existing since the beginning of time.
- **Aqueous**: Related to or resembling water.
- **Writhes**: Twists and turns in a contorted manner.
- **Precipice**: A very steep cliff or edge.
- **Oblivion**: A state of being forgotten or ceasing to exist.

The Hidden Tomb of Genghis Khan

Shrouded in veils of secrecy and legend, the final resting place of Genghis Khan remains one of history's most elusive enigmas. The great Mongol conqueror, whose empire stretched from the Pacific Ocean to the heart of Europe, vanished into the folds of time upon his death in 1227. His burial site, concealed with deliberate subterfuge, is rumored to be nestled deep within the desolate expanse of Mongolia's Khentii Mountains—its precise location obliterated by the hooves of a thousand horses, trampling the earth to erase any trace of his sepulcher. According to lore, the funeral procession slaughtered all who beheld the site, ensuring its eternal secrecy. Over the centuries, clandestine expeditions have scoured the steppe, employing satellites and ground-penetrating radar to pierce the veil of earth and myth. Yet, the grave remains untouched, as if guarded by the spirits of the steppes. Whether hidden beneath an unassuming mound or within a subterranean mausoleum, the tomb of Genghis Khan endures as a ghostly whisper in history—a monument unseen, yet towering in its legend.

Key Vocabulary:
- **Sepulcher**: A tomb or burial chamber.
- **Subterfuge**: Deceptive maneuvering or secrecy.
- **Obliterated**: Completely destroyed or erased.
- **Clandestine**: Conducted in secrecy.
- **Mausoleum**: A grand, above-ground tomb.

The Road That Disappears Underwater Twice a Day

Beneath the shifting tides of France's Bay of Bourgneuf lies a vanishing marvel—Passage du Gois, a causeway that disappears beneath the ocean's embrace twice a day. This cobbled artery, stretching over four kilometers, connects the mainland to the storied isle of Noirmoutier, but only for a fleeting window. When the tide recedes, the road emerges, glistening with residual brine, beckoning the intrepid to traverse its ephemeral path. Yet, as the waters return, the passage is devoured in a relentless cycle, swallowed whole beneath the Atlantic's inexorable tide. Warning signs stand as silent sentinels, cautioning against misjudged crossings, but each year, reckless souls find themselves stranded, forced to cling to rescue towers as the sea reclaims its dominion. The road is both a bridge and a trap—a capricious artery of land and water, where time and tide dictate passage, and where those who linger too long may find themselves engulfed in the ocean's indifferent grasp.

Key Vocabulary:
- **Causeway**: A raised road across water or wet ground.
- **Ephemeral**: Lasting for only a short time.
- **Brine**: Saltwater, especially seawater.
- **Inexorable**: Impossible to stop or resist.
- **Capricious**: Unpredictable and changeable.

The Island Where People Have Lived for 60,000 Years Without Contact with the Outside World

In the vastness of the Indian Ocean, North Sentinel Island remains a fortress of time, its inhabitants untouched by the ceaseless march of civilization. For over 60,000 years, the Sentinelese people have dwelled upon its verdant shores, their existence a living relic of prehistory. They reject all external contact with fervent hostility, loosing arrows upon approaching vessels, warding off intrusions with the ferocity of a people untainted by modernity. Attempts at diplomacy have been rebuffed with unwavering defiance, and those who dared trespass—missionaries, castaways, and explorers—have met grim fates upon its shores. The Indian government, acknowledging the inviolate nature of their sovereignty, has imposed a strict exclusion zone, sealing the island from the encroaching grasp of globalization. North Sentinel remains a bastion of humanity unaltered—a place where time stands still, where languages unheard by outsiders echo in the dense foliage, and where ancient people persist in defiant isolation.

Key Vocabulary:
- **Cerulean**: Deep blue in color.
- **Verdant**: Green and lush with vegetation.
- **Fervent**: Displaying passionate intensity.
- **Inviolate**: Untouched, unharmed, or sacred.
- **Encroaching**: Intruding gradually upon something.

The Cliffside Village That Was Abandoned Overnight for Unknown Reasons

Perched upon a precipitous escarpment, cradled by the silent sentinels of the Apennine Mountains, lies the forsaken hamlet of Craco—an Italian ghost town frozen in eerie abandonment. Once a thriving medieval settlement, its cobbled streets now wind through spectral ruins, their skeletal facades whispering of a mass exodus whose cause remains shrouded in ambiguity. Official records cite treacherous landslides, the earth itself betraying its inhabitants, yet whispers persist of darker omens—plague, superstition, or the unseen hand of fate. The village, suspended in haunting desolation, has become a siren's call to explorers and filmmakers alike, its decaying majesty immortalized in cinema. Time has claimed Craco, yet its mystery lingers, embedded in the crumbling walls, the abandoned chapels, and the echoing corridors where the ghosts of its past still roam.

Key Vocabulary:
- **Precipitous**: Extremely steep.
- **Escarpment**: A steep slope or long cliff.
- **Hamlet**: A small village.
- **Exodus**: A mass departure.
- **Desolation**: A state of emptiness or ruin.

The 'Door to Hell' That Has Been Burning for Over 50 Years

In the barren expanse of Turkmenistan's Karakum Desert, an infernal maw gapes wide—a smoldering chasm known as the "Door to Hell." This abyss, a crater born of human folly, has burned with unrelenting fury since 1971, when Soviet geologists, in their quest for natural gas, inadvertently unleashed an underground reservoir of methane. Fearing an ecological catastrophe, they ignited the gas, expecting it to extinguish within days. Decades later, the flames still rage, licking the darkness with tongues of liquid fire, casting an eerie glow upon the desolate terrain. The crater has become a paradoxical pilgrimage site, where the reckless ambitions of man have forged a perpetual beacon of destruction. Its ceaseless blaze defies logic, an eternal pyre in the heart of the desert, where the Earth itself breathes fire, refusing to be tamed.

Key Vocabulary:
- **Infernal**: Relating to hell or something fiery.
- **Maw**: A deep, gaping hole or mouth-like opening.
- **Abyss**: A seemingly bottomless pit.
- **Ecological**: Related to the environment or nature.
- **Pyre**: A fire, often for burning bodies or rituals.

The Deepest Cave in the World That Could Fit the Empire State Building Inside

Hidden beneath the rugged limestone terrain of Abkhazia, Georgia, the Krubera Cave plunges into the bowels of the Earth, a chasm so deep that it could swallow the Empire State Building whole and still have room to spare. With a staggering depth of over 2,197 meters, this labyrinthine abyss remains one of the most formidable and least explored subterranean landscapes on the planet. Its descent is treacherous, a vertical maze of sheer drops, flooded tunnels, and claustrophobic passageways where the weight of the world presses in from all sides. Explorers must brave bone-chilling darkness, oxygen-deprived air, and an eerie silence punctuated only by the distant drip of water echoing through unseen corridors. It is a world untouched by time, where prehistoric fossils are entombed in ancient rock, and blind cave-dwelling creatures navigate the abyss without ever knowing the light. Few have dared reach its nadir, for the journey requires weeks of relentless descent, carrying provisions, roping down yawning voids, and squeezing through rock crevices barely wide enough for a human body. The deeper one goes, the more the weight of existence itself feels fragile, insignificant against the immeasurable vastness of the underworld.

Key Vocabulary:
- **Chasm**: A deep, gaping hole in the earth.
- **Labyrinthine**: Complicated and maze-like.
- **Subterranean**: Existing beneath the earth's surface.
- **Nadir**: The lowest point.
- **Claustrophobic**: Uncomfortably confined or restricted.

The Underground Salt Cathedral Built by Miners

In Colombia, beneath the town of Zipaquirá, miners have created a truly unique underground marvel: a salt cathedral. The cathedral, carved into the heart of a salt mine, reminds us of the ingenuity and devotion of the miners who built it. The structure includes intricate altars, chapels, and sculptures, all made from the salt of the mine itself. The cathedral's cool, dimly lit atmosphere adds to the mystical and spiritual feeling that pervades the space. It has become one of Colombia's most famous tourist attractions, drawing visitors from around the world who come to marvel at the craftsmanship and the sheer scale of the project. The underground salt cathedral is of course an architectural wonder but also a reflection of the region's deep cultural and religious roots. It remains a symbol of resilience, a sacred space that was built through hard labor and determination.

Key Vocabulary:
- **Marvel**: Something that is extraordinary or impressive, often in a way that inspires admiration or wonder.
- **Ingenuity**: The quality of being clever, original, or inventive, especially in finding solutions to difficult problems.
- **Intricate**: Very detailed and complex, often referring to designs, patterns, or structures that require careful attention to detail.
- **Permeates**: Spreads throughout or influences every part of something, often used to describe an atmosphere or feeling that fills a space.
- **Resilience**: The capacity to recover quickly from difficulties or adversity, often referring to a person, community, or structure.

The Village That Experiences Two Months of Darkness Every Year

In the far northern reaches of Norway, there exists a village called Tromsø, located within the Arctic Circle, where residents experience an extraordinary natural phenomenon. For nearly two months each year, the sun never rises, and the village is plunged into a constant twilight. This is known as the Polar Night, a period where the Earth's tilt causes the sun to remain below the horizon, leaving the village in complete darkness for an extended time. While this can be challenging for some, the locals have adapted to the darkened months, embracing the beauty of the starry nights and the Northern Lights that illuminate the winter skies. The prolonged darkness also brings a unique opportunity for quiet reflection and deep connection with nature, allowing for a rare sense of peace. Tromsø is a popular destination for those seeking to witness the Northern Lights, and the village thrives despite the long, dark winters, demonstrating the resilience and adaptability of its inhabitants.

Key Vocabulary:
- **Phenomenon**: An unusual or remarkable event or fact that can be studied and observed.
- **Twilight**: The soft, dim light that occurs just before sunrise or after sunset, often characterized by a sense of mystery or calm.
- **Plunged**: To fall or dive quickly and dramatically, often into a state of darkness or uncertainty.
- **Adapted**: To adjust or modify in response to new conditions or challenges.
- **Resilience**: The ability to withstand or recover from difficult conditions, demonstrating strength and persistence.

The Mystery of the Moving Islands in Lakes

In various lakes around the world, an intriguing natural phenomenon occurs: floating islands that drift across the water's surface. These islands, known as "tussocks" or "sudds," are actually masses of vegetation, soil, and organic matter that have broken free from the shoreline or lake bottom. Covered in trees and other plants, these islands slowly drift with wind and water currents. The phenomenon is particularly well-documented in places like Lake Bokodi in Hungary and Lake Upemba in the Democratic Republic of the Congo. Scientists understand that these islands form when plant roots and organic material create a buoyant mat that can support soil and vegetation. Wind patterns and water currents influence their movement, while gas buildup from decomposing plant matter can affect their buoyancy. Despite being well-studied, these floating islands continue to captivate observers and serve as unique ecosystems, supporting various plant and animal species. Local communities near such lakes often incorporate these wandering islands into their cultural stories and traditional knowledge.

Key Vocabulary:

- **Tussock**: A floating mat of vegetation and organic matter that has broken free from its original location.
- **Buoyant**: Able to float or stay afloat in water due to upward force exerted by the fluid.
- **Decomposition**: The natural process by which organic material breaks down into simpler forms of matter.
- **Ecosystem**: A biological community of interacting organisms and their physical environment.
- **Vegetation**: Plants considered collectively, especially those found in a particular area or habitat.

How an Entire City Was Carved Into a Mountain in Turkey

In the heart of Cappadocia, Turkey, lies one of the most astonishing examples of human ingenuity and architectural prowess—the ancient underground city of Derinkuyu. This city, carved entirely into the soft volcanic rock of a mountain, stretches several levels below the surface and could once accommodate tens of thousands of people. Thought to have been created by early civilizations as a refuge from invading forces, the city features an elaborate network of tunnels, chambers, ventilation shafts, and storage areas, all carefully designed to provide comfort and security for its inhabitants. The city was self-sufficient, with its own wells, stables, and places of worship, making it a thriving underground hub. Even today, parts of the city remain untouched, offering a glimpse into the remarkable resourcefulness and resilience of its creators. Derinkuyu shows the extraordinary lengths that people went to in order to survive and thrive in an unforgiving world, where the mountain itself became both a shield and a home.

Key Vocabulary:

- **Ingenuity**: The ability to invent or devise clever solutions, often in a creative and resourceful way.
- **Prowess**: Exceptional skill, ability, or expertise in a particular field or endeavor.
- **Elaborate**: Involving many careful details or intricate design, often showing complexity and thoroughness.
- **Self-sufficient**: Able to meet one's needs independently, without relying on external resources or support.
- **Resourcefulness**: The ability to find quick and clever ways to overcome difficulties, using available resources effectively.

The Place on Earth That Looks Like Mars

On the barren plains of the Atacama Desert in Chile, there exists a place so desolate and unearthly that it is often compared to the surface of Mars. The Valle de la Luna, or Valley of the Moon, is a landscape of salt flats, towering rock formations, and sweeping sand dunes that resemble the Martian terrain in every way. The extreme dryness of the desert and the unusual geological formations create an otherworldly atmosphere, making it the perfect analog for the red planet. Scientists have even used the Valle de la Luna as a testing ground for Mars exploration missions, as its conditions closely mimic those found on Mars. The valley is devoid of plant life, and only the hardiest of animals, such as rodents and lizards, manage to survive in this harsh environment. Despite the harshness, the Valley of the Moon draws travelers from around the world who come to witness the surreal beauty of the landscape and experience a slice of Mars on Earth.

Key Vocabulary:
- **Desolate**: Empty, bleak, and devoid of life or activity, often evoking feelings of isolation or abandonment.
- **Otherworldly**: Not of this world; something that appears strange, mysterious, or supernatural.
- **Analog**: A comparison or similarity between two things,

often used to highlight their shared characteristics.
- **Mimic**: To imitate or resemble something closely, often in order to replicate its qualities or features.
- **Harshness**: The severity or difficulty of a situation or environment, often characterized by extreme conditions or unpleasantness.

The World's Largest Living Organism That Covers an Entire Forest

In the Malheur National Forest of Oregon, an extraordinary organism lies hidden beneath the forest floor. The largest living organism on Earth, a fungus known as Armillaria ostoyae, spans over 2,385 acres and is thought to be thousands of years old. This massive fungal colony lives underground, with only its network of mycelium—the threadlike structures that make up the fungal body—visible to the naked eye. The fungus is the largest, but also one of the oldest living organisms, having grown and spread beneath the soil for centuries. While the above-ground mushrooms it produces are visible to hikers, the true scale of the organism is revealed only to those who understand the vastness of the mycelial network. The fungus feeds on the trees in the forest, decomposing dead matter and recycling nutrients back into the ecosystem. Despite its size and age, it remains largely unnoticed by the public, quietly sustaining the forest's delicate balance. The Armillaria ostoyae serves as a reminder of the incredible interconnectedness of life and the mysteries that lie hidden beneath the surface.

Key Vocabulary:
- **Mycelium**: The network of threadlike structures that form the body of a fungus, typically found underground.
- **Spans**: To extend across a particular area or range, often referring to the scope or extent of something.
- **Decomposing**: The process of breaking down organic matter, often by the action of microorganisms or fungi.

- **Recycling**: The process of converting waste or dead matter into reusable materials, helping to maintain ecological balance.
- **Interconnectedness**: The state of being connected or related to one another, often in a complex or interdependent manner.

The Secret Underground City Built During the Cold War

In the heart of Germany, hidden beneath the surface, lies a secret city that was built during the Cold War era. Known as the Felsennest Bunker, this underground complex was designed as a highly secure, self-contained facility to protect civilians and military personnel in the event of a nuclear attack. The bunker is a labyrinth of concrete corridors, storage rooms, living quarters, and supply depots, all constructed to withstand the devastating force of a nuclear blast. Despite its strategic importance, the bunker was kept secret for decades, its existence known only to a select few. It wasn't until after the fall of the Berlin Wall that the Felsennest Bunker was declassified and made accessible to the public. Today, it serves as a historical site, offering a chilling glimpse into the paranoia and preparation that defined the Cold War era. The bunker's isolation, fortified walls, and underground tunnels stand as a silent monument to a time when the world teetered on the brink of nuclear annihilation.

Key Vocabulary:
- **Labyrinth**: A complex network of pathways or passages, often designed to confuse or disorient.
- **Self-contained**: Capable of functioning independently without external support or resources.
- **Declassified**: Officially released from secrecy or confidentiality, often allowing public access to previously restricted information.
- **Chilling**: Causing fear or discomfort, often through a sense of dread or unease.

- **Paranoia**: An irrational fear or suspicion, often characterized by an excessive concern for potential threats or dangers.

How the Sahara Desert Used to Be a Lush Green Paradise

The vast expanse of the Sahara Desert, now a barren and inhospitable region, was once a lush, vibrant paradise teeming with life. Thousands of years ago, the Sahara was a fertile landscape of lakes, rivers, and forests, supporting a rich diversity of flora and fauna. Evidence of this dramatic transformation is scattered across the desert in the form of ancient cave paintings, fossilized remains of prehistoric creatures, and dried riverbeds, all pointing to a time when the region had a much wetter and milder climate. Researchers believe that a combination of natural climatic shifts and Earth's axial tilt gradually altered the Sahara's environment, turning it from a verdant paradise into the arid desert we know today. This transition occurred over millennia, leaving behind a desert that seems to be an unchanging, eternal fixture of the landscape. The discovery of ancient water sources beneath the sand has sparked interest in potential underground aquifers, which may offer a glimpse into the Sahara's wetter past and provide insight into the planet's changing climates over time. The Sahara's transformation serves as a stark reminder of the delicate balance of Earth's ecosystems.

Key Vocabulary:
- **Expanse**: A vast area or stretch, often referring to a large, open, and unbroken region.
- **Teeming**: Overflowing or abundantly filled with life or activity.
- **Fossilized**: Preserved in a form that remains after the organic material has been replaced by minerals over time.

- **Axial tilt**: The angle at which the Earth tilts on its axis, affecting the planet's seasonal patterns and climate over long periods.
- **Aquifers**: Underground layers of rock or soil that contain water, often tapped for irrigation or drinking water.

The Ancient Ice Caves That Have Never Melted

Hidden deep beneath the earth's surface, the Ice Caves of Mount Rwenzori, located on the border between Uganda and the Democratic Republic of Congo, are among the most extraordinary natural wonders in the world. These ancient ice caves, whose existence dates back millennia, have remained frozen despite the surrounding tropical climate. The unique geographic location of the Rwenzori Mountains, coupled with their high altitude, has preserved the ice in these caves for generations, even as the planet's climate has warmed. Scientists have long been fascinated by the ice within these caves, as they contain layers of ancient ice that offer a glimpse into the Earth's climatic past. The preservation of these ice formations, despite the surrounding warm environment, challenges our understanding of climate systems and their resilience. However, with global warming accelerating, the ice caves are slowly shrinking, raising concerns about their future and the potential loss of a key natural archive. The Rwenzori Ice Caves serve as both a breathtaking marvel and a poignant reminder of the fragility of Earth's natural wonders in the face of climate change.

Key Vocabulary:
- **Geographic**: Relating to the physical features, location, and environment of the Earth.
- **Resilience**: The ability to withstand or recover from difficult conditions, often referring to natural systems or organisms.
- **Fascinated**: Deeply captivated or absorbed by something, often in a way that sparks curiosity or awe.

- **Breathtaking**: Strikingly beautiful or impressive, often in a way that leaves one in awe or wonder.
- **Poignant**: Evoking a strong sense of sadness or regret, often due to the recognition of a loss or inevitable change.

Zealandia: Earth's Eighth Continent

Scientists recognize Zealandia as a distinct continent, with approximately 94% of its landmass submerged beneath the Pacific Ocean. The visible portions include New Zealand and New Caledonia. This continent spans roughly 5 million square kilometers (1.9 million square miles) and has a unique geological composition that distinguishes it from the surrounding oceanic crust. Zealandia was once connected to the supercontinent Gondwana before tectonic processes caused it to break away and partially submerge between 85-130 million years ago. The recognition of Zealandia as a continent in 2017 came after decades of research that confirmed it met all criteria for continental status: distinctive geology, elevated and thickened crust, well-defined boundaries, and an area larger than 1 million square kilometers.

Key Vocabulary:

- **Continental crust**: The thick, less dense outer layer of Earth that makes up the continents, typically 30-50 kilometers thick
- **Tectonic**: Relating to the structure and movement of Earth's crust and upper mantle
- **Gondwana**: An ancient supercontinent that included most of the landmasses in today's Southern Hemisphere
- **Submerged**: Located or positioned underwater
- **Lithosphere**: Earth's rigid outer layer, consisting of the crust and upper mantle

The Lake That Vanishes Through a Hole

Nestled in Oregon's Mount Hood National Forest lies a peculiar natural wonder: Lost Lake, a body of water that performs an annual disappearing act. Each spring, this 85-acre lake dramatically drains like a giant bathtub, its waters swirling into a mysterious 6-foot-wide hole—actually an ancient lava tube formed by the region's volcanic past. As winter snows melt and spring rains fill the basin, Lost Lake stretches across a pristine forest clearing. But when warmer weather arrives, the water begins its mesmerizing descent into the volcanic drain.

The lava tube responsible for this phenomenon was created thousands of years ago when molten lava flowed through the area, leaving behind a natural tunnel in the basaltic rock. Today, this tunnel acts as a direct conduit into the porous volcanic terrain below. While scientists understand that the drained water likely feeds into the vast aquifer system beneath the Cascade Range, the exact path it takes remains unmapped.

During its dry phase, the lakebed transforms into a meadow. Local wildlife adapts to this cyclical change, with different species making use of the landscape in its wet and dry states. The U.S. Forest Service actively discourages attempts to plug the hole, as this natural drain is crucial to the area's ecological balance and represents a fascinating glimpse into the region's volcanic heritage.

Key Vocabulary:

- **Lava tube**: A natural tunnel formed by flowing lava that creates a covered channel
- **Basaltic**: Relating to basalt, a dark volcanic rock formed from rapidly cooling lava
- **Aquifer**: Underground layer of permeable rock that holds or transmits groundwater
- **Porous**: Full of tiny holes that allow water to pass

through
- **Ecological**: Relating to the relationships between living things and their environment
- **Cyclical**: Occurring in a regular pattern or cycle
- **Terrain**: The physical features of an area of land

The Ancient Trees and Their Secret Locations

Nestled within a protected grove in California's White Mountains stands one of the world's oldest known trees—an arboreal titan whose origins predate the rise and fall of empires. Methuselah, a bristlecone pine estimated to be over 4,800 years old, shares these arid slopes with an even older neighbor discovered in 2012, which surpasses 5,000 years in age. Yet neither holds the current record—that distinction belongs to "Gran Abuelo," a 5,400-year-old Patagonian cypress found in Chile. Like their ancient kin, these trees remain relatively diminutive, their gnarled and twisted forms shaped by centuries of relentless winds, frigid winters, and parched summers. Their precise locations are closely guarded secrets, a necessary precaution to protect them from vandalism or inadvertent harm by eager visitors. Their ancient rings serve as living archives, chronicling millennia of climatic shifts, volcanic eruptions, and ecological transformations. Scientists have long studied their resilient anatomy, seeking to understand how such organisms have withstood the inexorable march of time. Yet, despite their age, these ancient sentinels remain very much alive, continuing to unfurl new growth in their desolate landscapes. They are living relics of Earth's primordial past, silent witnesses to history whose longevity surpasses that of civilizations that once flourished and faded into oblivion.

Key Vocabulary:
- **Arboreal**: Relating to trees or tree-like growth forms

- **Diminutive**: Unusually small; compact in size
- **Gnarled**: Twisted and knotted, especially from age or exposure to elements
- **Inexorable**: Relentless; impossible to stop or prevent
- **Sentinel**: A guard or watchman; something that stands as a marker or monument
- **Primordial**: Existing from the beginning; ancient or prehistoric
- **Resilient**: Able to withstand difficult conditions and recover from challenges

The Town That Is Slowly Sinking into the Ocean

Far from the bustling metropolises of the world lies a town doomed by the encroaching sea. The coastal settlement of Kivalina, Alaska, perched precariously on a narrow barrier island, is succumbing to the inexorable grip of rising tides and coastal erosion. Once shielded by thick permafrost and resilient sea ice, the town now finds itself at the mercy of an increasingly volatile climate. The warming Arctic has accelerated the thawing of its frozen foundations, causing the land to crumble and collapse into the churning waters. Fierce tempests and relentless waves batter the town's fragile coastline, carving away chunks of land with each passing season. Despite desperate efforts to fortify the shorelines with sea walls and sandbags, the ocean's advance remains unyielding. The residents of Kivalina face an uncertain future, forced to reckon with the stark reality that their home may soon be swallowed whole. With relocation efforts proving both logistically and financially daunting, the town stands as a haunting reminder of the profound consequences of environmental change, a vanishing relic of a world reshaped by the tides.

Key Vocabulary:
- **Encroaching**: Gradually advancing or intruding upon

something.
- **Precariously**: Dangerously unstable or uncertain.
- **Tempests**: Violent storms with strong winds and heavy rain.
- **Unyielding**: Not giving way to pressure; stubbornly resistant.
- **Daunting**: Overwhelmingly difficult or intimidating.

LEGENDS AND MYTHS

The Lost City of Atlantis

The legend of Atlantis, first described by the ancient Greek philosopher Plato, has captivated imaginations for centuries. Atlantis was said to be a vast, technologically advanced island, larger than Libya and Asia combined, with a society that rivaled the gods. However, it allegedly sank into the sea in a cataclysmic event around 9,000 years ago. Despite centuries of speculation and exploration, no physical evidence has ever confirmed its existence. Some believe the story is merely an allegory, a warning about the dangers of hubris and the fragility of civilization. Others remain convinced that Atlantis lies hidden beneath the ocean, waiting to be rediscovered. Various theories abound, from it being located in the Mediterranean to the Caribbean, with many proposing that its destruction was caused by a volcanic eruption or tectonic shift. The allure of the lost city lies in its promise of forgotten knowledge and untold riches, as well as the mystery of whether it was real or simply a grand myth. The search for Atlantis continues, making it a symbol of mankind's eternal quest for the unknown.

Key Vocabulary:
- **Hubris**: Excessive pride or self-confidence, often leading to a downfall, particularly when one challenges divine authority.

- **Cataclysmic**: Relating to a violent, often destructive event, such as a natural disaster that causes widespread damage.
- **Allegory**: A narrative in which characters and events represent abstract ideas or moral lessons, often used to teach societal or philosophical concepts.
- **Tectonic**: Pertaining to the movement or structure of the Earth's crust, especially in relation to the shifting of tectonic plates.
- **Allure**: The power to attract or charm, often through mystery or fascination.

The Legend of the Fountain of Youth

The Fountain of Youth has been a legendary source of immortality for centuries, with tales of its discovery dating back to the Spanish explorer Ponce de León. According to the myth, the fountain was said to grant eternal youth to those who bathed in or drank from its waters. Ponce de León, motivated by his quest for everlasting life, embarked on an expedition to the New World in the early 16th century in search of the mystical spring. Though he never found it, the legend endured, with many speculating that the fountain was located somewhere in Florida. Over the centuries, the tale has become synonymous with the human desire to stave off aging and death, as well as the endless pursuit of youth. Even today, people continue to seek out the mythical fountain, hoping to uncover its secrets. The legend represents humanity's universal yearning for immortality and the lengths we would go to in order to avoid the inevitable.

Key Vocabulary:
- **Immortality**: The condition of living forever, often used in mythology to describe beings who never age or die.
- **Everlasting**: Lasting forever; eternal. Used to describe something that has no end or decay.
- **Stave off**: To prevent something from happening,

especially something negative or harmful, by taking action in advance.
- **Synonymous**: Closely associated with something, often to the point where the two terms can be used interchangeably.
- **Universal**: Applicable to or affecting all people or things in the world, often used to describe concepts or desires shared by everyone.

The Curse of the Hope Diamond

The Hope Diamond, a magnificent 45.52-carat blue diamond, has long been associated with a curse that causes misfortune and tragedy to its owners. Originating in India, the diamond was believed to have been stolen from a Hindu temple, which set off a chain of calamities for those who possessed it. Over the centuries, the diamond passed through the hands of various aristocrats and jewelers, each of whom faced misfortune, including death, financial ruin, and scandal. The most famous of these owners was Evalyn Walsh McLean, whose life was filled with personal tragedy. Despite the ominous legend surrounding the diamond, it was eventually donated to the Smithsonian Institution, where it is now displayed. The mystery of the Hope Diamond's curse continues to intrigue and terrify, raising questions about fate, superstition, and the power of objects in shaping our lives.

Key Vocabulary:
- **Calamity**: A sudden and disastrous event, often causing great damage or loss. Used to describe a catastrophic event that brings about widespread suffering.
- **Aristocrat**: A member of the aristocracy, or the upper class, often possessing inherited wealth, power, or privilege.
- **Ominous**: Giving the impression that something bad or unpleasant is going to happen; foreboding.
- **Superstition**: A belief or practice that is not based

on reason or scientific evidence, often rooted in fear or ignorance of the unknown.
- **Fate**: A predetermined course of events, often associated with the idea that certain outcomes are inevitable, regardless of human action.

The Ancient Myth of the Phoenix— The Bird That Rises from Ashes

The Phoenix, a legendary bird from ancient mythology, is said to live for hundreds of years before bursting into flames and dying in a fiery death. From its ashes, a new Phoenix is born, symbolizing the cyclical nature of life, death, and rebirth. This myth, found in cultures across the world, represents resilience and renewal. The Phoenix is often seen as a metaphor for overcoming adversity, rising stronger from the challenges and struggles one faces. In some traditions, the Phoenix is considered a sacred creature, symbolizing immortality, while in others, it embodies the promise of a new beginning. The Phoenix's symbolism continues to inspire those who seek hope and strength in times of hardship, reminding them that even in the face of destruction, there is always the possibility of transformation and renewal.

Key Vocabulary:
- **Cyclical**: Happening in a repeating, circular pattern, often referring to events that go through phases or stages that repeat over time.
- **Resilience**: The ability to recover or bounce back from adversity, hardship, or difficulty, often used to describe emotional or psychological strength.
- **Adversity**: Difficulties or misfortune, often used to describe challenges that test a person's endurance or resolve.
- **Metaphor**: A figure of speech that compares two unlike things without using "like" or "as," often to create a deeper meaning or understanding.

- **Transformation**: A complete change or conversion in form, appearance, or character, often implying a significant improvement or shift.

The Story of King Arthur and His Mysterious Sword

King Arthur, a famous figures in British legend, is often depicted as a noble ruler who united the kingdom of Camelot. His legendary sword, Excalibur, is said to have been bestowed upon him by the Lady of the Lake, giving him unparalleled power and strength. The sword is often seen as a symbol of Arthur's rightful claim to the throne, as well as his bravery and honor. The mystery surrounding Excalibur's origins has captivated storytellers for centuries, with various versions of the tale suggesting different ways Arthur obtained it. Some say that he pulled the sword from a stone, proving his worth as king, while others suggest it was given to him in a more mystical ceremony. Regardless of its origin, Excalibur remains one of the most iconic weapons in mythological history, representing the ideals of chivalry, justice, and the eternal battle between good and evil.

Key Vocabulary:
- **Unparalleled**: Having no equal or rival; unmatched in quality or achievement.
- **Bestowed**: Given as a gift or honor, often used in the context of something valuable or significant.
- **Chivalry**: The medieval knightly code of conduct, emphasizing bravery, honor, and respect for women and the weak.
- **Mystical**: Relating to the supernatural, spiritual, or mysterious, often associated with things that are beyond ordinary understanding.
- **Ideals**: Standards of perfection or excellence, often used to describe the highest values or principles that one strives to achieve.

The Hidden Secrets of the Bermuda Triangle

The Bermuda Triangle, also known as the "Devil's Triangle," is a region in the North Atlantic Ocean where numerous ships and aircraft have mysteriously vanished over the centuries. Stretching between Miami, Bermuda, and Puerto Rico, the area has become infamous for the inexplicable disappearances of vessels and planes, some of which seemed to vanish without a trace. Various theories have been proposed to explain the phenomena, ranging from natural explanations such as magnetic anomalies and methane gas eruptions to more fantastical ideas like alien abductions or underwater civilizations. Some believe that the triangle harbors a rift in space and time, where the normal rules of physics do not apply. Others claim that the lost souls of ships and planes haunt the area, causing further disappearances. Despite extensive investigations, no single explanation has been universally accepted, and the Bermuda Triangle continues to captivate and mystify the public. The mystery surrounding this area symbolizes humanity's fear of the unknown and our constant search for meaning in inexplicable events, no matter how seemingly irrational.

Key Vocabulary:
- **Inexplicable**: Impossible to explain or account for, often referring to something that defies logical understanding or conventional reasoning.
- **Phenomena**: Observable events or occurrences, particularly those that are unusual or extraordinary. Used to describe things that cannot be easily explained or understood.
- **Rift**: A break or opening, often referring to a significant division or separation, whether physical or metaphorical. In this context, it refers to a possible tear in the fabric of reality.
- **Underwater**: Located or occurring beneath the surface

of the water, often used to describe things hidden or submerged.
- **Haunt**: To appear in a disturbing or ghostly way, often used to describe the persistent presence of a spirit or memory.

The Myth of the Loch Ness Monster—Fact or Fiction?

The Loch Ness Monster, affectionately known as "Nessie," has been a part of Scottish folklore for centuries. Described as a large, serpent-like creature with a long neck and humps on its back, Nessie is said to reside in the depths of Loch Ness, a large freshwater lake in the Scottish Highlands. The first recorded sighting of the monster dates back to the 6th century, but the myth gained significant attention in the 20th century following a series of photographs and videos purporting to show the creature. Despite numerous expeditions and scientific investigations, no conclusive evidence of Nessie's existence has been found, leading many to dismiss the creature as a hoax or the product of overactive imaginations. However, others believe that the monster is simply elusive, perhaps a relic from prehistoric times, hiding in the lake's deep, murky waters. The Loch Ness Monster represents a symbol of mystery and wonder, embodying the human desire to uncover the unknown and to seek out creatures that defy explanation.

Key Vocabulary:
- **Affectionately**: With fondness or tenderness, often used to describe actions or attitudes that show warmth or love.
- **Serpent-like**: Having the appearance or qualities of a snake; long, sinuous, and winding. Often used to describe creatures or figures that resemble snakes in shape or movement.
- **Expedition**: A journey or voyage undertaken for a specific purpose, particularly one that involves exploration or investigation.

- **Elusive**: Difficult to find, catch, or understand, often used to describe something that seems to escape detection or comprehension.
- **Relic**: An object or artifact from the past that holds historical or cultural significance, often associated with ancient or long-gone civilizations or practices.

The Legend of El Dorado—The City of Gold

The legend of El Dorado, often referred to as the "City of Gold," has lured explorers and treasure hunters to the Americas for centuries. According to the myth, El Dorado was a wealthy city hidden deep in the jungles of South America, where gold and precious stones were abundant. Early Spanish conquistadors, including Francisco Pizarro and Hernán Cortés, heard rumors of this city from indigenous people and embarked on perilous journeys to find it. They believed that the ruler of El Dorado, known as the Golden Man, would be covered in gold dust and lead them to unimaginable riches. However, despite numerous expeditions, the city was never found. Some historians believe that El Dorado was never a city at all but rather a metaphor for the vast wealth that existed in the New World. Others argue that it was a real place that was destroyed or hidden over time. The legend of El Dorado lives on, symbolizing humanity's insatiable greed and desire for wealth, as well as the dangers of blind ambition and the relentless pursuit of elusive dreams.

Key Vocabulary:
- **Lured**: Attracted or tempted, often by something enticing or desirable.
- **Perilous**: Full of danger or risk, often used to describe journeys or situations that are hazardous and life-threatening.
- **Conquistador**: A Spanish or Portuguese explorer, particularly those who conquered large areas of the Americas in the 15th and 16th centuries.
- **Insatiable**: Impossible to satisfy; a never-ending desire or

hunger for something, often used to describe cravings or ambitions that can never be fully fulfilled.
- **Relentless**: Unyielding or persistent in pursuing something, often without stopping or letting up, no matter the difficulty or opposition.

The Story Behind the Trojan Horse

The Trojan Horse is one of the most famous stories from Greek mythology, a tale of deception and cunning that led to the fall of the ancient city of Troy. According to the myth, after a long and fruitless siege, the Greeks constructed a massive wooden horse and left it at the gates of Troy as a supposed offering to the gods. Inside the horse, however, hid a group of Greek soldiers. The Trojans, believing the horse to be a gift, brought it into the city, where it was celebrated as a symbol of victory. That night, the soldiers emerged from the horse and opened the city gates, allowing the Greek army to enter and destroy Troy. The story of the Trojan Horse is often used as a metaphor for trickery and strategic thinking, representing the idea that appearances can be deceiving, and sometimes the greatest threats come from the most unexpected places.

Key Vocabulary:
- **Deception**: The act of deceiving or misleading someone, often used to describe trickery or falsehoods meant to manipulate or control.
- **Cunning**: Skill in achieving one's goals through cleverness, deceit, or ingenuity, often used to describe someone who is sly or crafty in their methods.
- **Siege**: A military operation in which forces surround a place, cutting it off from essential supplies, with the aim of forcing surrender or capturing the location.
- **Metaphor**: A figure of speech in which a word or phrase is applied to an object or action to which it is not literally applicable, often to imply a deeper meaning.
- **Unexpected**: Not anticipated or foreseen; surprising

in nature, often describing events that happen out of the blue or without warning.

The Mystery of the Hanging Gardens of Babylon

The Hanging Gardens of Babylon, one of the Seven Wonders of the Ancient World, are shrouded in mystery. Described by ancient historians as an incredible feat of engineering, the gardens were said to have been built in the city of Babylon, located in present-day Iraq. The gardens were reputed to consist of tiered terraces filled with lush greenery and exotic plants, creating an oasis in the desert. However, no definitive archaeological evidence has ever been found to confirm their existence, leading many to question whether the gardens were real or simply a myth. Some believe they were constructed by King Nebuchadnezzar II for his wife, Amytis, who longed for the green hills of her homeland. Others argue that the gardens were never in Babylon at all, but instead were located in Nineveh, the capital of the Assyrian Empire. Despite the uncertainty surrounding their location and existence, the Hanging Gardens remain a symbol of human ingenuity and the quest for beauty in the face of harsh, barren environments.

Key Vocabulary:
- **Shrouded**: Covered or concealed, often used to describe something that is hidden or kept secret.
- **Feats**: Remarkable achievements or actions, often requiring great skill, strength, or bravery.
- **Tiered**: Arranged in layers or levels, often used to describe structures or arrangements that have multiple levels stacked on top of each other.
- **Exotic**: Unusual or strikingly different, often used to describe things that are foreign, rare, or out of the ordinary.
- **Ingenuity**: The quality of being clever, original, and inventive, particularly in solving problems or creating solutions.

The Myth of Icarus and His Wings of Wax

The myth of Icarus is a tale from ancient Greek mythology about a young man who flew too close to the sun. Icarus's father, Daedalus, was an inventor and craftsman who created wings made of feathers and wax for himself and his son to escape from the island of Crete. Despite his father's warnings, Icarus became overwhelmed with the thrill of flight and soared higher and higher, getting closer to the sun. The heat from the sun caused the wax in his wings to melt, and Icarus plummeted into the sea and drowned. His story has come to symbolize human ambition and the dangers of overreach, as well as the tragic consequences of ignoring wise counsel. The myth serves as a reminder of the balance between freedom and caution, and the consequences of losing sight of one's limits.

Key Vocabulary:
- **Thrill**: A feeling of excitement or exhilaration, often associated with risky or daring activities.
- **Overwhelmed**: Overcome with emotions or sensations to the point of being unable to control them.
- **Plummeted**: Fell quickly and steeply, often with a sense of uncontrollable speed.
- **Plight**: A difficult or unfortunate situation, often one that involves suffering or hardship.
- **Counsel**: Advice or guidance, especially from someone experienced or knowledgeable.

The Legend of the Kraken—The Sea Monster of Old

The Kraken is a mythical sea monster said to dwell off the coast of Norway and Greenland. Described as a giant, tentacled creature, it was believed to be capable of dragging entire ships and their crews into the depths of the ocean. Sailors from centuries ago warned of the Kraken's presence, and its legend became a popular subject in literature and folklore. Some believed the monster was so large that its tentacles would wrap around entire ships, pulling them under the water. The Kraken was often portrayed as a creature of the deep, hiding beneath the surface until it emerged to wreak havoc. While the Kraken's existence has never been confirmed, the myth may have been inspired by sightings of giant squid, which can grow to impressive sizes. In modern times, the Kraken has been immortalized in films, books, and video games, continuing to captivate audiences with its terrifying and mysterious presence.

Key Vocabulary:
- **Tentacled**: Having long, flexible appendages, like the tentacles of a squid or octopus.
- **Drag**: To pull something along the ground or through the water, often with force or effort.
- **Wreak**: To cause damage or harm, often in a violent or destructive way.
- **Immortalized**: Made famous or remembered forever, often through art, literature, or media.
- **Captivate**: To attract and hold the attention or interest of someone, often in a fascinating or charming way.

The Story of the Yeti—The Abominable Snowman

The Yeti, also known as the Abominable Snowman, is a legendary creature said to inhabit the remote mountain ranges of the Himalayas. Described as a large, ape-like being covered in thick white fur, the Yeti is often depicted as a reclusive and elusive creature, rarely seen by humans. The myth of the Yeti has been passed down for generations, with various reports of sightings from local inhabitants and mountaineers. While no concrete evidence has ever been found to confirm the Yeti's existence, some believe that the creature may be a type of undiscovered animal, possibly a primate or bear-like species. Others argue that the Yeti is a symbolic representation of the wild, untamed nature of the Himalayas, a place that is both awe-inspiring and dangerous. Despite the lack of scientific proof, the legend of the Yeti continues to capture the imagination of adventurers and cryptozoologists alike, fueling expeditions in search of the elusive creature.

Key Vocabulary:
- **Reclusive**: Avoiding the company of others; solitary and withdrawn.
- **Elusive**: Difficult to find, catch, or understand.
- **Concrete**: Based on actual facts or reality; solid or definite.
- **Cryptozoologist**: A person who studies animals whose existence is unproven or disputed, often focusing on mythical creatures.
- **Expedition**: A journey undertaken for a specific purpose, especially one involving exploration or research.

The Myth of Pandora's Box—The Story That Warned Humanity

The myth of Pandora's Box is a cautionary tale in Greek mythology. Pandora was the first woman created by the gods, and she was given a jar (often misinterpreted as a box) that contained all the evils of the world. She was warned by the gods never to open it, but driven by curiosity, Pandora eventually unlocked the jar, releasing the countless miseries—disease, death, jealousy, and strife—into the world. However, as she quickly closed the jar, the only thing that remained inside was hope. This story explains the origins of human suffering and the presence of both good and evil in the world. The myth highlights the dangers of curiosity and the unintended consequences of actions, while also suggesting that hope remains a crucial force even in the darkest times. Over time, Pandora's Box has become a symbol for the consequences of meddling with things that should be left undisturbed. In modern interpretations, the story is often used to remind people of the fragile balance between knowledge and ignorance. It serves as a warning to respect boundaries and to be mindful of the impact our actions can have on the world around us.

Key Vocabulary:
- **Cautionary**: Intended to warn or advise against certain actions or behaviors.
- **Miseries**: Great suffering, unhappiness, or discomfort.
- **Strife**: Bitter conflict or disagreement, often involving violence.
- **Unintended**: Not planned or meant; accidental.
- **Fragile**: Easily broken, damaged, or harmed; delicate.

The Legend of Robin Hood—The Outlaw Who Stole from the Rich

Robin Hood is a famous figures in English folklore, known for his skills in archery and his defiant stand against injustice. Living in Sherwood Forest with his band of Merry Men, including loyal companions like Little John and Friar Tuck, Robin Hood became a symbol of resistance against oppressive rulers. The legendary outlaw is said to have stolen from the rich to give to the poor, challenging the corrupt authorities of his time. His story, often set during the reign of King Richard the Lionheart and his brother Prince John, reflects the tension between the monarchy and the common people in medieval England. Robin Hood's acts of bravery and fairness made him a hero among the downtrodden, and his legend has been adapted into numerous books, films, and plays. Over time, the figure of Robin Hood has become a symbol of social justice, representing the fight against inequality and tyranny. His actions resonate as a reminder of the power of individuals to challenge authority and advocate for the marginalized. Though the historical existence of Robin Hood is debated, his legend continues to inspire generations to fight for what is right, regardless of the odds. In the modern world, Robin Hood's tale remains a narrative of defiance, justice, and altruism.

Key Vocabulary:
- **Defiant**: Showing resistance or bold opposition to authority or an established rule.
- **Altruism**: Selfless concern for the well-being of others; generosity.
- **Tyranny**: Cruel and oppressive government or rule.
- **Resonate**: To evoke a strong feeling or memory, often in a way that feels relevant or meaningful.
- **Marginalized**: Treated as insignificant or peripheral, often by social, political, or economic forces.

The Mystery of the Holy Grail

The Holy Grail is one of the more enduring symbols of mystery and spiritual quest in Western culture. In Christian mythology, the Grail is said to be the cup used by Jesus Christ during the Last Supper, and it is believed to have miraculous powers, including the ability to heal the sick and grant eternal life. The Grail's significance in legend goes beyond its religious associations, as it is often portrayed as an object of an epic search in the Arthurian legends. Knights of the Round Table, including Sir Lancelot and Sir Galahad, embarked on perilous quests to find the Grail, each of them hoping to unlock its divine power. The quest for the Holy Grail is often viewed as a symbol of the search for truth, enlightenment, and spiritual fulfillment. In modern interpretations, the Grail has been used to explore themes of self-discovery, personal transformation, and the pursuit of unattainable ideals. While the actual existence of the Holy Grail remains unproven, its legend continues to inspire countless writers, filmmakers, and adventurers to explore the mystery behind it. The Grail's allure is in its promise of something greater than the mundane world —a beacon of hope, redemption, and divine intervention. Whether as a religious artifact or a symbol of human striving, the Grail remains one of the most intriguing and powerful myths in history.

Key Vocabulary:
- **Miraculous**: Extraordinary and unexplainable, often involving divine or supernatural intervention.
- **Perilous**: Full of danger or risk; hazardous.
- **Enlightenment**: The state of gaining deeper knowledge or wisdom, often associated with spiritual or intellectual growth.
- **Unattainable**: Impossible to achieve or reach.
- **Allure**: The quality of being powerfully attractive or fascinating.

The Story of Medusa and the Gorgon Sisters

Medusa is a tragic figures in Greek mythology, a Gorgon whose terrifying appearance could turn anyone who looked into her eyes to stone. She was originally a beautiful maiden, but after being cursed by the goddess Athena, Medusa's transformation into a monster began. The curse was a punishment for being violated by Poseidon in Athena's temple, an act that angered the goddess. As a result, Medusa's hair turned into writhing snakes, and her once-beautiful face became a horrific sight. She was banished to a remote island, where she lived in isolation, terrifying anyone who dared approach her. Medusa's tragic story takes a turn when the hero Perseus is sent on a quest to slay her. Armed with a reflective shield from Athena and a sword from Hermes, Perseus was able to approach Medusa without looking directly at her, using the shield's reflection to avoid her deadly gaze. He successfully beheaded Medusa, but the myth does not end there. From her severed neck sprang the winged horse Pegasus, symbolizing the link between life and death. Medusa's legacy lives on as a symbol of transformation, vengeance, and the consequences of divine punishment. Her story explores themes of beauty, power, and victimization, as well as the complex relationships between gods and mortals.

Key Vocabulary:
- **Writhing**: Twisting or squirming, often in a way that suggests discomfort or agitation.
- **Banished**: Forced to leave a place or group, often as a punishment.
- **Quest**: A long and challenging journey in search of something important, often involving a hero's trials.
- **Severed**: Cut off from the rest, especially referring to body parts.
- **Vengeance**: The act of seeking revenge or retribution for a wrong or injustice.

The Origins of the Werewolf Myth

The werewolf, or "man-wolf," is an iconic creatures in Western folklore, with origins that date back to ancient times. The myth of the werewolf is rooted in the fear of transformation, particularly the idea of a human changing into a dangerous, uncontrollable beast. Ancient Greek and Roman writers mention shape shifting beings that could change into wolves, often associated with divine punishment. However, the modern concept of the werewolf is more closely tied to medieval Europe, where it was believed that certain people had the ability to transform into wolves either through dark magic or as a curse. In these regions, werewolves were often seen as outcasts, feared by communities who believed they were capable of wreaking havoc, especially during the full moon. The idea of a person transforming into a wolf was also tied to the belief in lycanthropy, a psychological condition where an individual believes they can turn into an animal. Over the centuries, the werewolf myth evolved, becoming a staple of horror literature and films. The transformation itself, marked by physical pain and uncontrollable rage, became a symbol of inner conflict and the loss of humanity. Werewolves were often portrayed as tragic figures, caught between their human and monstrous sides, adding a layer of psychological depth to the myth. Today, werewolves remain a popular subject in horror fiction, symbolizing the darker aspects of human nature and the fear of the unknown.

Key Vocabulary:
- **Shapeshifting**: The ability to change physical form, often into another creature.
- **Lycanthropy**: The mythical condition of being able to transform into a wolf or other animal.
- **Outcasts**: People who are rejected or excluded from society.
- **Wreaking havoc**: Causing widespread destruction or chaos.
- **Tragic**: Marked by sorrow or misfortune, often leading to a downfall.

The Myth of Charon—The Ferryman of the Underworld

In ancient Greek mythology, Charon is the ferryman of the Underworld, tasked with transporting the souls of the dead across the River Styx to the realm of the dead. Charon is often depicted as a grim, somber figure, sometimes with a skeletal appearance, ferrying souls in his boat through the dark waters. According to myth, the souls of the deceased must pay Charon for passage, usually with an obolus or a coin placed in their mouth upon burial. This payment was essential, as it ensured that the soul would be able to reach its final resting place. Those who were not given a proper burial or lacked the coin to pay Charon were said to wander the banks of the Styx for eternity, unable to cross into the afterlife. Charon's role in the myth highlights the ancient Greeks' belief in the importance of honoring the dead and the rituals surrounding death and burial. The ferryman's grim task symbolized the inevitability of death, with no one able to escape his service. Charon's presence also reflects the ancient Greeks' understanding of the afterlife as a place of separation and transition, where souls could not return to the world of the living. Over time, Charon's figure became a powerful symbol of the inescapable journey into death, appearing in literature, art, and later in modern films and stories. His portrayal continues to evoke themes of death, passage, and the crossing into the unknown.

Key Vocabulary:
- **Ferryman**: A person who operates a boat or ferry, especially one that transports souls in mythology.
- **Obolus**: A small coin, often used as payment in ancient times.
- **Styx**: A river in Greek mythology that separates the world of the living from the Underworld.
- **Somber**: Dark, serious, or melancholy in tone.
- **Inevitable**: Certain to happen, unavoidable.

The Tale of the Minotaur and the Labyrinth

The Minotaur is one of the most famous creatures in Greek mythology, a fearsome monster with the body of a man and the head of a bull. According to the myth, the Minotaur was born to Queen Pasiphae of Crete, who, through a curse from the gods, fell in love with a sacred bull. The resulting creature, half-human and half-bull, was so monstrous that it could not be allowed to roam freely. The Minotaur was confined to a maze-like structure called the Labyrinth, built by the skilled craftsman Daedalus on the island of Crete. The Labyrinth was designed to be so complex that anyone who entered would become hopelessly lost, making it impossible to escape. Every year, Athens was required to send a group of young men and women as tribute to the Minotaur, who would devour them. The story of the Minotaur reaches its climax when the hero Theseus volunteers to enter the Labyrinth and slay the beast. With the help of Princess Ariadne, who gives him a ball of thread to mark his path, Theseus manages to find the Minotaur and defeat it. The tale of the Minotaur and the Labyrinth is key myth of Greek mythology, symbolizing the struggle between human bravery and monstrous evil, and the triumph of intelligence over overwhelming danger. The Labyrinth itself represents both the complexity of human challenges and the fear of being trapped by fate.

Key Vocabulary:
- **Tribute**: A payment made by one group or nation to another, often in the form of goods or people, as a sign of submission.
- **Maize-like**: Having a design that is complex and difficult to navigate, symbolizing entrapment.
- **Slay**: To kill in a violent or brutal way.
- **Complex**: Complicated, made of many interconnected parts.
- **Climax**: The most intense or exciting point in a story or narrative.

The Curse of the Mummy's Tomb

The curse of the mummy's tomb is a legend steeped in mystery, superstition, and the allure of ancient Egypt. The myth centers on the idea that those who disturb the tombs of mummies, particularly the tombs of pharaohs, will be cursed, suffering misfortune or even death as a result. This legend became especially popular after the discovery of the tomb of Tutankhamun in 1922 by archaeologist Howard Carter. After the tomb's opening, several members of the expedition, including Lord Carnarvon, who funded the excavation, died under mysterious circumstances, leading to rumors of a curse. The idea of a mummy's curse plays on the fear of the unknown, particularly the belief that the ancient Egyptians placed great importance on protecting their tombs and their treasures from grave robbers and intruders. According to the myth, the curse was invoked by the gods to punish those who desecrated sacred resting places. In addition to the death of the expedition members, other people connected to the discovery of Tutankhamun's tomb also experienced misfortune, further fueling the legend. While modern archaeologists dismiss the idea of a curse, the tale persists as part of the mystique surrounding ancient Egypt. The mummy's curse has been featured in countless films, books, and stories, making it one of the more enduring myths of the 20th century. Its popularity perhaps reflects society's fascination with ancient history, superstition, and the fear of the unknown.

Key Vocabulary:
- **Desecrated**: Treated with disrespect, especially something sacred or holy.
- **Superstition**: A belief or practice resulting from fear of the unknown or belief in magic.
- **Mystique**: An air of mystery or fascination surrounding something or someone.
- **Expedition**: A journey undertaken for a specific purpose, often for exploration or research.
- **Curse**: A solemn utterance intended to bring bad luck or misfortune to someone or something.

The Story of the Basilisk—The Snake That Could Kill with a Glance

The basilisk is a legendary creature from European folklore, often depicted as a giant serpent or lizard with deadly powers. It is said that the basilisk's gaze alone could kill anyone who met its eyes. In some versions of the myth, the creature's breath or venom is also poisonous enough to bring death. The basilisk's origins are traced back to ancient Greece, where it was described as the king of serpents. In medieval Europe, it became a symbol of terror, thought to reside in dark caves or hidden corners of the world. To combat the basilisk, mythological heroes used mirrors or reflective shields to avoid its deadly stare. The creature became a symbol of destructive power and the danger of temptation, where even a momentary weakness could lead to death. Today, the basilisk remains a powerful symbol of fear and danger in fantasy literature and popular culture.

Key Vocabulary:
- **Glance**: A quick look.
- **Venom**: A poisonous substance secreted by certain animals.
- **Terror**: Intense fear.
- **Reflective**: Capable of reflecting light or images.
- **Temptation**: The desire to do something, especially something wrong or unwise.

The Mystery of the Chupacabra

The chupacabra, meaning "goat-sucker" in Spanish, is a creature of modern legend originating from Latin America. Described as a reptilian monster with spines along its back or sometimes as a hairless dog-like creature, the chupacabra is said to drain the blood of livestock, particularly goats. The first reported sightings occurred in Puerto Rico in the 1990s, where several animals were found dead, their blood mysteriously drained. Over time, the legend of the chupacabra spread to other parts of the Americas, including Mexico and the southwestern United States. Some believe it to be an alien or a mutant creature, while others argue that it is a misidentified animal, like a coyote suffering from mange. Despite investigations, no concrete evidence of the chupacabra's existence has ever been found. The creature's mystery continues to fascinate, and it has become a staple of modern folklore, often appearing in stories, films, and TV shows. The chupacabra is a reminder of how legends can take on a life of their own, fueled by fear and imagination.

Key Vocabulary:
- **Reptilian**: Having characteristics of a reptile.
- **Sucker**: Someone or something that takes in or absorbs something.
- **Mange**: A skin disease affecting animals, often causing hair loss.

- **Misidentified**: Incorrectly identified.
- **Folklore**: Traditional beliefs, myths, or stories passed down through generations.

The Tale of the Banshee—The Harbinger of Death

In Irish mythology, the banshee is a ghostly figure whose wail is believed to foretell the death of a family member. The name "banshee" comes from the Irish words "bean sídhe," meaning "woman of the fairy mound," reflecting her connection to the spirit world. The banshee is often depicted as a pale woman with long, flowing hair, wearing a white or gray gown. Her scream is said to be so mournful and chilling that it sends fear through anyone who hears it. The banshee's role in Irish folklore is as a harbinger of death, warning of impending tragedy, particularly within certain families. While her appearance is often seen as a sign of doom, some myths suggest that her cry is a form of mourning, expressing sorrow for the loss of a loved one. The legend of the banshee has influenced many stories of spirits and death omens, remaining a powerful figure in Irish and Celtic culture. It symbolizes the deep connection between the living and the dead, and the inevitability of mortality.

Key Vocabulary:
- **Wail**: A long, high-pitched cry of sorrow or pain.
- **Harbinger**: A sign or indication of something to come.
- **Fairy mound**: A burial mound or hill associated with fairy or spirit activity in Celtic mythology.
- **Mournful**: Full of sadness or grief.
- **Inevitable**: Certain to happen, unavoidable.

The Myth of the Doppelgänger—An Omen of Doom

The doppelgänger is a supernatural entity that appears as an identical double of a person. Originating from German folklore, the word "doppelgänger" literally means "double-goer," and the myth suggests that encountering one's doppelgänger is a bad omen. In many stories, seeing one's double is said to precede misfortune or even death. The doppelgänger is often depicted as a mirror image, but with an unsettling or malevolent presence. Some believe that the doppelgänger is a harbinger of doom, while others suggest it is a manifestation of a person's darker, hidden self. Throughout history, numerous reports of doppelgänger sightings have stirred fear, particularly when they are seen by loved ones or close friends. The myth continues to captivate writers and filmmakers, who use the concept of the doppelgänger to explore themes of identity, fate, and the human psyche. Its recurring presence in literature and film shows our fascination with the unknown and the unsettling idea of facing one's own reflection in a sinister form.

Key Vocabulary:
- **Doppelgänger**: A ghostly or supernatural double of a living person.
- **Unsettling**: Causing anxiety or discomfort.
- **Malevolent**: Having or showing a desire to harm others.
- **Manifestation**: The act of making something appear, especially something abstract or hidden.
- **Fate**: The course of events that are believed to be beyond a person's control.

The Legend of the Djinn—Ancient Spirits of Fire and Smoke

The djinn, or genies, are supernatural beings mentioned in pre-Islamic Arabian mythology, but they later became a prominent feature in Islamic culture as well. Traditionally, djinn are considered spirits of fire, capable of shape-shifting and inhabiting various forms, including animals or humans. They are said to possess great powers, including the ability to grant wishes, but also to cause mischief or even harm to those who encounter them. The most famous depiction of the djinn comes from the tale of "Aladdin," where a genie grants the protagonist three wishes. However, the original myth of the djinn is far darker, with many stories warning of their dangerous and unpredictable nature. In Islamic belief, djinn are said to live in a parallel world to humans and have free will, much like humans do. They can be benevolent, malevolent, or neutral, depending on the individual djinn. The legend of the djinn has captivated the imagination of many cultures, and they continue to be a popular figure in folklore, literature, and movies.

Key Vocabulary:
- **Djinn**: Supernatural beings, often associated with granting wishes or causing trouble.
- **Shape-shifting**: The ability to change form or appearance.
- **Benevolent**: Well-meaning and kindly.
- **Mischief**: Behavior that causes trouble or harm, often in a playful way.
- **Parallel**: Existing alongside, but separate or different.

The Mystery of the Lost Colony of Roanoke

The Lost Colony of Roanoke is one of America's more vexing historical mysteries. In 1587, a group of English settlers established a colony on Roanoke Island, but when a supply ship returned three years later, the entire settlement had vanished without a trace. All that remained was the word "Croatoan" carved into a tree, suggesting that the settlers may have relocated to a nearby island or been absorbed into the local indigenous tribes. Various theories about their fate include starvation, attacks by Native Americans, or integration into other communities. The mystery deepens as no definitive evidence has been found to explain what happened to the settlers. Some believe they may have been lost to time or even wiped out in a storm. Over the centuries, the story of Roanoke has captured the imagination of many, fueling speculation and debate. The Lost Colony remains a symbol of the unknown in early American history.

Key Vocabulary:
- **Tribe**: A group of people sharing common customs, traditions, and language, often with a social structure.
- **Speculation**: The act of guessing or forming theories without sufficient evidence.
- **Definitive**: Providing a clear and final answer or solution.
- **Symbol**: An object, mark, or concept that represents something else, often an idea or quality.

The Legend of Bigfoot—The Elusive Forest Giant

Bigfoot, also known as Sasquatch, is a creature that has captured the imagination of people across North America for centuries. Described as a large, hairy, human-like being, Bigfoot is often said to inhabit remote forests, particularly in the Pacific Northwest. The legend of Bigfoot has deep roots in Indigenous folklore, with various Native American tribes telling stories of wild, human-like creatures living in the woods. These stories were passed down through generations, long before European settlers arrived in North America. Bigfoot sightings began to gain widespread attention in the 20th century, with photographs, videos, and footprints allegedly documenting the creature's existence. While there is no definitive proof of Bigfoot's existence, many people continue to search for evidence, convinced that the creature remains hidden in the vast forests of the American wilderness. Skeptics argue that the sightings could be explained by hoaxes, misidentifications of other animals, or even the human tendency to see patterns in nature. Yet, despite the lack of concrete evidence, the Bigfoot legend has become a fixture of popular culture, with numerous documentaries, books, and TV shows dedicated to exploring the mystery. Bigfoot's story represents the fascination with the unknown, the wilderness, and the possibility of creatures that may exist just beyond the edges of our understanding. Whether seen as a cryptid or a myth, Bigfoot continues to be a symbol of both the unexplored and the supernatural.

Key Vocabulary:
- **Elusive**: Difficult to find, catch, or understand.
- **Indigenous**: Native to a particular region or environment.
- **Hoaxes**: Deceptive tricks or false claims intended to mislead people.
- **Skeptics**: People who doubt or question accepted beliefs or claims.
- **Cryptid**: A creature whose existence is unsubstantiated by scientific evidence.

The Story of Thor and His Mighty Hammer

Thor, the Norse god of thunder, is one of the most well-known figures in Norse mythology, symbolizing strength, protection, and bravery. Thor is the son of Odin, the king of the gods, and is often depicted wielding his mighty hammer, Mjölnir, which has the power to summon lightning and thunder. According to myth, Thor's primary role is to protect the gods and humans from the giants (Jotnar), who are the enemies of the gods. One of the most famous tales of Thor is the story of his journey to the land of the giants to retrieve his stolen hammer. In this tale, Thor is forced to disguise himself as a bride in order to trick the giant king Thrym, who had stolen Mjölnir and demanded the goddess Freyja as his bride in exchange for its return. In the end, Thor regains his hammer by outwitting the giants, using both his strength and cunning. Thor's hammer, Mjölnir, is a weapon but also serves as a symbol of fertility, protection, and the power to ward off evil. The thunder god's adventures are also filled with humor, as Thor's sometimes brash and impulsive behavior often leads to chaotic, yet victorious, outcomes. Thor's stories reflect the values of Norse culture, emphasizing courage, loyalty, and the triumph of order over chaos. In modern times, Thor has become an iconic figure in popular culture, especially through the Marvel comic books and films, where he is portrayed as a superhero with both human vulnerability and divine power. The ongoing popularity of Thor's legend speaks to the timeless appeal of stories about gods and heroes.

Key Vocabulary:
- **Mjölnir**: Thor's magical hammer, often depicted as a weapon capable of generating thunder and lightning.
- **Jotnar**: The giants in Norse mythology, often in opposition to the gods.
- **Cunning**: Skill in achieving one's goals through cleverness or deceit.
- **Brash**: Bold or audacious, often in a way that is too forward or disrespectful.
- **Vulnerability**: The state of being open to harm or attack, often seen as a weakness.

The Myth of the Wendigo—The Spirit of Cannibalism

The Wendigo is a terrifying creature from Algonquian folklore, particularly associated with the cold, desolate forests of the northern United States and Canada. Described as a spirit or monster with an insatiable hunger for human flesh, the Wendigo embodies the horrors of cannibalism and the loss of humanity. According to legend, a person who resorts to cannibalism during a time of extreme hunger is cursed and transformed into a Wendigo, forever driven by an endless craving for human flesh. The Wendigo is often depicted as a gaunt, emaciated figure with glowing eyes, long claws, and an unsettling, hollow voice. The myth of the Wendigo serves as a warning against the extremes of greed and desperation, especially in times of famine. It is also a symbol of the dangers of losing one's moral compass and succumbing to primal instincts. The Wendigo is a creature of physical horror but also represents the mental and spiritual corruption that can result from isolation and deprivation. Over time, the Wendigo myth has become a popular figure in horror stories, films, and television, often representing the darker side of human nature. In contemporary interpretations, Wendigo's tale continues to resonate as a symbol of the dangers of unchecked desire and the consequences of moral decay. Its legend reminds us of the delicate balance between survival and the loss of humanity.

Key Vocabulary:
- **Insatiable**: Impossible to satisfy; having an unquenchable desire.
- **Emaciated**: Extremely thin or weak, often due to hunger or illness.
- **Craving**: A strong desire for something, especially something unhealthy or forbidden.
- **Primal**: Relating to the basic instincts or behaviors of early humans and animals.
- **Deprivation**: The state of lacking something essential, such as food, sleep, or emotional support.

The Legend of the Headless Horseman

The Headless Horseman is a legendary figure from American folklore, most famously featured in Washington Irving's The Legend of Sleepy Hollow. According to the tale, the Headless Horseman is the ghost of a soldier who was decapitated during the American Revolutionary War. He is said to haunt the village of Sleepy Hollow, riding through the night in search of his missing head. The figure of the Headless Horseman is both terrifying and tragic, embodying the restless spirit of a man who has not found peace after death. The story's protagonist, Ichabod Crane, encounters the Headless Horseman during his travels, and the ghostly rider chases him, throwing a pumpkin (which is mistaken for the decapitated head) at him. The legend of the Headless Horseman has become a symbol of fear and the supernatural, but it also taps into deeper themes of war, death, and unresolved conflict. The Horseman's pursuit of Ichabod Crane can be seen as a manifestation of the dangers of meddling with forces beyond human understanding, as well as the lingering trauma of the past. Over time, the tale of the Headless Horseman has become a staple of Halloween folklore, with adaptations in films, television, and literature. The mysterious nature of the story and its eerie atmosphere continue to captivate audiences, making the Headless Horseman a timeless figure in American mythology.

Key Vocabulary:
- **Decapitated**: Beheaded; the act of removing someone's head.
- **Restless**: Unable to find peace or settle; constantly agitated.
- **Manifestation**: A clear or tangible expression of something abstract, such as a feeling or spirit.
- **Meddling**: Interfering in something, often in a way that is unwelcome or harmful.
- **Staple**: A basic or essential element of something, often repeated or commonly used.

The Myth of the Chimera—A Beast of Many Creatures

In Greek mythology, the Chimera is a fearsome creature composed of multiple animals. Typically described as having the body of a lion, the head of a goat rising from its back, and a serpent's tail, it was a terrifying force to be reckoned with. The Chimera was said to breathe fire, making it nearly invincible. It was eventually slain by the hero Bellerophon, who rode the winged horse Pegasus into battle. In their encounter, Bellerophon used a spear tipped with lead, which melted when exposed to the Chimera's fire, suffocating the beast. The Chimera represents the idea of chaos and the unnatural combination of different creatures into one being. It has come to symbolize challenges that seem insurmountable, as well as the potential for great strength in unity. Today, the Chimera remains a prominent symbol in art, literature, and popular culture.

Key Vocabulary:
- **Fearsome**: Causing fear or dread due to its strength or appearance.
- **Invincible**: Impossible to defeat or overcome.
- **Suffocate**: To die or cause someone to die due to a lack of air or oxygen.
- **Chaos**: Complete disorder or confusion.
- **Symbolize**: To represent something with a particular meaning or idea.

The Story of Excalibur—The Sword of Destiny

Excalibur, the legendary sword of King Arthur, is one of the most iconic weapons in mythology. It is said to have been forged by the Lady of the Lake, a mythical figure who granted Arthur the sword as part of his destiny to become a great king. Excalibur's power was unmatched, and it symbolized Arthur's divine right to rule. The sword's magical properties were said to include the ability to cut through anything, even the toughest armor. After Arthur's death, Excalibur was returned to the Lady of the Lake, ensuring its mystique lived on. The sword has come to represent strength, leadership, and the idea of destiny shaping the future. Many stories and adaptations have kept Excalibur alive in both folklore and modern media, linking it to Arthurian legends. The tale of Excalibur continues to inspire those who seek a symbol of hope and the eternal struggle for justice.

Key Vocabulary:
- **Iconic**: Widely recognized and symbolic of a particular idea or theme.
- **Forged**: Created or shaped through intense heat or pressure.

- **Mystique**: An air of mystery, beauty, or charm.
- **Divine**: Of or relating to a god or supreme being.
- **Eternal**: Lasting forever, without end.

The Legend of the Naga—The Snake Gods of Asia

In many Asian cultures, the Naga is a powerful and revered mythical creature, often depicted as a serpent or dragon-like being with divine qualities. In Hindu and Buddhist traditions, Nagas are believed to be semi-divine, possessing both human and serpent features. They are guardians of water sources such as rivers and lakes, and their presence is often associated with fertility and prosperity. Some stories portray the Naga as protectors of sacred knowledge or treasure, while others describe them as vengeful beings who can bring disasters if angered. In Southeast Asia, Nagas are also believed to have the ability to shape-shift, becoming human or other forms at will. The Naga is considered a symbol of power, mystery, and the balance of nature. In addition to their role in religion and myth, the Naga is a significant figure in art and architecture, often seen in temples and shrines. The legend of the Naga continues to inspire spiritual beliefs and cultural practices across Asia.

Key Vocabulary:
- **Revered**: Deeply respected or admired.
- **Semi-divine**: Partly divine, with some god-like qualities.
- **Guardian**: A protector or defender.
- **Vengeful**: Seeking revenge or punishment for a wrong.
- **Shape-shift**: To transform into a different form or appearance.

The Tale of the Pied Piper—The Man Who Stole the Children

The legend of the Pied Piper of Hamelin is one of the most well-known and eerie folk tales. It begins with the town of

Hamelin, which is overrun by rats. Desperate to rid themselves of the vermin, the townspeople hire a mysterious piper who promises to lead the rats away with his enchanted music. True to his word, the piper plays his pipe, and the rats follow him into the Weser River, where they drown. However, when the piper returns to collect his fee, the townspeople refuse to pay him, breaking their agreement. In retaliation, the piper plays his pipe once more, this time leading the children of the town away. The children follow him through the town and into a cave, where they disappear, never to be seen again. Some versions of the story claim that the children were taken to a faraway land, while others say they were lost forever. The tale of the Pied Piper has been interpreted as a warning about the consequences of dishonesty and betrayal. The mysterious figure of the piper remains a symbol of retribution and the idea that broken promises can lead to irreversible consequences.

Key Vocabulary:
- **Overrun**: To be filled or overwhelmed with something, often in an undesirable way.
- **Enchanted**: Filled with magic or charm.
- **Retaliation**: The act of returning an injury or wrong with another act of harm.
- **Retribution**: Punishment for a wrong or crime.
- **Irreversible**: Not able to be undone or changed.

The Myth of the White Lady—A Ghostly Apparition Seen Worldwide

The White Lady is a common apparition in folklore across many cultures and countries, each with its own interpretation of the spirit. Generally depicted as a woman dressed in white, she is often linked to tragedy or loss, particularly in connection to love. Some versions of the legend say that the White Lady is the ghost of a woman who died tragically, such as from an unfulfilled love or a violent death. In many stories, she appears to warn people of impending death or disaster, often foretelling an accident or death of someone close. The White Lady is also said to haunt certain locations, such as roadsides, graveyards, or castles, where her presence is felt as an omen of doom. Across the world, she has been spotted by travelers, and her sightings are often described as eerie and unsettling. The legend of the White Lady reflects the universal human fear of death and the unknown, as well as the belief that spirits continue to exist after death. Some cultures see her as a protective figure, offering guidance to the lost, while others view her as a malevolent force. The mystery of the White Lady has endured over the centuries, captivating those who hear her tale and inspiring countless ghost stories and urban legends. The stories of the White Lady continue to be passed down, a haunting reminder of the unknown that lurks just beyond the veil of life.

Key Vocabulary:
- **Apparition**: A ghostly figure or manifestation of a spirit.
- **Omen**: A sign or event that is believed to predict the future.
- **Unsettling**: Causing discomfort or unease.
- **Malevolent**: Having or showing a desire to cause harm or evil.
- **Veil**: A thin, transparent covering that often symbolizes the boundary between life and death.

The Legend of the Thunderbird— The Giant Bird of the Skies

The Thunderbird is a powerful figure in Native American mythology, particularly among tribes such as the Algonquian and Sioux. It is described as a massive bird, so large that it can create storms by flapping its wings. The Thunderbird is said to live in the sky, often dwelling in high mountain peaks or clouds, where it controls the weather and protects the natural world. Some stories portray the Thunderbird as a divine being, sent to guard the earth from evil or to restore balance when it is disturbed. In some versions, the Thunderbird is a fierce protector of the people, striking down enemies with bolts of lightning from its eyes or claws. The bird's power is often seen as a symbol of strength, power, and divine wrath. The legend of the Thunderbird has transcended its Native American origins, influencing popular culture and becoming a symbol of American pride. It is often depicted in art and literature, where it represents both the might of nature and the spiritual connection between the earth and the heavens. Many modern-day interpretations of the Thunderbird continue to emphasize its role as a symbol of hope, resilience, and protection.

Key Vocabulary:
- **Massive**: Extremely large or heavy.
- **Transcended**: Went beyond or surpassed something.
- **Divine**: Of or relating to a god or supreme being.
- **Bolt**: A sudden flash of light, often associated with lightning.
- **Resilience**: The ability to recover from or adapt to difficult situations.

The Mystery of the Alchemist's Philosopher's Stone

The Philosopher's Stone is a legendary substance in alchemy, believed to have the power to transform base metals into gold and grant immortality through the Elixir of Life. Alchemists, particularly during the Middle Ages, sought to create the stone as the pinnacle of their craft, believing it could unlock the secrets of the universe. Many famous alchemists, such as Nicolas Flamel, were rumored to have discovered the stone, though no concrete evidence exists to support these claims. The stone itself was often described as a red or orange gem with magical properties, able to perform feats that defied the laws of nature. The search for the Philosopher's Stone became a metaphor for humanity's desire to attain eternal life and ultimate knowledge. Some believed the stone's discovery would lead to enlightenment, while others saw it as a path to great wealth and power. Over time, the Philosopher's Stone became a symbol of unattainable wisdom and the dangers of obsessive pursuit. In modern times, it has been immortalized in works of fiction, such as Harry Potter and the Philosopher's Stone, where it continues to captivate the imagination. The mystery of the Philosopher's Stone remains one of the more intriguing tales in the history of alchemy and mysticism.

Key Vocabulary:
- **Alchemist**: A person who practices alchemy, a medieval forerunner of chemistry.
- **Pinnacle**: The highest point or peak of something.
- **Concrete**: Based on actual facts or evidence.
- **Feats**: Achievements or accomplishments, especially ones that are impressive or difficult.
- **Aspiration**: A strong desire or ambition to achieve something.

The Myth of the Cursed Black Pearl

The Black Pearl is a legendary and cursed treasure, often associated with pirates and the sea. The myth surrounding the Black Pearl speaks of a cursed ship, its crew doomed to sail the oceans forever, never able to set foot on land. The legend suggests that anyone who possesses the Black Pearl will be cursed with bad luck and misfortune, and that the treasure will bring nothing but tragedy to those who seek it. In many stories, the curse is tied to a great betrayal or a wrongful act, often involving greed or lust for power. The Black Pearl itself is said to be a priceless gem, with an otherworldly glow that attracts treasure hunters and pirates alike. Some versions of the myth claim that the Black Pearl was forged by dark magic or that it is the soul of a pirate captain who made a deal with the devil. Over time, the Black Pearl has become synonymous with the idea of cursed treasure and the inevitable downfall of those who seek it. The tale of the Black Pearl has been popularized in movies, books, and folklore, where it is portrayed as a symbol of the dangers of greed and the consequences of defying fate. Whether as a literal treasure or a metaphor for temptation, the Black Pearl serves as a reminder that some things are best left untouched. The mystery of the Black Pearl endures, captivating the imagination of adventurers and dreamers alike.

Key Vocabulary:
- **Doomed**: Destined to fail or suffer a negative fate.
- **Betrayal**: The act of being disloyal or treacherous to someone.
- **Misfortune**: Bad luck or an unlucky event.
- **Allure**: The quality of being attractive or tempting.
- **Defying**: Resisting or challenging authority or expectations.

The Story of Baba Yaga—The Witch of the Woods

Baba Yaga is a formidable figure in Slavic folklore, revered as both a wise woman and a terrifying witch. She is depicted as an old, haggard crone with iron teeth, living in a hut that stands on chicken legs deep in the forest. According to legend, Baba Yaga possesses the ability to control the elements, manipulating winds and storms with a mere wave of her hand. Some tales describe her as a figure who imparts wisdom to those brave enough to seek her counsel, though her advice often comes at a steep price. However, she is just as well-known for her cruelty, particularly in her tendency to devour those who fail to meet her expectations. Baba Yaga's connection to death and rebirth has made her a symbol of duality: she embodies both the life-giving power of nature and the destructive forces that govern it. Her role in folklore varies, but she is often seen as a test for heroes, forcing them to prove their worthiness before she bestows her aid. The most striking characteristic of Baba Yaga is her dual nature, capable of great kindness or dreadful malevolence depending on her whims. As the embodiment of the untamed wilderness, she is often associated with the mysterious and dangerous aspects of the natural world. Baba Yaga's legend endures, her image shifting to reflect humanity's fears and desires, while remaining an iconic figure of folklore.

Key Vocabulary:
- **Formidable**: Inspiring fear or respect due to the large amount of power or ability.
- **Haggard**: Appearing worn out, gaunt, or tired, often due to age or stress.
- **Crone**: An old, often evil woman, especially in folklore.
- **Imparts**: To give or bestow, especially in relation to knowledge.
- **Malevolence**: The desire to cause harm or evil to others.

The Legend of the Golem—A Creature Made of Clay

The Golem is a mythical creature from Jewish folklore, often depicted as a giant humanoid figure created from clay or mud. The most famous tale involves a Rabbi in Prague, who, in an effort to protect the Jewish community from persecution, forms a Golem to defend them. This creature, brought to life through mystical rituals and inscribed with sacred words, becomes an instrument of divine vengeance, acting according to its creator's commands. The Golem, however, is an inherently flawed creation—its obedience becomes difficult to control, and it can spiral into uncontrollable violence. Some versions of the story suggest that the Golem's mindlessness is what causes it to eventually become dangerous. The creature's eventual destruction, either through its disobedience or the removal of the sacred word that animated it, marks the tragic end of its existence. While the Golem is sometimes seen as a protector, the legend underscores the dangers of attempting to control life and death through human hands. This tale is often interpreted as a cautionary warning against hubris—the arrogance of humans thinking they can command forces beyond their understanding. The Golem's legacy as a symbol of both creation and destruction has inspired countless works of literature and film. Through the Golem, we are reminded of the eternal tension between the power of human ingenuity and the uncontrollable forces of nature.

Key Vocabulary:
- **Humanoid**: Having characteristics or qualities that resemble a human being.
- **Persecution**: Hostility or ill-treatment, often due to race, religion, or political beliefs.
- **Vengeance**: The act of seeking revenge, often with a desire to inflict harm or punishment.
- **Hubris**: Excessive pride or self-confidence, often leading to downfall.
- **Ingenuity**: The quality of being clever, original, and inventive.

The Story of the Valkyries—The Choosers of the Slain

The Valkyries are powerful and revered figures in Norse mythology, known for their role in the selection of warriors who will die in battle and those who will be honored in Valhalla. They are often depicted as beautiful, fierce women riding winged horses, who carry the souls of fallen warriors to the afterlife. Their name, meaning "choosers of the slain," reflects their pivotal role in determining the fate of the dead. The Valkyries serve Odin, the chief of the gods, and their task is to select only the bravest and most worthy soldiers, bringing them to Valhalla to fight in the final battle during Ragnarok. While the Valkyries are sometimes seen as agents of fate, they also represent the warriors' aspirations for glory and honor. The myths surrounding the Valkyries reflect the Norse belief in the importance of battle and honor in the afterlife, where only those who die valiantly are worthy of joining Odin's hall. Their ethereal beauty, combined with their warrior prowess, has made them iconic figures in literature and art, often serving as symbols of strength and bravery.

Over time, the Valkyries have come to symbolize the complex and sometimes contradictory nature of war, where glory and death are inseparably intertwined. Their role in the mythology suggests that life and death are not arbitrary but governed by higher powers, whose decisions are both mysterious and final. Through the Valkyries, the Norse people celebrated the valor of warriors while acknowledging the inevitable fate that awaits all.

Key Vocabulary:
- **Revered**: Highly respected or admired.
- **Pivotal**: Of crucial importance in the development or success of something.
- **Valhalla**: The hall of the slain in Norse mythology, where warriors chosen by the Valkyries go after death.
- **Ethereal**: Extremely delicate and light in a way that seems too perfect for this world.
- **Contradictory**: Involving or having a conflict between two or more things.

The Myth of the Seven Wonders of the Ancient World

The Seven Wonders of the Ancient World represent the pinnacle of human achievement in the classical era, showcasing both architectural brilliance and the ingenuity of ancient civilizations. These monuments were celebrated by ancient travelers who marveled at their grand scale and the remarkable skills required to construct them. Among the most famous wonders was the Great Pyramid of Giza, the only one of the original Seven Wonders that still stands today, a symbol of Egypt's ancient glory. Other wonders, such as the Hanging Gardens of Babylon and the Statue of Zeus at Olympia, have been lost to time, their exact locations or existence debated by scholars. The myth surrounding these wonders often emphasizes their almost supernatural nature, as they seemed to defy the limitations of technology and imagination of their time. Each wonder carried its own distinct significance, from religious devotion to the representation of imperial power. The stories surrounding their construction and eventual destruction evoke a sense of both awe and melancholy, as they symbolize the transience of human endeavor. The Seven Wonders reflect the aspirations of ancient peoples to immortalize their achievements, though the passage of time has rendered many of these monuments mere shadows of their former selves. Today, the wonders continue to captivate the human imagination, inspiring not just historians and archaeologists but artists, writers, and dreamers. Through the myth of the Seven Wonders, we glimpse the eternal pursuit of greatness, as well as the inevitable decay of all things built by human hands.

Key Vocabulary:
- **Pinnacle**: The highest point or peak, often used metaphorically for the height of achievement.
- **Ingenuity**: The ability to invent and create through cleverness and resourcefulness.
- **Transience**: The state of being temporary or fleeting; not lasting forever.
- **Awe**: A feeling of reverential respect mixed with fear or wonder.
- **Melancholy**: A deep, persistent sadness, often without clear reason.

EXTRAORDINARY PEOPLE

The Man Who Climbed Mount Everest Solo Without Oxygen

In 1978, Reinhold Messner and Peter Habeler together achieved an extraordinary feat that left the world in awe: they became the first people to climb Mount Everest without supplemental oxygen. Later that same year, Messner accomplished another historic first by making a solo ascent of Everest without oxygen. These monumental achievements were not just triumphs of physical endurance but testaments to the expansion of human potential. Most climbers rely on oxygen tanks to survive the thinning air at Everest's higher altitudes, where oxygen levels are roughly one-third of those at sea level in what's known as the "death zone" above 8,000 meters (26,000 feet).

Messner's and Habeler's decision to tackle the mountain without supplemental oxygen was heavily criticized by the medical community, who predicted it would result in permanent brain damage. Many considered it impossible for humans to survive at such altitudes without assistance. However, their success, followed by Messner's solo climb, fundamentally changed our understanding of human physiology and adaptation at extreme altitudes.

These historic ascents represented both physical and psychological victories over exhaustion, fear, and extreme conditions. Messner and Habeler's achievement opened a new chapter in mountaineering history, though it's worth noting that climbing without supplemental oxygen remains extremely dangerous and is attempted by only a small percentage of Everest climbers. To this day, their accomplishment stands as one of the most significant breakthroughs in high-altitude mountaineering, demonstrating how perceived human limitations can be transcended through preparation, determination, and understanding of human physiology.

Key Vocabulary:

- **Adaptation**: The process of adjusting to new conditions or environments.
- **Physiology**: The study of how living organisms and their parts function.
- **Supplemental**: Additional or extra, often referring to something that serves as a complement to something else.
- **Altitude**: Height above sea level, particularly relevant in mountaineering.
- **Pioneering**: Being among the first to explore or develop new areas or methods.

The First Human to Travel into Space

In 1961, Soviet cosmonaut Yuri Gagarin made history as the first human to travel into space. His spacecraft, Vostok 1, lifted off from Earth and orbited the planet at an altitude of over 100 miles. For nearly 108 minutes, Gagarin floated in space, witnessing the curvature of the Earth for the first time. This extraordinary feat was not just a triumph of human ingenuity but also a significant step in the space race between the United States and the Soviet Union. As Gagarin orbited Earth, he became an instant hero, a symbol of Soviet achievement and technological superiority. His successful mission marked the beginning of human space exploration, paving the way for future missions that would lead to the moon landing and beyond. Despite the risks involved, Gagarin's flight was a major victory for the Soviet space program. However, he remained humble about his achievement, stating that he was merely the first to make the journey but not the last. Gagarin's mission forever altered the course of human history, opening the door to exploration beyond our planet. His name is forever etched in the annals of space exploration.

Key Vocabulary:
- **Cosmonaut**: A Russian or Soviet astronaut; someone trained and certified for space travel by the Russian or Soviet space program.
- **Ingenuity**: The quality of being clever, original, and inventive, especially in solving problems. It is often associated with creative and resourceful thinking.
- **Triumph**: A great victory or achievement, often resulting from effort, perseverance, or skill. It implies overcoming obstacles to reach success.
- **Orbit**: The curved path taken by a celestial body or spacecraft as it moves around another body, such as the Earth or the Moon.
- **Annals**: A record of events, often historical, that are documented in chronological order. Commonly used to refer to official or formal records.

The Story of the Deepest Free Diver in the World

In 2019, Herbert Nitsch, an Austrian freediver, set a world record by diving to a depth of 831 feet (253.2 meters) without the aid of breathing equipment. This astounding achievement was accomplished in the Ionian Sea off the coast of Greece, where Nitsch plunged deeper than any human before him, surpassing his previous records. His dive, which lasted just over 4 minutes, required immense physical strength but also mental fortitude, as freediving is a discipline that demands perfect control of one's breath and mind. The pressure at such a depth is overwhelming, and even the slightest miscalculation could lead to fatal consequences. Nitsch's record was achieved in the discipline of No Limits, where divers can use a weighted sled to descend rapidly and a lift bag to return to the surface. Nitsch's accomplishment was a testament to his preparation, focus, and years of training. The world of free diving had never seen such a feat, and his record remains a pinnacle in the sport. He is considered the "deepest man on Earth" for his unparalleled achievement. Nitsch's dive left experts in awe, as he pushed the limits of human potential in the face of extreme danger. His record was a defining moment in the world of extreme sports.

Key Vocabulary:
- **Fortitude**: Mental and emotional strength in facing adversity, danger, or difficulty with courage and resolve.
- **Sled**: A vehicle used to slide over snow or ice, or in this case, a mechanical device used by free divers to help them descend quickly.
- **Miscalculation**: An error in judgment, calculation, or planning, especially when the consequences are significant.
- **Pinnacle**: The highest point or peak of achievement, success, or development. It often refers to the ultimate or most outstanding moment in a field or endeavor.
- **Testament**: A proof or confirmation of something, often used to describe evidence of something's truth or strength, such as a person's achievements.

The Man Who Memorized 100,000 Digits of Pi

Akira Nakai, a Japanese prodigy, is renowned for memorizing an astounding 100,000 digits of Pi, a feat that baffles mathematicians and memory experts alike. His ability to recall an infinite sequence of numbers without error has earned him worldwide recognition. Nakai's accomplishment was not just a test of his memory, but a profound demonstration of cognitive discipline. The training required to achieve this remarkable feat involved countless hours of rote memorization and mnemonic techniques. For years, he meticulously broke down Pi's digits into manageable chunks, utilizing patterns and associations that enabled him to recall them with ease. His mental dexterity challenges conventional understandings of memory, as most people can only memorize a handful of digits before losing track. To this day, Nakai's record remains unchallenged, as few have the patience or perseverance to rival his mental endurance. His achievement continues to inspire those fascinated by the limits of human memory and cognitive capacity. It serves as a testament to the boundless potential of the human mind when subjected to intense focus and dedication. Nakai's feat is a reminder that, with unwavering resolve, the impossible may be within reach.

Key Vocabulary:
- **Prodigy**: A person, especially a young one, endowed with exceptional talents or abilities.
- **Rote**: Mechanical or habitual repetition of something to be learned, often without understanding the underlying meaning.
- **Mnemonic**: A device or technique used to aid memory retention, such as a pattern or association.
- **Dexterity**: Skill and agility in physical or mental tasks, especially involving precision and coordination.
- **Endurance**: The capacity to withstand hardship or stress over a prolonged period, particularly in physical or mental contexts.

The Story of the Woman Who Won a Nobel Prize Twice

Marie Curie is the only person to have won two Nobel Prizes in different scientific fields—Physics and Chemistry—solidifying her place as one of history's most groundbreaking scientists. Her first award, in 1903, was shared with her husband

Pierre Curie and Henri Becquerel for their pioneering research on radioactivity. However, her second Nobel Prize, awarded in 1911, was an individual achievement for her discovery of the elements radium and polonium. Curie's unwavering dedication to scientific inquiry, coupled with her relentless pursuit of knowledge, transcended the gender biases of her time, allowing her to make extraordinary contributions to science. Despite facing immense personal and professional challenges, including the death of her beloved husband, she never wavered in her commitment to research. Her work revolutionized the understanding of atomic science and laid the foundation for advancements in medicine, particularly in the field of cancer treatment. Curie's legacy continues to inspire generations of scientists, especially women in STEM fields, who follow in her footsteps. She is remembered not just for her academic achievements but also for her perseverance in the face of adversity. Marie Curie's life embodies the spirit of intellectual curiosity and resilience, qualities that transcend time and remain relevant to this day. Her twice-earned Nobel Prizes stand as a lasting testament to the power of determination and innovation.

Key Vocabulary:
- **Groundbreaking**: Innovating or pioneering; introducing new and significant ideas or methods.
- **Relentless**: Unyielding in intensity or determination, often to the point of being uncompromising or unremitting.
- **Transcended**: To rise above or go beyond the limits of something, surpassing the normal boundaries.
- **Perseverance**: Steadfastness in doing something despite difficulty or delay in achieving success.
- **Resilience**: The capacity to recover from difficulties or challenges, maintaining a positive and productive state.

The Man Who Walked a Tightrope

Between Two Skyscrapers

On August 7, 1974, Philippe Petit, a French high-wire artist, performed an unauthorized walk between the Twin Towers of New York's World Trade Center. After spending nearly six years planning the feat, which he called "le coup," Petit and his team covertly accessed the towers at night, using a bow and arrow to first string a cable between them. Starting at 7:15 AM, Petit walked on a 3/4" steel cable stretched 1,350 feet above the ground between the North and South towers. Over 45 minutes, he made eight passes along the wire, during which he walked, danced, laid down on the cable, and knelt to salute onlookers.

The 24-year-old performer had no safety harness or net as he crossed the 140-foot gap between the towers. Hundreds of onlookers gathered on the streets below, and traffic came to a halt as people watched his performance. When Petit finally stepped off the wire onto the South Tower's roof, he was arrested by NYPD officers. However, due to public acclaim for his artistic achievement, the charges were dropped in exchange for him performing a free show for children in Central Park.

This was not Petit's first high-profile wire walk. In 1971, he had walked between the towers of Notre Dame Cathedral in Paris, and in 1973, he crossed between the pylons of the Sydney Harbour Bridge. The World Trade Center walk was documented in the Oscar-winning 2008 film "Man on Wire" and later dramatized in the 2015 film "The Walk."

Key Vocabulary:

- **Unauthorized**: Done without official permission or approval
- **Covertly**: Done in a way that is not openly acknowledged or displayed
- **Wire walk**: The act of walking on a suspended cable or rope

- **Pass**: One complete crossing from one end to the other
- **Harness**: Safety equipment used to protect against falls

The Story of the Human Computer

Shakuntala Devi (1929-2013), an Indian mathematician and mental calculator, earned the nickname "human computer" due to her extraordinary ability to perform complex calculations mentally. She could multiply, divide, and find roots of large numbers with remarkable speed and accuracy. Her mathematical abilities were first demonstrated publicly in her childhood when her father, a circus performer, showcased her skills in calculating shows.

Devi performed calculations around the world, often competing against computers. On June 18, 1980, at Imperial College London, she demonstrated her most famous feat: correctly multiplying two 13-digit numbers (7,686,369,774,870 × 2,465,099,745,779) in 28 seconds. This achievement was recorded in the 1982 Guinness Book of World Records. Her answer of 18,947,668,177,995,426,462,773,730 was verified by the computer at the university.

Although she lacked formal mathematical education beyond elementary school, Devi wrote several books about mathematics, astrology, and puzzles. She was also an author of novels and books about homosexuality (including "The World of Homosexuals" published in 1977, which advocated for greater understanding and acceptance). Beyond her mathematical abilities, she was known as an astrologer and gave lectures on analytical and memory development techniques.

Devi firmly believed that mathematical ability was present in everyone and could be developed through practice and proper techniques. She created methods for rapid mental calculation that she shared through her books and lectures. Her work continues to interest those studying mental calculation and mathematical cognition.

Key Vocabulary:

- **Mental calculator**: Someone who can perform complex mathematical calculations in their head
- **Multiplication**: The mathematical operation of adding a number to itself a specified number of times
- **Calculate**: To determine by mathematical processes
- **Mathematical**: Relating to mathematics
- **Analytical**: Using or skilled in using analysis or logical reasoning

The Man Who Held His Breath Underwater for 24 Minutes

Stig Severinsen, a Danish freediver, astonished the world when he set a record for holding his breath underwater for 24 minutes, a feat that pushes the limits of human physiology. Severinsen's achievement was not the result of chance but of years of intense physical and mental preparation. Freediving, the art of diving without breathing apparatus, requires the body to adapt to extreme conditions, and Severinsen trained his lungs and cardiovascular system to tolerate the lack of oxygen for extended periods. His record-breaking breath-hold was accomplished through a combination of relaxation techniques, controlled breathing, and extreme mental focus. Severinsen's body, through years of conditioning, had learned to reduce oxygen consumption and enhance the efficiency of his organs. His remarkable feat challenges the conventional understanding of human endurance and capacity for adaptation to extreme environments. In addition to his diving achievements, Severinsen has worked to raise awareness about the importance of breath control in physical and mental health. His story serves as an inspiration to those seeking to push the boundaries of their own capabilities, showing that with practice and discipline, seemingly impossible feats can become reality. Severinsen's record stands as a testament to the power of human resilience and the potential of the body when trained to its maximum limits. His story encourages individuals to explore the untapped power within themselves, seeking to accomplish extraordinary feats.

Key Vocabulary:
- **Freediving**: The practice of diving into water without the use of breathing equipment, relying on holding one's breath.
- **Physiology**: The branch of biology that deals with the normal functions of living organisms and their parts.
- **Cardiovascular**: Relating to the heart and blood vessels, particularly the circulatory system.
- **Endurance**: The ability to endure difficult physical conditions or prolonged exertion without giving in to fatigue.
- **Resilience**: The capacity to recover quickly from difficulties, remaining adaptable in challenging situations.

The Person Who Survived Being Struck by Lightning Seven Times

Roy Sullivan, a U.S. park ranger, is often referred to as "The Human Lightning Rod" for his unbelievable survival of seven lightning strikes over a span of 35 years. Despite the odds, he endured each strike with astonishing resilience, never succumbing to the lethal effects that would typically prove fatal. Each time, Sullivan's body absorbed the electrical energy, resulting in severe burns and injuries, yet he miraculously recovered. Lightning strikes, especially multiple ones, are extraordinarily rare, and most individuals struck even once do not survive. Sullivan's extraordinary endurance and survival became the subject of worldwide fascination, with people marveling at his improbable streak of near-death experiences. His case defied scientific expectations, leaving experts questioning the intricate ways in which the human body can withstand such extreme forces. Though he later suffered mental anguish, his incredible story became a symbol of human tenacity. Sullivan's saga exemplified the fine line between fate and resilience, where his persistence in surviving these strikes was nothing short of remarkable. His legacy challenges conventional understandings of mortality and the resilience of the human form. Sullivan's improbable survival remains one of the most bizarre and awe-inspiring accounts of human endurance.

Key Vocabulary:
- **Resilience**: The capacity to recover quickly from difficulties or traumatic events.
- **Succumbing**: To yield to pressure, illness, or a dangerous situation, often resulting in defeat.
- **Endurance**: The ability to endure prolonged stressful conditions or physical hardship without giving in.
- **Fascination**: A deep and intense interest or attraction to something or someone.
- **Tenacity**: The quality of being determined and persistent, often in the face of challenges.

The Man Who Lived on a Raft in the Ocean for Over a Year

Alexander Selkirk, a Scottish sailor, became the inspiration for Daniel Defoe's novel Robinson Crusoe after surviving alone on Más a Tierra (now called Robinson Crusoe Island) off the coast of Chile for four years and four months (1704-1709). Selkirk was marooned on the uninhabited island after a dispute with his ship's captain over the vessel's seaworthiness. Rather than risk sailing on what he believed was an unseaworthy ship, he requested to be put ashore.

During his solitary existence, he survived using supplies left by the ship (including some clothing, bedding, a musket, gunpowder, tools, and a Bible) as well as his own resourcefulness. The isolation proved to be a severe test of his mental and physical endurance. Selkirk built two huts from pimento trees, hunted feral goats for food and clothing, and gathered wild turnips and other edible plants. He had to maintain constant vigilance against Spanish ships, as he was a British privateer and would have been imprisoned if discovered.

When he was finally rescued by privateer Woodes Rogers in February 1709, Selkirk had become so agile at running and hunting that he could outrun and catch goats with his bare hands. His remarkable survival story captivated the British public when he returned home, and his experience became emblematic of human resilience and the will to endure. Though his years of isolation affected him deeply – he initially struggled to speak clearly and preferred to drink his liquids from a coconut shell – his story became an iconic narrative of survival that inspired Defoe's novel, published in 1719.

Key Vocabulary:

- **Marooned**: To be stranded in an isolated place with no means of escape
- **Seaworthiness**: The state of a ship being fit and safe for voyage
- **Solitary**: Existing alone; separated from others
- **Vigilance**: Careful observation or attention; being alert to danger
- **Agile**: Able to move quickly and easily
- **Emblematic**: Serving as a symbol or representation of something

The Man Who Walked Around the World with His Dog

On April 2, 2015, Tom Turcich embarked on an extraordinary journey that would make him the 10th documented person to walk around the world. His motivation stemmed from profound personal loss - the death of his close friend Ann Marie at age 17, which sparked his realization about life's brevity and led to this ambitious undertaking.

Early in his journey, while passing through Austin, Texas, Turcich adopted a puppy he named Savannah, who would become his loyal companion and the first dog documented to walk around the world. Together, they traversed approximately 25,000 miles across six continents and 38 countries, pushing a cart containing their supplies and equipment. The journey was made possible in part through sponsorship from Philadelphia Sign Company, though they still often relied on the kindness of strangers along their route.

Over the course of 7 years and 3 months, Turcich and Savannah encountered diverse cultures, landscapes, and challenges. They crossed deserts, mountains, and cities, experiencing both the harsh realities and beautiful moments of life on foot. Through extreme weather, physical exhaustion, and various obstacles, they pressed forward, documenting their experiences for others to follow.

The journey ended triumphantly on July 9, 2022, when Turcich and Savannah returned home. Their walk had evolved beyond mere physical achievement into a profound exploration of human connection, personal growth, and the deep bond between human and dog. Through his journey, Turcich demonstrated that extraordinary achievements often begin with a single step - and sometimes, a faithful four-legged friend.

Key Vocabulary:

- **Documented**: Recorded or verified through evidence
- **Traverse**: To travel across or through
- **Ambitious**: Requiring great effort and aspiring to significant achievement
- **Triumph**: A great success or achievement
- **Bond**: A strong connection or relationship between people or animals

The First Woman to Fly Solo Across the Atlantic

Amelia Earhart's pioneering spirit led her to become the first woman to fly solo across the Atlantic Ocean, marking a historic achievement in aviation. In 1932, amidst societal skepticism and gender-based limitations, Earhart defied expectations by flying a custom-built Lockheed Vega from Newfoundland to Ireland, a journey that took over 13 hours. The feat was a testament to her skill as a pilot but also to her determination to break barriers for women in fields traditionally dominated by men. During her flight, Earhart faced numerous challenges, including unpredictable weather, mechanical issues, and the fatigue of flying alone for such an extended period. Despite these obstacles, her unwavering resolve allowed her to land safely, earning her worldwide acclaim. Earhart's flight made her a national hero and also highlighted the possibilities for women to excel in areas previously and incorrectly thought to be inaccessible to them. Her triumph in aviation encouraged countless young girls to pursue careers in science, technology, and engineering, fields that had long been male-dominated. Amelia Earhart's story became an indelible part of history, inspiring future generations to challenge limitations and push the boundaries of what was considered possible. Her legacy lives on as a beacon of courage, perseverance, and groundbreaking achievement. Earhart's accomplishments transcended her era, solidifying her status as an icon of empowerment and trailblazing innovation.

Key Vocabulary:
- **Pioneering**: Leading the way in a particular field or endeavor, often through innovation.
- **Defied**: To openly resist or challenge something, such as authority or expectations.
- **Skepticism**: A lack of belief or doubt about the validity of something.
- **Unwavering**: Steady and resolute, not changing or yielding in the face of challenges.
- **Indelible**: Impossible to forget or erase; permanent in nature.

The Story of the Woman Who Lived to Be 122 Years Old

The extraordinary life of Jeanne Louise Calment, who lived to the age of 122 years and 164 days, has fascinated scientists and historians alike. Born in Arles, France, on February 21, 1875, and passing away on August 4, 1997, her longevity surpassed all verified human records. Throughout her life, she witnessed tremendous historical changes, from the completion of the Eiffel Tower to the dawn of the internet age. She even met Vincent van Gogh in her youth, describing him as "dirty, badly dressed, and disagreeable" when he visited her uncle's shop in 1888.

Calment led an active lifestyle, taking up fencing at age 85 and continuing to ride her bicycle until age 100. She maintained her independence well into her later years, living on her own until age 110. Her lifestyle included habits that would surprise modern health enthusiasts - she smoked cigarettes until age 117 and regularly ate chocolate. She attributed her longevity to olive oil, which she used on her food and skin, along with drinking port wine and maintaining a sense of humor.

Her case has been extensively studied by gerontologists and demographic researchers, particularly Jean-Marie Robine and Michel Allard, who meticulously verified her age through historical documentation. Calment maintained remarkably clear cognition and memory until late in life, able to vividly recall details from her youth even past age 120. Her exceptional longevity has provided valuable insights into the potential limits of human lifespan, though researchers continue to debate the various factors that contributed to her long life.

Key Vocabulary:
- **Longevity**: Long life, particularly when lived in good health
- **Gerontologists**: Scientists who study aging and the elderly
- **Demographic**: Relating to the study of populations and their characteristics
- **Cognition**: Mental processes including thinking, understanding, and remembering
- **Meticulously**: With extreme attention to detail and accuracy

STRANGE EVENTS

Rain of Fish in Honduras

In the remote town of Yoro, Honduras, a bewildering phenomenon has captivated locals and scientists for over a century—the alleged rain of fish. Known as Lluvia de Peces, this peculiar occurrence manifests during torrential storms between May and July, when hundreds of small silver fish mysteriously appear on the rain-soaked ground. While no scientific team has directly observed fish descending from the heavens, the aftermath has been well-documented by witnesses and media outlets, including National Geographic.

The prevailing scientific hypothesis suggests that powerful waterspouts might lift aquatic life from nearby water bodies, a phenomenon documented in other parts of the world. However, a curious detail challenges this theory—the fish found in Yoro are consistently of the same small, silver variety and appear remarkably fresh, hinting at a more localized origin. Some researchers propose that the fish might emerge from underground streams during heavy rainfall, though this explanation remains unverified.

Local lore traces the phenomenon's origins to the 1850s and the prayers of Father José Manuel Subirana, a Spanish missionary whose supplications allegedly summoned the first piscine shower. The events consistently occur in a specific valley near Yoro, rather than randomly throughout the region, lending a geographic pattern to the mystery. Each new occurrence reinvigorates scientific curiosity while deepening the town's singular legacy. Whether explained by hidden hydrological systems or atmospheric phenomena, the rain of fish in Yoro persists as one of nature's most enigmatic displays, bridging the realms of scientific inquiry and cultural folklore.

Key Vocabulary:

- **Phenomenon**: A remarkable occurrence or circumstance.
- **Hydrological**: Relating to the movement, distribution, and quality of water.
- **Torrential**: (of rain) falling in rapid and abundant quantities.
- **Endemic**: Native and restricted to a particular place.
- **Lore**: A body of traditions and knowledge held by a specific group.

The Taos Hum—A Mystery Sound Heard by Few

In the tranquil town of Taos, New Mexico, an auditory anomaly afflicts approximately 2% of its inhabitants. The Taos Hum, first reported in the early 1990s, manifests as a persistent, low-frequency droning that remains inaudible to the vast majority of residents. Those who detect it often describe it as reminiscent of a distant diesel engine or a deep rumble emanating from an indeterminate source. Despite a comprehensive 1993 investigation by experts from the University of New Mexico, alongside numerous other scientific inquiries, no definitive acoustic source has been identified.

Theories abound, ranging from industrial equipment and electrical grid infrastructure to atmospheric conditions and variations in individual auditory sensitivity. Some researchers postulate that certain individuals possess heightened sensitivity to specific frequencies typically imperceptible to human hearing, while others suggest connections to tinnitus or unique auditory processing conditions. The phenomenon extends beyond Taos's borders, with similar mysterious hums reported in locations worldwide, including Windsor, Ontario and Bristol, UK.

Unlike many sensationalized accounts, the Hum appears to be location-specific—those who relocate from Taos typically report cessation of the sound, though they may encounter similar phenomena in other known "hum" locations. Whether an unrecognized environmental frequency or a complex interplay of acoustic and physiological factors, the Taos Hum endures as one of the world's most perplexing scientific mysteries, residing at the intersection of acoustics, psychology, and environmental science.

Key Vocabulary:

- **Anomaly**: Something that deviates from the norm or expectation.
- **Imperceptible**: Impossible or nearly impossible to detect.
- **Frequency**: The rate at which a sound wave oscillates, determining its pitch.
- **Physiological**: Relating to the normal functions of living organisms and their parts.
- **Acoustic**: Relating to sound or the sense of hearing.

A Ghost Ship Found Drifting with No Crew

In 1872, the Mary Celeste was discovered adrift in the Atlantic, its sails intact but eerily void of its crew. The ship's cargo of alcohol remained untouched, personal belongings lay undisturbed, and there were no signs of violence or struggle. The lifeboat was missing, suggesting a hurried evacuation, yet the vessel was completely seaworthy. Some theorized a rogue wave had swept the crew away, while others believed they fell victim to an undetected mutiny or even supernatural forces. The ship's log offered no insight beyond its last recorded position, leaving investigators baffled. To this day, the fate of the ten souls aboard remains an enigma, adding to the annals of maritime mysteries. Legends have since embellished the tale, with whispers of ghostly figures seen aboard the Mary Celeste in later years. Attempts to explain the event range from carbon monoxide poisoning to seaquake-induced hallucinations. Yet, no theory fully accounts for why an experienced crew would abandon a perfectly navigable ship in open waters. The Mary Celeste remains a quintessential phantasmagoria of the sea, its unanswered questions drifting through time like the ship itself.

Key Vocabulary:
- **Phantasmagoria**: A sequence of real or imaginary images, often dreamlike or eerie in nature.
- **Enigma**: A person or thing that is mysterious, puzzling, or difficult to understand.
- **Embellish**: To add details, often exaggerated or fictitious, to make a story more interesting.
- **Seaworthy**: In a condition fit for sailing; capable of enduring a voyage.
- **Hallucination**: A perception of something not actually present, often caused by illness or extreme conditions.

The Voynich Manuscript—A Medieval Mystery

The Voynich Manuscript, discovered by rare book dealer Wilfrid Voynich in 1912, remains one of history's most enigmatic texts. Written in an unknown script and filled with colorful illustrations of unidentifiable plants, astronomical diagrams, and what appear to be medicinal drawings, the manuscript has defied comprehensive decryption despite decades of scholarly analysis.

Radiocarbon dating places the manuscript's vellum pages between 1404 and 1438, during Europe's late medieval period. The manuscript's known provenance includes ownership by Emperor Rudolf II of Habsburg in the late 16th century and later by Georg Baresch, a Prague alchemist. The text currently resides at Yale University's Beinecke Rare Book and Manuscript Library.

Statistical analysis of the manuscript's text reveals patterns consistent with natural languages, including Zipf's law—a feature typically found in meaningful communication rather than random sequences. This suggests the text likely represents either an unknown language or an encrypted message rather than meaningless symbols.

The manuscript contains approximately 240 pages organized into apparent sections: botanical, astronomical, balneological (relating to medicinal baths), pharmaceutical, and continuous text. Its illustrations include elaborate botanical drawings of plants that don't match known species, celestial diagrams, and figures in what appear to be medicinal baths.

While numerous theories about its origin and purpose exist—ranging from medieval medical treatise to esoteric philosophical text—none have been definitively proven. Modern analysis techniques, including multispectral imaging and computational linguistics, continue to reveal new details about its physical construction and linguistic properties, though its contents remain undeciphered.

Key Terms:
- **Vellum**: A fine parchment made from animal skin, commonly used for medieval manuscripts
- **Provenance**: The chronology of ownership and transmission of a historical object
- **Zipf's law**: A linguistic pattern where the frequency of any word is inversely proportional to its rank in the frequency table
- **Balneological**: Relating to the therapeutic use of baths and bathing
- **Multispectral imaging**: A technique that captures image data at specific wavelengths across the electromagnetic

spectrum

The Devil's Footprints—The Mystery of Devon's Snow Tracks

On February 8th, 1855, residents across Devon, England, awoke to a bewildering sight after a night of snowfall. Stretching across multiple towns and villages were mysterious tracks in the snow, each print measuring roughly 4 inches long. The tracks appeared in a peculiar single-file line, as if made by a two-legged creature, and were reported to traverse unusual paths—over garden walls, across rooftops, and through farmyards.

Local newspapers documented the phenomenon extensively, and the story quickly captured public imagination. Some religious residents, gripped by fear, attributed the prints to the Devil himself, while others searched for more earthly explanations. The tracks were investigated by respected naturalists of the time, including Reverend George Musgrave, who published detailed observations of the event.

Though often exaggerated in retellings, the tracks did cover significant distances, appearing in multiple locations across South Devon. While they didn't literally cross rivers as some accounts claim, they were found on both sides of waterways. Contemporary witnesses noted that the prints appeared to go over and under obstacles in ways that seemed difficult to explain by known wildlife behavior.

Various natural explanations have been proposed over the years. Some scientists suggested wood mice hopping through the snow, while others theorized about escaped kangaroos or experimental hot air balloons dragging chains. A more recent theory suggests that multiple animals, combined with peculiar weather conditions, might have created the illusion of a single set of continuous tracks.

Today, the Devil's Footprints remain one of Victorian England's most intriguing unsolved mysteries. While the supernatural explanations have largely been dismissed, the true cause of these unusual tracks continues to generate debate among historians and scientists alike.

Key Vocabulary:

- **Bewildering**: Confusing or perplexing
- **Contemporary**: Belonging to or occurring in the same period of time
- **Naturalist**: A person who studies or is expert in natural history
- **Phenomenon**: A remarkable or unusual occurrence
- **Attribution**: The action of regarding something as being caused by a person or thing

The Green Children of Woolpit—A Medieval Mystery

In the 12th century, two medieval chroniclers—Ralph of Coggeshall and William of Newburgh—recorded a remarkable tale from the English village of Woolpit in Suffolk. According to their accounts, villagers discovered two children with green-tinted skin who emerged from the local wolf pits (deep ditches used to trap wolves). The children, described as a brother and sister, wore unfamiliar clothing and spoke an unknown language. The chronicles report that they would only eat beans, refusing all other food initially offered to them.

The historical records tell us that the boy fell ill and died, while the girl survived, gradually lost her green coloring, and learned to speak English. According to Ralph of Coggeshall's account, she explained that she and her brother came from a twilight land called "St. Martin's Land," where everything was green.

Modern historians and researchers have proposed several compelling explanations for this medieval tale. One medical theory suggests the children may have suffered from hypochromic anemia, a condition that can cause a greenish tint to the skin when combined with malnutrition. Historian Paul Harris has proposed they might have been Flemish orphans, abandoned during a period of persecution of Flemish immigrants in England during the reign of King Stephen—their strange language possibly being Flemish.

The story contains elements common to medieval British folklore, including the motif of mysterious beings emerging from caves or pits. Some scholars suggest it may be an allegorical tale about the interaction between different cultures in medieval England, while others view it as a classic example of how unusual events were interpreted through a medieval worldview.

Key Terms:

- **Chronicle**: A factual written account of important events in the order of their occurrence
- **Hypochromic anemia**: A type of anemia that can cause pallor with a greenish tint
- **Wolf pit**: A deep ditch used in medieval England to trap wolves
- **Allegorical**: Having hidden symbolic meaning
- **Medieval worldview**: The way people in the Middle Ages understood and interpreted events

The Mystery of the Final Calls

In 2008, a devastating collision between a Metrolink commuter train and a freight train in Chatsworth, California claimed 25 lives. Among the victims was Charles Peck, whose story would become particularly notable due to an unexplained technological phenomenon that followed.

For hours after the crash, Peck's family members received approximately 35 calls from his cell phone. Each time they answered, they heard only static. Rescue workers used these signals to help locate Peck's body nearly 12 hours after the crash, but medical examiners determined he had died on impact. When investigators examined his phone, they found no record of outgoing calls during this period.

While some view this as an unsettling mystery, telecommunications experts have proposed several possible explanations. In catastrophic events, damaged phones can exhibit unusual behavior - circuits may short out, causing random activations. Network infrastructure damage can also create communication anomalies. Additionally, rescue operations themselves, involving heavy machinery and debris movement, could potentially trigger phone activity.

This isn't the only documented case of phones making calls after their owners have died. Similar incidents have occurred in other accidents, though most have eventually been attributed to technical malfunctions or environmental factors. The phenomenon highlights how modern technology can behave in unexpected ways under extreme conditions.

The case of Charles Peck's final calls remains a sobering reminder of both the 2008 tragedy and the mysteries that can emerge when technology behaves in ways we don't fully understand. While various technical explanations exist, none have been definitively proven, leaving the true cause of these calls an open question.

Key Terms:
- **Anomaly**: A deviation from the expected norm or standard behavior
- **Circuit**: The complete path through which electricity flows in an electronic device
- **Infrastructure**: The fundamental facilities and systems serving a country, city, or area
- **Signal**: An electrical or electromagnetic pulse used to transmit information
- **Technical malfunction**: A failure or irregularity in the

way a device operate.

Animal Behavior Before Natural Disasters: What We Know

During the 2004 Indian Ocean earthquake and tsunami, several documented reports emerged of unusual animal behavior. According to eyewitness accounts from Khao Lak, Thailand, elephants were observed breaking their chains and moving to higher ground before the tsunami struck. In Sri Lanka's Yala National Park, wildlife officials noted that no large animal carcasses were found after the tsunami, suggesting possible evacuation.

Scientists have since investigated the mechanisms that could explain such behavior. Many animals can hear infrasound (very low-frequency sounds) that humans cannot detect. Some species can sense minor changes in air and water pressure, while others may detect preliminary tremors that are too subtle for humans to feel. These natural capabilities could potentially alert animals to impending disasters before humans notice any signs.

While there are numerous anecdotal reports of animals behaving unusually before earthquakes and other natural disasters, obtaining rigorous scientific evidence has been challenging. One notable verified case occurred in Peru, where researchers documented unusual behavior in toads, which left their breeding site five days before a magnitude 6.3 earthquake in 2009. However, most other reported cases lack systematic documentation or controlled observation conditions.

Scientists are currently conducting more rigorous research to understand these phenomena. For instance, researchers in Germany are monitoring animal behavior patterns alongside seismic data to establish whether there are consistent correlations between animal activity and earthquakes. This ongoing research aims to separate coincidence from genuine predictive behavior and understand the specific mechanisms that might allow animals to detect impending natural disasters.

Key Vocabulary:

- **Infrasound**: Sound waves with frequencies below the lower limit of human hearing
- **Seismic**: Relating to earthquakes or other vibrations of the earth
- **Anecdotal evidence**: Information from personal accounts rather than scientific studies
- **Correlation**: A mutual relationship or connection between two or more things

A Book That Predicted the Sinking of the Titanic—Years Before It Happened

In 1898, a little-known novella titled Futility by Morgan Robertson was published, telling the tale of a ship called the Titan, which was described as "unsinkable" and was tragically doomed to sink after striking an iceberg in the North Atlantic. Thirteen years later, in 1912, the Titanic—a real ship with striking similarities to Robertson's fictional vessel—met a horrifying fate when it sank after colliding with an iceberg. The striking coincidence between the two events sent shockwaves through the public, with many wondering if Robertson had somehow foreseen the disaster. The novella's details, including the ship's size, the number of lifeboats, and even the time of the collision, were eerily similar to those of the Titanic, leading some to speculate that the author may have had an almost prescient vision of the ship's doomed voyage. Some claim that Robertson's experience as a sailor gave him a unique understanding of the risks involved in shipbuilding, while others propose more supernatural explanations. The tale of Futility remains one of the most unsettling and prophetic coincidences in literary history. Robertson's premonition, whether the result of intuition, chance, or something more mystical, continues to fascinate and puzzle historians, literary critics, and conspiracy theorists alike.

Key Vocabulary:
- **Horrifying**: Causing fear, shock, or dread.
- **Coincidence**: A remarkable occurrence of events or circumstances without apparent causal connection.
- **Prescient**: Having knowledge of events before they happen; prophetic.
- **Unsettling**: Causing discomfort or unease.
- **Premonition**: A strong feeling or sense that something is about to happen, especially something negative.

A Bridge That Makes Dogs Jump to Their Deaths

High above a misty gorge in Milton, Scotland, the Victorian-era Overtoun Bridge has earned a troubling reputation due to a perplexing phenomenon: dogs seem strangely drawn to leap from its walls, often to their deaths. The concerning occurrences began in the 1950s, when local residents started reporting that their dogs, without warning, would suddenly bolt toward the bridge's parapet and jump into the ravine 50 feet below.

Unnerving reports came from residents who had witnessed these incidents, describing their dogs' behavior as unusually focused, as if drawn by something they couldn't see. While initial investigations by animal behaviorists and engineers found the bridge structurally sound, the phenomenon demanded deeper study. Research eventually revealed several potential explanations: the bridge's thick granite walls obscure dogs' vision of the drop below, while strong scents of mink and other small mammals in the gorge may trigger their hunting instincts.

The terrain and bridge design create unique sensory conditions that appear to disorient dogs. With an estimated 50-100 incidents over several decades, the bridge continues to intrigue researchers studying the intersection of animal behavior and architectural design. Many locals now take precautions, keeping their dogs leashed while crossing. The Overtoun Bridge, with its documented history of tragic incidents, stands as a testament to how seemingly ordinary structures can create unexpected and dangerous situations for our four-legged companions.

Key Vocabulary:

- **Perplexing**: Confusingly difficult to understand or explain
- **Parapet**: A protective wall or barrier at the edge of a bridge
- **Sensory**: Relating to physical senses like smell, sight, and hearing
- **Disorient**: To cause someone or something to lose their bearings
- **Testament**: A proof or demonstration of something

The Wow! Signal: An Astronomical Mystery

On August 15, 1977, astronomer Jerry Ehman detected an unusual signal while working at Ohio State University's Big Ear radio telescope. The signal lasted for 72 seconds - the maximum time the telescope could observe a fixed point in the sky. The event became known as the "Wow! Signal" because Ehman wrote "Wow!" on the computer printout when he saw the signal's characteristics.

What made the signal notable was its frequency (around 1420 MHz) and strength. This frequency is significant because it's in a range that scientists had predicted might be useful for interstellar communication, as it's associated with neutral hydrogen. The signal appeared to come from the direction of the constellation Sagittarius.

Despite multiple attempts over the decades, the signal has never been detected again. While various explanations have been proposed - including both natural phenomena and artificial sources - none have been conclusively proven. Scientists have investigated possible sources such as satellites, aircraft, and celestial bodies, but the true origin remains unknown.

The Wow! Signal continues to be studied and debated in the scientific community. While some researchers have suggested it as a possible candidate for extraterrestrial origin, others work to identify potential natural explanations. The signal remains one of the most discussed events in radio astronomy, though its nature is still uncertain.

Key Vocabulary:

- **Radio telescope**: An instrument used to detect radio waves from space
- **Frequency**: The number of waves that pass a fixed point in a given time
- **Signal**: A detectable transmission or variation in a physical quantity
- **Constellation**: A group of stars forming a recognized pattern
- **Radio astronomy**: The study of celestial objects using radio waves
-

A Girl Who Survived a Plane Crash in the Jungle Alone

In 1971, a young girl named Juliane Koepcke found herself stranded in the dense Amazon rainforest after surviving a horrific plane crash. The plane, struck by lightning mid-flight, plummeted to the earth, killing everyone aboard except for Juliane, who was only 17 at the time. Miraculously, she was ejected from the wreckage and fell into the thick jungle below, sustaining only minor injuries. Despite being disoriented and alone in the vast wilderness, Juliane's survival instincts kicked in. She trekked for days, relying on her knowledge of the rainforest and her sheer determination to stay alive. She managed to find a river, which eventually led her to a research station, where she was rescued after nearly two weeks in the jungle. Her story became a symbol of human resilience, an incredible example of the power of the human spirit. In interviews, Juliane explained that it was her belief in the importance of survival that kept her going. Her remarkable ordeal remains one of the most extraordinary tales of survival in the history of aviation. Despite the traumatic experience, she later became a biologist, dedicating her life to studying the rainforest she had once wandered in alone.

Key Vocabulary:
- **Dense**: Having a compact structure or close-packed elements.
- **Resilience**: The ability to recover quickly from difficulties.
- **Instincts**: Innate behaviors or responses, often subconscious.
- **Trekking**: A long, arduous journey, especially on foot.
- **Ordeal**: A difficult or painful experience.

THE EVERYDAY WORLD

The Science of Why We Yawn

Yawning is a ubiquitous yet perplexing behavior that has long captivated scientists and philosophers alike. Despite its seemingly innocuous nature, the act of yawning is intriguingly complex and serves a variety of physiological functions. It is most commonly associated with tiredness or boredom, yet studies reveal that yawning may also help to regulate the temperature of the brain, keeping it cool and functioning at its optimal capacity. The contagious nature of yawning is equally enigmatic—seeing or hearing someone yawn can prompt an involuntary response in others, suggesting that yawning may also play a role in fostering social bonds. While the precise neurological mechanisms behind yawning remain largely speculative, it is believed to involve the brain's regulation of various chemicals, such as dopamine and serotonin. Some research posits that yawning may be a form of evolutionary communication, signaling a state of alertness or readiness within a group. Interestingly, other animals, including dogs and even certain reptiles, exhibit similar yawning behaviors, further suggesting that it serves an essential biological function. Despite its universal prevalence, yawning remains an enigma, with many aspects of its origins and purpose still shrouded in mystery. Understanding this seemingly mundane act may offer profound insights into the inner workings of the human brain.

Thus, the science of yawning is far from being a trivial pursuit —its implications reach deep into the realms of psychology, physiology, and evolutionary biology.

Key Vocabulary:
- **Intriguingly**: In a manner that arouses curiosity or interest.
- **Contagious**: Likely to spread or be transmitted to others.
- **Evolutionary**: Pertaining to the gradual development of species over time.
- **Mystery**: Something that is difficult or impossible to understand or explain.
- **Physiology**: The study of the functions and processes of living organisms.

How Mushrooms Communicate Like a Forest Internet

The mycelium, the underground network of fungal threads that make up mushrooms, has recently been recognized for its remarkable similarity to the Internet. This vast subterranean system enables mushrooms to communicate and exchange information, nutrients, and even warnings across large expanses of forest. Through a process called "nutrient sharing," mycelium links trees, plants, and other organisms, ensuring the mutual survival of the ecosystem. The mycelial network is capable of transmitting chemical signals that alert neighboring plants to potential threats such as pests or disease, prompting them to bolster their defenses. This intricate form of communication mirrors the way humans use the Internet to exchange data instantaneously across vast distances. Moreover, recent studies have shown that mycelium can even redirect resources to plants that are in need, ensuring the overall health of the forest. In this sense, mycelium acts as a natural internet, facilitating the exchange of vital information and resources in ways that scientists are only beginning to comprehend. The notion that mushrooms play a central role in ecosystem communication challenges our traditional understanding of plant and animal networks. As research into mycology continues to evolve, the fascinating parallels between fungi and technology offer a new perspective on the complex web of life. The discovery of this hidden "forest Internet" underscores the profound interconnectedness of all living organisms.

Key Vocabulary:
- **Mycelium**: The vegetative part of fungi, consisting of a mass of branching, thread-like hyphae.
- **Vast**: Very great in size, amount, or extent.
- **Communication**: The exchange of information between organisms.
- **Central**: Of primary importance or fundamental to the system.
- **Mycology**: The scientific study of fungi.

The Secret Language of Cats

Cats have long been regarded as aloof and enigmatic creatures, but beneath their seemingly indifferent exterior lies a highly sophisticated system of communication. While many people are familiar with the familiar "meow," this vocalization serves a far more nuanced purpose than simply seeking attention or food. Cats use a wide range of sounds—purring, chirping, and even growling—to convey emotions, intentions, and needs, depending on the context. Studies have shown that domestic cats are capable of tailoring their vocalizations specifically for their human companions, employing a unique "human-directed" meow that is often higher-pitched and more persistent. In addition to vocal communication, cats also rely on body language—tail movements, ear positioning, and even the dilation of their pupils—to convey their moods. A slow blink, for instance, is often referred to as a "cat kiss" and is interpreted as a sign of trust and affection. Interestingly, cats have been found to have a complex repertoire of scent-marking behaviors, using their pheromones to establish territory and communicate with other felines. Though their vocal language may appear minimal compared to that of other animals, the subtleties of feline communication demonstrate a highly developed system of interaction. Understanding these signals allows humans to form deeper, more meaningful connections with their feline companions. In essence, the secret language of cats is as multifaceted as the creatures themselves, an example of the intricate bond between humans and their pets.

Key Vocabulary:
- **Communication**: The exchange of messages or information.
- **Emotions**: Strong feelings such as joy, anger, or sadness.
- **Body Language**: Non-verbal cues that express feelings and intentions.
- **Complex**: Involving many different components or aspects.
- **Pheromones**: Chemical substances used by animals to communicate.

Why People Walk in Circles When Lost

When people become disoriented and lost, it is not uncommon for them to unknowingly walk in circles. This curious phenomenon, known as "circular error," has baffled researchers for centuries. One of the primary reasons for this behavior is that humans are heavily reliant on visual cues to navigate their environment, and in unfamiliar terrain, these cues can be misleading. Without recognizable landmarks, the brain struggles to maintain a consistent sense of direction, and as a result, individuals may unknowingly turn slightly to the left or right over time, gradually spiraling in a circular motion. Interestingly, studies have shown that people tend to favor one direction over the other—most often the right—when they become disoriented, leading to a gradual deviation from their intended path. Additionally, factors such as wind, uneven terrain, or the lack of a clear path can exacerbate the situation, making it even harder to maintain a straight trajectory. Some researchers argue that the phenomenon may be rooted in evolutionary biology, as early humans had to rely on their internal sense of direction to survive in the wild. Modern technology, such as GPS, has largely rendered this instinct obsolete, yet the underlying mechanism of circular movement persists in situations of extreme disorientation. This strange phenomenon highlights the complexities of human navigation and our innate dependence on external cues for orientation. Although walking in circles may seem like an odd and futile response, it is an involuntary survival mechanism that has evolved over millennia.

Key Vocabulary:
- **Disoriented**: Confused or unsure of one's surroundings or direction.
- **Misleading**: Giving the wrong idea or impression.
- **Gradual**: Occurring slowly over time.
- **Exacerbate**: To make a situation worse or more intense.
- **Instinct**: An innate, typically fixed pattern of behavior in animals and humans.

How Trees Secretly Help Each Other Survive

In the dense underbrush of ancient forests, an invisible network of trees is quietly at work, exchanging vital resources to ensure their collective survival. Trees are far from solitary giants; in fact, they participate in a highly interdependent system where they share nutrients, water, and even chemical signals through their roots. This process is facilitated by the "Wood Wide Web," a complex mycorrhizal network that connects trees and other plants underground, allowing them to communicate and support one another. When one tree is in need of nutrients, perhaps due to environmental stress or pest damage, nearby trees can send resources through their shared root systems, aiding in the distressed tree's recovery. In addition to nutrient sharing, trees also transmit warnings about potential threats, such as insect infestations or droughts, via chemical signals that alert surrounding plants to prepare their defenses. This mutualistic behavior extends beyond individual species, as trees of different kinds may share resources to ensure the health of the broader ecosystem. Research suggests that older, larger trees—often referred to as "mother trees"—play a particularly important role in the survival of younger saplings, guiding their growth and offering protection. Despite their seemingly silent existence, trees are capable of intricate social interactions that exemplify the cooperative nature of life. The notion that trees, seemingly solitary in their towering majesty, are so deeply interconnected challenges our understanding of nature's complexity. Indeed, the forest is a place of profound cooperation, where life thrives through mutual aid.

Key Vocabulary:
- **Interdependent**: Mutually reliant on each other.
- **Mycorrhizal**: Relating to the symbiotic association between fungi and plant roots.
- **Silent**: Not making any noise; in this context, hidden or unnoticed.
- **Cooperative**: Involving mutual assistance in working toward a common goal.
- **Ecosystem**: A biological community of interacting organisms and their physical environment.

The Science Behind Why We Get Goosebumps

Goosebumps are an involuntary response that humans experience when faced with intense emotions, cold, or certain physical sensations. Known as piloerection, this phenomenon occurs when the tiny muscles at the base of our hair follicles contract, causing the hairs to stand upright. This response is a remnant of our evolutionary past, where our ancestors relied on the sudden puffing up of body hair to appear larger and more intimidating to predators. When we experience extreme cold, goosebumps serve as a defense mechanism, helping to trap air close to the skin for warmth, although this effect is largely insignificant in modern humans with sparse body hair. The emotional triggers for goosebumps, such as listening to music or watching a particularly moving scene in a movie, can be attributed to the brain's activation of certain areas responsible for processing intense emotions. The physical sensation associated with goosebumps is deeply tied to the body's autonomic nervous system, a network that controls involuntary bodily functions. Though goosebumps are a commonplace experience, their biological significance is often overlooked. Scientists continue to study the intricate interplay between emotion, physiology, and evolutionary survival that leads to this seemingly trivial, yet fascinating, reaction. From an evolutionary standpoint, this seemingly minor phenomenon is a powerful reminder of the complexity of the human body. Goosebumps serve as a vestige of our past, reminding us that our physiological responses are deeply intertwined with our emotional and environmental stimuli.

Key Vocabulary:
- **Piloerection**: The physiological process of hair standing on end.
- **Ancestors**: Early generations from which individuals or species descend.
- **Insignificant**: Too small or unimportant to be worth consideration.
- **Activation**: The process of initiating or triggering a response.
- **Commonplace**: Ordinary or frequently encountered.

How Birds Navigate Thousands of Miles Without Getting Lost

The incredible migratory journeys undertaken by birds each year have long baffled scientists, who have marveled at their seemingly innate ability to travel thousands of miles without losing their way. Birds use a combination of sensory cues and remarkable navigational instincts to chart their courses across continents. One of the primary tools birds rely on is the Earth's magnetic field, which they can detect using special proteins in their eyes that allow them to sense magnetic forces. This geomagnetic sense provides birds with a compass to orient themselves, ensuring they stay on course even in unfamiliar landscapes. Birds also use the position of the sun, stars, and landmarks to guide their journey, a complex system of navigation that requires both precision and adaptability. In addition to visual cues, birds are thought to possess an extraordinary sense of smell, which may help them recognize certain environmental features that are critical for navigation. Recent studies suggest that some birds may even detect the Earth's electromagnetic pulses, giving them an added layer of navigational awareness. Despite the variety of methods birds employ, their ability to navigate with such precision remains a marvel of nature. Researchers continue to uncover new insights into the ways birds interact with their environment, but one thing is clear: the ability to navigate vast distances is deeply ingrained in their biology. Birds' extraordinary migratory abilities exemplify the intricacies of animal navigation, offering new perspectives on the interconnectedness of life on Earth.

Key Vocabulary:
- **Sensory**: Relating to the senses or sensation.
- **Geomagnetic**: Pertaining to the Earth's magnetic field.
- **Environmental**: Relating to the surroundings or conditions in which something exists.
- **Marvel**: A wonderful or astonishing thing.
- **Navigational**: Related to the process of determining one's position or course.

Why Certain Smells Bring Back Old Memories

The phenomenon of scent-triggered memory is one of the most striking examples of how deeply our senses are interwoven with our emotional experiences. The human sense of smell is intricately linked to the brain's limbic system, which is responsible for emotions, memory, and behavior. This unique connection allows smells to evoke vivid memories of people, places, and events from our past with startling clarity. One of the key reasons for this strong association between smell and memory is that the olfactory bulb, which processes odors, is directly connected to the hippocampus, a brain region critical for memory formation. Because of this neuroanatomical link, smells can bypass our conscious awareness and trigger deep emotional responses tied to our personal histories. Research has shown that certain scents, like the fragrance of a loved one's perfume or the smell of freshly baked cookies, can elicit strong feelings of nostalgia, comfort, or longing. This nostalgic effect is particularly powerful because it bypasses the rational brain, tapping into the emotional centers that are more easily swayed by sensory input. Interestingly, scent-triggered memories tend to be more vivid and emotionally intense than those triggered by other senses, further underscoring the profound connection between smell and memory. Understanding this connection has profound implications for therapeutic practices, as scent-based therapies are being used to help patients with memory loss or emotional trauma. Ultimately, the science of scent offers a fascinating glimpse into the complexities of human cognition and emotion.

Key Vocabulary:
- **Striking**: Remarkably impressive or noticeable.
- **Neuroanatomical**: Relating to the structure of the nervous system.
- **Nostalgic**: A sentimental longing for the past.
- **Vivid**: Producing powerful feelings or clear images in the

mind.
- **Olfactory**: Relating to the sense of smell.

The Hidden World Inside a Single Drop of Water

Beneath the surface of a seemingly simple drop of water exists a microcosm teeming with life and complex interactions. Through the lens of a microscope, what appears to be a clear, unassuming droplet becomes an entire universe, rich with microorganisms such as bacteria, algae, and protozoa. These minute organisms interact in a dynamic ecosystem that mirrors the complexities of larger ecological systems. The water drop serves as a habitat, a nurturing environment where these tiny life forms thrive, compete for resources, and evolve. Microbes within a drop of water engage in intricate food webs, where some organisms consume others, and others break down organic matter to recycle nutrients. These organisms also play pivotal roles in the global nutrient cycles, contributing to the health of ecosystems far beyond the boundaries of a single droplet. The sheer diversity of life forms within such a small volume of water offers a glimpse into the invisible world that exists around and within us. By studying these miniature ecosystems, scientists gain a deeper understanding of the interconnectedness of life. From the simplest bacteria to the more complex protozoa, every organism within a drop of water contributes to the delicate balance of life on Earth. This hidden world, though invisible to the naked eye, shows the richness of life that exists in even the most seemingly insignificant places.

Key Vocabulary:
- **Microcosm**: A miniature representation of a larger system.
- **Ecosystem**: A community of living organisms and their environment.
- **Nurturing**: Providing care and encouragement for growth.

- **Interconnectedness**: The state of being connected with each other.
- **Invisible**: Not able to be seen.

The Physics of Why Buttered Toast Falls Face Down

The phenomenon of buttered toast invariably falling face down has been a topic of both humorous and serious inquiry. The answer to this seemingly mundane mystery lies in the physics of torque and the center of gravity. When toast is dropped, the force of gravity acts upon it, pulling it downward, while the toast rotates in the air. Due to the uneven weight distribution, especially when the toast is buttered, the side with the butter tends to be heavier, causing the toast to flip mid-air. This rotation occurs rapidly, and because the toast typically falls from a height of just a few feet, there isn't enough time for it to complete a full rotation and land butter-side up. Additionally, the surface tension and density of the butter create a momentum that encourages the toast to settle with the butter facing downward. The physics of this phenomenon involves principles of angular momentum, which dictates how an object rotates and moves in response to external forces. While this behavior might seem trivial, it offers a fascinating glimpse into the unpredictability of everyday physics. In some ways, the dropping of buttered toast serves as a demonstration of the laws of motion and gravity in action, underscoring how even the simplest events are governed by the complexities of the physical world.

Key Vocabulary:
- **Humorous**: Causing laughter or amusement.
- **Torque**: A twisting force that causes rotation.
- **Heavier**: Having more weight or mass.
- **Momentum**: The force that keeps an object moving.
- **Angular Momentum**: The quantity of rotation of an object, taking into account its mass and rotational velocity.

How Plants Can "Hear" the Sound of Water

Plants have long been thought of as passive organisms, rooted firmly in place, unable to interact with the world around them in any dynamic way. However, recent studies suggest that plants possess a remarkable ability to detect sound, particularly the sound of water. Through specialized mechanoreceptors, plants can sense vibrations in their environment, including the subtle sounds of water flowing or dripping nearby. This ability likely evolved as a survival mechanism, allowing plants to identify sources of water even in dark or crowded environments. The sound of water prompts plants to adjust their growth patterns, reaching toward the source to take advantage of the moisture. This phenomenon, known as hydropathy, is an incredible example of how plants interact with their environment in ways that were once unimaginable. The sensitivity of plants to sound and vibration has also been observed to extend to other stimuli, including the sound of nearby insects, which may signal the presence of a potential pollinator or pest. The auditory capabilities of plants suggest a level of environmental awareness that challenges our conventional understanding of plant behavior. In light of this new evidence, plants are beginning to be seen not just as passive entities, but as complex organisms capable of detecting and responding to the world in ways that mirror the behaviors of more mobile creatures.

Key Vocabulary:
- **Detect**: To become aware of or identify something.
- **Mechanoreceptors**: Sensory receptors that respond to mechanical pressure or distortion.
- **Reaching**: Stretching out toward something, often in search of something.
- **Hydropathy**: The study of the interaction of water with other substances, or in this case, how plants respond to

water.
- **Auditory**: Relating to the sense of hearing.

Why Laughter Is Contagious

Laughter, that universal human response to humor or joy, is more than just a reaction to funny situations—it's a social phenomenon that is deeply contagious. Research has shown that hearing someone laugh triggers a neural response in the brain that encourages us to laugh as well. This contagious nature of laughter likely evolved as a social bonding mechanism, facilitating group cohesion and fostering positive social connections. Laughter helps to lower stress, enhance mood, and create a sense of shared joy, making it an essential part of human interaction. The contagiousness of laughter may also be tied to our empathy—the ability to sense and mirror the emotions of others. Studies have found that when we hear laughter, our brain's mirror neurons become active, encouraging us to mimic the sound and action of laughing. This mimicry serves to strengthen social ties, as it is inherently reassuring and promotes feelings of belonging. Laughter's ability to spread rapidly through a group, like an infectious virus, underscores its importance in facilitating communication and connection. It is a reminder that laughter is not just a solitary act, but a shared experience that transcends individual barriers and strengthens our bonds with others. The science of why laughter is contagious reveals the deep social and emotional threads that connect us all.

Key Vocabulary:
- **Contagious**: Capable of being transmitted from one person to another.
- **Neural**: Relating to nerves or the nervous system.
- **Enhance**: To improve or increase in quality or intensity.
- **Empathy**: The ability to understand and share the feelings of another.
- **Belonging**: The sense of being accepted or included in a

group.

How the Moon Affects Human Behavior

The moon has long been a subject of fascination and superstition, with many believing that its phases influence human behavior. From ancient times, the moon has been thought to affect everything from sleep patterns to mood swings. Modern science has found some evidence to support these claims, suggesting that the lunar cycle can impact human circadian rhythms, which govern our sleep-wake cycles. During the full moon, people may experience disruptions in sleep quality, with increased restlessness and difficulty falling asleep. Moreover, studies have indicated that the moon's gravitational pull, though minuscule compared to the Earth's, can have subtle effects on human behavior, including an increase in accidents or even heightened aggression in some individuals. The connection between the moon and human behavior is thought to stem from a deep-rooted, biological sensitivity to the cycles of nature. Some theories propose that the moon's influence dates back to prehistoric times, when early humans relied on the moon's phases for navigation and timekeeping. Additionally, the emotional impact of the moon, particularly during lunar eclipses, has been linked to increased anxiety and heightened stress levels. While much of this remains speculative, the moon's role in shaping human experience continues to captivate and intrigue scientists and laypeople alike. Its cycles, as they rhythmically unfold, seem to stir something primal in the human psyche.

Key Vocabulary:
- **Circadian Rhythms**: The natural cycles of the body that regulate sleep, eating, and other functions.
- **Biological**: Relating to living organisms and their physical processes.
- **Emotional**: Relating to feelings or the experience of

emotions.
- **Gravitational**: Pertaining to the force of gravity, especially between celestial bodies.
- **Lunar Eclipse**: An astronomical event where the Earth blocks sunlight from reaching the moon.

The Reason Why Time Feels Faster as We Age

As we grow older, many people experience the curious sensation that time seems to pass more quickly than it did in their youth. This perception of time speeding up is linked to both psychological and neurological factors. As children, time feels long and expansive because everything is novel, and our brains are processing new experiences at a rapid pace. However, as we age and accumulate more experiences, the brain tends to process familiar events more efficiently, making time seem to pass by more swiftly. This change in perception is also influenced by the ratios of time: as we grow older, each year represents a smaller fraction of our total life. For instance, to a 10-year-old, one year is 10% of their life, whereas for a 50-year-old, it's only 2%. This ratio effect makes time feel like it's accelerating as we age. Additionally, the brain's slowing of information processing over time contributes to the feeling that life is flying by. The loss of novelty and routine can make days and years blend together, leaving us with a sense of time slipping away unnoticed. This psychological phenomenon is an example of how our perception of time is shaped by our experiences, cognitive processes, and the way our minds interact with the world around us. As we age, we may find ourselves longing for the long, drawn-out days of childhood, when time seemed to stretch endlessly before us.

Key Vocabulary:
- **Perception**: The way we interpret and understand sensory information.
- **Efficiently**: Accomplishing something with minimal waste of time or resources.

- **Ratios**: The relative proportion of one quantity compared to another.
- **Familiar**: Well-known or easily recognized.
- **Flying**: Moving quickly or passing rapidly.

The Secret Ingredients That Make Rain Smell So Good

The delightful scent of rain, often referred to as "petrichor," has captivated our senses for centuries. This distinctive aroma, which fills the air after a fresh rainfall, is the result of a complex interaction between the atmosphere, the earth, and a variety of natural compounds. One key component is ozone, which is produced when lightning strikes, giving rainstorms their characteristic fresh, sharp scent. Another contributor to the earthy fragrance is a compound called geosmin, which is released by soil-dwelling microbes when it rains, creating the unmistakable earthy smell. Additionally, plants and trees contribute to the rain's aroma through the release of aromatic oils, which are absorbed by rainwater and then released into the air. These compounds, combined with the cooling effect of the rain, create a scent that is both refreshing and grounding. Interestingly, the smell of rain may also have psychological benefits, evoking feelings of calmness and nostalgia. The scent of rain often triggers positive memories, creating an emotional connection to nature and the environment. The complexity of the rain's scent is a reminder of how much the natural world influences our sensory experiences. With each rainfall, nature creates a unique and ephemeral fragrance that we can enjoy, breathe in, and connect with on a deeper level.

Key Vocabulary:
- **Distinctive**: Recognizably different or unique.
- **Ozone**: A gas composed of three oxygen atoms, often associated with the fresh smell after a storm.
- **Geosmin**: An organic compound that gives soil its earthy smell.
- **Aromatic**: Having a strong, pleasant scent.

- **Connection**: A bond or association between two things, often on an emotional or intellectual level.

How Music Can Change the Taste of Food

The relationship between our senses of taste and sound is more profound than many realize, with music playing an unexpected role in how we perceive food. Research has shown that certain types of music can enhance or alter the taste of what we eat, influencing everything from sweetness to bitterness. Fast, high-pitched music, for instance, can make food taste sweeter, while slower, lower-pitched sounds can intensify bitterness. This phenomenon occurs because music has the ability to influence our mood and psychological state, which in turn affects our sensory experience of food. When we listen to upbeat music, our emotions are elevated, and we tend to perceive food as more pleasant, possibly due to a heightened sense of enjoyment. Conversely, more melancholic or somber music can make food seem less appetizing, altering our experience of even the most delicious dishes. The connection between sound and taste is so powerful that researchers have even explored using music as a tool in the food industry to influence consumer preferences and behavior. Certain restaurants and food brands have embraced this idea by curating specific soundtracks to complement the dining experience, aiming to evoke particular feelings that enhance the flavor of their dishes. In essence, music can transform a meal from a simple act of eating into a multi-sensory experience, where sound and taste are inextricably intertwined.

Key Vocabulary:
- **Enhance**: To improve or increase the quality of something.
- **Sweeter**: Having a more pleasant, sugary taste.
- **Mood**: A temporary state of mind or feeling.
- **Somber**: Serious, grave, or dark in tone.

- **Inextricably**: Impossible to separate or untangle.

Why We Dream and What It Might Mean

Dreaming is one of the most perplexing and mystifying aspects of the human experience. While science has made great strides in understanding the physical processes behind dreaming, the purpose of dreams remains an enigma. Theories abound, ranging from the idea that dreams are the brain's way of processing emotions and experiences to the belief that they serve as a method of preparing us for future challenges. Some psychologists argue that dreams are a manifestation of our unconscious mind, bringing repressed thoughts and desires to the surface in symbolic form. Others propose that dreams serve a more practical function, such as aiding in memory consolidation or problem-solving. The vivid nature of certain dreams, which can feel strikingly real, suggests that they have a profound impact on our emotional state, often reflecting or amplifying our waking concerns and anxieties. Throughout history, dreams have been interpreted as divine messages, foretelling the future or offering insights into one's destiny. Yet, despite extensive study, the true significance of dreams remains elusive, with many scientists acknowledging that we may never fully comprehend their role in our lives. What is certain, however, is that dreams continue to fascinate and mystify, offering a window into the hidden realms of the human psyche.

Key Vocabulary:
- **Purpose**: The reason something exists or happens.
- **Unconscious**: The part of the mind not accessible to conscious thought, often housing repressed memories or desires.
- **Vivid**: Intensely deep or clear, often used to describe highly detailed or striking dreams.
- **Manifestation**: The act of bringing something into existence or revealing it.

- **Elusive**: Difficult to define, grasp, or understand.

The Strange Science of Why We Feel Deja Vu

Déjà vu, the eerie sensation that we've experienced before, is a phenomenon that has intrigued both scientists and mystics alike for centuries. While its exact cause remains unclear, researchers have proposed several theories to explain this perplexing sensation. One leading theory suggests that déjà vu occurs when the brain processes a new experience in two parts: first, it registers the information, and then it mistakenly identifies the second processing as a memory, creating the illusion of having lived through the event before. This misfiring of the brain's memory system is thought to be linked to the hippocampus, the part of the brain responsible for storing and recalling memories. Some theories also point to the possibility of microseconds of delay between the brain's perception of an event and its conscious recognition, causing the brain to interpret the present as a past memory. Another theory posits that déjà vu is a form of neurological glitch, where the brain briefly experiences a crossover between different memory circuits. Despite the multitude of explanations, déjà vu continues to elude a definitive answer, remaining a fascinating and mysterious aspect of human experience. Some even suggest that it might have metaphysical or spiritual significance, though this view is far from scientifically accepted. Regardless of its origins, déjà vu remains one of the most intriguing cognitive phenomena in neuroscience.

Key Vocabulary:
- **Theories**: Ideas or explanations based on research or reasoning.
- **Hippocampus**: A part of the brain involved in forming and storing memories.
- **Neurological**: Related to the nervous system and its diseases or functions.

- **Glitch**: A small, temporary malfunction or error in a system.
- **Crossover**: The process of things mixing or merging.

The Hidden Patterns in Everyday Traffic Jams

Anyone who has sat in traffic knows how frustrating it can be, but there are surprising patterns at work in these daily bottlenecks that are often unnoticed. Traffic jams, though seemingly chaotic, often follow predictable rhythms. One key pattern is the phenomenon known as the traffic wave, where a small disruption at the front of the line can ripple through the entire flow of traffic, causing a backup that seems disproportionate to the initial cause. These waves can be triggered by something as minor as a car braking unexpectedly or a driver changing lanes. Interestingly, traffic jams tend to form at certain times of the day, often during peak hours when everyone is commuting to or from work. In addition, research has found that driver behavior plays a significant role in the flow of traffic. For instance, if a driver brakes too suddenly, it can create a chain reaction that slows down the entire lane, even though there may be no obvious obstacle ahead. Traffic engineers use sophisticated models to predict and alleviate traffic congestion by understanding these patterns. By using sensors and real-time data, they can monitor traffic in real time and adjust traffic signals to prevent bottlenecks. The study of traffic flow is a fascinating example of how human behavior interacts with complex systems in ways that can be both unpredictable and, at times, disturbingly predictable.

Key Vocabulary:
- **Predictable**: Able to be anticipated or expected based on patterns.
- **Traffic Wave**: A ripple effect in traffic caused by disruptions at the front of the line.
- **Certain**: Known or established without doubt.

- **Models**: Simulations or representations used to study or predict real-world phenomena.
- **Human Behavior**: The actions or reactions of individuals in response to stimuli, often influenced by social and psychological factors.

How Bees Recognize Human Faces

Bees, those industrious little creatures that pollinate our crops, possess a surprisingly sophisticated ability: they can recognize and remember human faces. This capability was uncovered through a series of experiments in which researchers trained bees to associate a particular face with a sugary reward. The bees learned to recognize the faces but also retained this information for several days. This phenomenon is particularly fascinating because, unlike humans who rely on a complex combination of facial features, bees recognize faces by processing configurations of elements, such as the arrangement of eyes, nose, and mouth. This suggests that bees, despite their small brains, possess a remarkable level of cognitive processing. Their ability to discern faces may have evolved as a means to navigate their environment and interact with other members of their colony. This ability also allows them to distinguish between flowers, as they associate specific flowers with memories of previous encounters. In a broader sense, this research demonstrates that cognitive abilities in animals can be much more advanced than previously thought, with bees exemplifying the surprising complexities of animal intelligence. Understanding how bees process faces may even have implications for improving machine learning and artificial intelligence, as researchers continue to explore the ways in which small-brained creatures outperform expectations.

Key Vocabulary:
- **Experiments**: Controlled tests conducted to discover or validate scientific theories.

- **Configurations**: The arrangement of elements or components in a particular pattern.
- **Encounters**: Meetings or interactions, often with unfamiliar entities.
- **Advanced**: Highly developed or sophisticated.
- **Machine Learning**: A type of artificial intelligence where systems learn from data to improve performance.

Why We Get "Brain Freeze" from Ice Cream

The phenomenon of "brain freeze," that sharp, sudden pain in the head after consuming cold food or drinks, occurs when something cold makes contact with the roof of the mouth. This causes the blood vessels in the mouth to constrict rapidly in response to the extreme cold, only to dilate quickly afterward. The change in blood flow is believed to trigger the pain receptors in the brain, leading to the sensation of a headache. This sudden shift in temperature may cause the brain to interpret the pain as coming from the head, even though the source of the discomfort is in the mouth. The medical term for brain freeze is "sphenopalatine ganglioneuralgia," but most people prefer the colloquial term.

Interestingly, this intense pain is typically brief, often subsiding within seconds, although it can feel much longer. The phenomenon is thought to be more common in individuals who consume cold substances rapidly, as the brain is given less time to acclimatize to the change in temperature. While brain freeze is harmless, it serves as a reminder of the sensitive and complex nature of our nervous system, which can misinterpret stimuli in fascinating ways. Understanding this process also sheds light on the interconnectedness of our body's systems and the fine-tuned reactions that allow us to navigate an often challenging environment.

Key Vocabulary:
- **Dilate**: To expand or open wider.

- **Pain Receptors**: Nerve cells that detect pain stimuli.
- **Sphenopalatine Ganglioneuralgia**: The medical term for brain freeze.
- **Colloquial**: Informal or conversational language.
- **Complex**: Intricate or consisting of many interconnected parts.

The Way Colors Can Influence Our Mood

Color has a profound impact on human psychology, influencing emotions and even behavior. Scientists have long studied the ways in which different colors can evoke specific psychological responses, with certain hues being linked to particular emotions. For instance, the color red is often associated with passion, excitement, or anger, while blue tends to induce feelings of calmness and tranquility. Yellow, a bright and energizing color, can evoke feelings of happiness or optimism, while green is frequently tied to nature and feelings of renewal. Interestingly, colors can also have an effect on our physical responses, such as heart rate and blood pressure, indicating that they may influence both the emotional and physiological states of individuals. Some researchers have suggested that the color of a room or environment can impact our productivity, with blue spaces fostering focus and concentration, while red spaces might encourage energy but also stress. The impact of color on mood is not universally experienced, however, as cultural and personal associations with colors can differ significantly from person to person. Despite these differences, the psychology of color remains an essential field of study in design, marketing, and even mental health, with the potential to shape how we experience and interact with the world around us.

Key Vocabulary:
- **Specific**: Clearly defined or identified.
- **Optimism**: A hopeful or positive outlook on the future.
- **Productivity**: The efficiency of producing goods or

completing tasks.
- **Differ**: To be unlike or distinct from something else.
- **Psychology**: The scientific study of behavior and mental processes.

How the Shape of Your Ear Affects What You Hear

The shape of your ears plays a crucial role in how you perceive sound, acting as an important part of your auditory system. Each ear has a unique structure, with folds and contours that help to capture and direct sound waves into the ear canal. The ear's pinna, the external part of the ear, helps to amplify certain frequencies while attenuating others, shaping the way sound is heard. In particular, the shape of the ear can affect our ability to localize sound, or determine its direction. The folds of the pinna can reflect sound waves, which helps us detect where sounds are coming from, even if we can't directly see the source. This is crucial for spatial awareness, as the brain processes the time it takes for sound to reach each ear to triangulate its location. Changes or abnormalities in the shape of the ear can alter this process, potentially leading to difficulty in distinguishing between sounds or identifying their origin. Additionally, research has shown that the shape of the ear can also influence the perception of pitch, with certain ear shapes being more sensitive to higher or lower frequencies. This intricate relationship between ear shape and sound perception demonstrates the body's remarkable adaptability and the complex processes involved in hearing.

Key Vocabulary:
- **Pinna**: The external, visible part of the ear.
- **Attenuating**: Reducing the force, effect, or strength of something.
- **Identifying**: Recognizing or establishing the identity of something.
- **Pitch**: The highness or lowness of a sound.
- **Auditory**: Related to hearing or the sense of sound.

Why Some People Can "Taste" Words

Some individuals have a fascinating condition called synesthesia, where they experience cross-wired sensory perceptions. One of the more intriguing forms of synesthesia is when people can "taste" words. These individuals perceive specific words or sounds as distinct flavors, colors, or textures. The phenomenon occurs due to an unusual connection between the brain's sensory pathways, where stimuli from one sense activate those of another. For example, someone might taste chocolate when hearing a certain word or experience a tangy sensation while reading a particular sentence. While synesthesia has long been viewed as a curiosity, modern neuroscience suggests that this condition might involve heightened neuroplasticity, where the brain's wiring is more adaptable and interconnected than in the general population. Synesthesia can sometimes provide artistic inspiration, as individuals can perceive music or language in an intensely sensory manner. The prevalence of this condition is thought to be rare, with only a small percentage of the population experiencing it. Despite its rarity, synesthesia offers a unique window into the complexities of the brain and its ability to intertwine different sensory experiences. Further research into this condition could provide deeper insights into how our brains interpret and process the world around us, as well as how we construct meaning from the stimuli we encounter.

Key Vocabulary:
- **Flavors**: Distinct tastes perceived by the tongue.
- **Connection**: A relationship or link between two or more elements.
- **Neuroplasticity**: The brain's ability to reorganize and adapt by forming new neural connections.
- **Prevalence**: The state of being widespread or common in a particular area.
- **Stimuli**: Something that causes a reaction or response in

the body or brain.

The Secret Lives of Dust Mites in Your Bed

The humble dust mite, invisible to the naked eye, leads a surprisingly complex and somewhat disconcerting life in the comfort of our own beds. These microscopic creatures thrive in the warmth and moisture of bedding, feeding on dead skin cells shed by humans and animals. Despite their small size, dust mites play an outsized role in the ecosystem of your mattress, contributing to the decomposition of organic material. However, their presence is not entirely benign. Dust mites are a major source of indoor allergens, as their waste products can trigger respiratory issues like asthma and allergic reactions. Studies have shown that even a seemingly clean bed can host thousands of these mites, making them a constant but largely unnoticed presence in our lives. Their population grows exponentially in environments that are humid, as they rely on moisture for survival. Interestingly, dust mites are not the only creatures that inhabit your bed; other microscopic organisms such as bacteria and fungi also thrive in these warm, dark environments. Despite their negative connotations, dust mites are part of the natural cycle of life, playing an integral role in the breakdown of organic materials. However, for those with allergies, the presence of dust mites can be an ongoing source of discomfort. Controlling humidity and regularly washing bedding are effective ways to limit their numbers.

Key Vocabulary:
- **Disconcerting**: Causing confusion or concern.
- **Dead Skin Cells**: Cells shed from the skin as part of its natural renewal process.
- **Respiratory**: Relating to the process of breathing or the organs involved in it.
- **Humid**: Containing a high level of moisture, especially in the air.

- **Microorganisms**: Organisms too small to be seen by the naked eye, such as bacteria and fungi.

How Cities Create Their Own Microclimates

Cities are known for their distinctive energy, bustling with people, traffic, and industry. Yet, this vibrant activity can also lead to the creation of urban microclimates—localized climate variations that differ from the surrounding natural environment. These microclimates occur due to the dense concentrations of buildings, roads, and human activity, which absorb and retain heat. This phenomenon, known as the "urban heat island" effect, results in cities often being significantly warmer than their rural counterparts, especially during the night. The materials used in urban construction, such as concrete and asphalt, are excellent at trapping heat, which can exacerbate the temperature differences. Furthermore, cities often have reduced greenery, leading to less evaporative cooling from plants and trees. The limited airflow and high levels of pollution further contribute to the warmth, trapping heat in the atmosphere. The creation of microclimates can also influence local weather patterns, leading to altered precipitation levels and more intense storms. While urban microclimates may seem like an unavoidable byproduct of modern living, some cities have begun implementing green roofs, urban parks, and reflective materials to mitigate the effects. These efforts aim to balance the ecological impact of cities while improving their inhabitants' quality of life.

Key Vocabulary:
- **Distinctive**: Characteristic of a particular person, thing, or group.
- **Precipitation**: Any form of water—liquid or solid—that falls from the atmosphere, including rain, snow, and sleet.
- **Greenery**: Vegetation, especially when it is lush and abundant.

- **Ecological**: Relating to the environment and the relationships between organisms and their surroundings.
- **Exacerbate**: To make a situation worse or more intense.

The Physics Behind Why Your Reflection Flips Horizontally but Not Vertically

When you look into a mirror, the reflection you see is reversed, but not in the way you might expect. The most common misconception is that mirrors flip images left to right; in reality, they only flip them front to back. This occurs due to the orientation of light rays that bounce off the mirror. When you stand in front of a mirror, the light reflecting off your body travels toward the reflective surface. The mirror doesn't reverse the image horizontally or vertically but reflects it along an axis perpendicular to the surface. This gives the illusion that the left side of your body is on the right in the reflection, and vice versa. The reason for the perceived "horizontal" flip is due to the way we interpret the spatial relationship between objects in our environment. Our brains are wired to associate a left-to-right relationship with physical movement, but mirrors only reverse the direction of depth—front to back. This phenomenon is deeply rooted in the fundamental principles of optics and the behavior of light, which follows predictable laws of reflection. This seemingly simple concept illustrates the complexity of how we perceive reality, often making us aware of the mysterious ways in which the world around us can be distorted.

Key Vocabulary:
- **Orientation**: The position or alignment of something relative to its surroundings.
- **Horizontally**: In a manner parallel to the horizon, from left to right.
- **Reverse**: To turn something in the opposite direction.
- **Optics**: The branch of physics that deals with the behavior of light.

- **Mysterious**: Something that is difficult to understand or explain.

Why Some People's Voices Sound Different in Recordings

Have you ever been startled to hear your voice in a recording, only to wonder why it sounds so different from what you hear when you speak? This phenomenon is rooted in the complex science of sound transmission. When you speak, the sound waves travel through the air and into your ears, where they are processed by your brain. However, the sound you hear is not the same as what others perceive because of the resonance that occurs within your head. The vibrations caused by your voice travel through the bones of your skull, enriching the sound with lower frequencies that make it sound fuller to you. In contrast, when recorded, your voice is captured purely through airwaves, lacking these bone-conducted vibrations. Additionally, the recording equipment itself can affect the sound, distorting it or emphasizing certain tones, which may make it sound higher-pitched or thinner. The result is often an unfamiliar version of your voice, which may seem less melodious or more nasally than you expect. This discrepancy is a fascinating example of how our perception of sound is influenced by the environment and the mediums through which it is transmitted. Over time, people may become more accustomed to hearing their recorded voice and learn to accept it, but the initial reaction is usually one of surprise or discomfort.

Key Vocabulary:
- **Sound Transmission**: The process by which sound moves through different mediums.
- **Resonance**: The amplification or enrichment of sound due to vibration.
- **Bone-Conducted**: Referring to the way sound vibrations travel through bones in the body.

- **Melodious**: Having a pleasant or harmonious sound.
- **Discrepancy**: A difference or inconsistency between two things.

The Science Behind Why Some People Are Morning or Night Owls

Are you an early riser or a night owl? Whether you're alert and active in the early morning or find your energy peaks at night, the science behind your internal clock is governed by your circadian rhythm, a natural 24-hour cycle that regulates various physiological processes. This rhythm is controlled by the brain's suprachiasmatic nucleus, which receives input from light and darkness, signaling to your body when to wake up and when to rest. Morning people, or "larks," tend to have a genetic predisposition to wake early, while night owls are wired to feel most awake during the evening hours. These differences in sleep-wake cycles are linked to variations in melatonin production, a hormone responsible for regulating sleep. The timing of melatonin release can be influenced by lifestyle choices, environmental factors, and even your genetic makeup. Interestingly, your circadian rhythm can be shifted, especially in response to external stimuli such as light exposure or social obligations. Disruptions to this rhythm, like those caused by shift work or jet lag, can lead to significant physical and mental fatigue. Understanding the science behind these cycles can help individuals optimize their productivity and well-being, aligning their routines with their natural sleep patterns.

Key Vocabulary:
- **Circadian Rhythm**: The internal biological clock that governs sleep-wake cycles.
- **Suprachiasmatic Nucleus**: A small part of the brain that controls circadian rhythms.
- **Melatonin**: A hormone that regulates sleep patterns.
- **Predisposition**: A genetic or environmental tendency

toward a certain condition or behavior.
- **Shifted**: Changed or altered, particularly in reference to a sleep schedule.

How Certain Animals Can See Colors We Can't

While humans are capable of perceiving a wide array of colors, there are some animals that possess the extraordinary ability to see a broader spectrum, far beyond what we can imagine. Many animals, such as certain species of birds and insects, can perceive ultraviolet (UV) light, a range of colors invisible to the human eye. This heightened color perception is due to the specialized structure of their eyes, which contain additional photoreceptor cells that can detect wavelengths outside the visible spectrum. For example, butterflies and honeybees are able to see UV patterns on flowers that help them identify nectar sources, a feature completely invisible to humans. Some fish, reptiles, and birds also have tetrachromacy, a condition that enables them to perceive four primary colors, compared to the three colors humans can distinguish. This expanded color vision aids in navigation and mate selection, enhancing survival and reproductive success. The presence of such visual abilities highlights the incredible diversity of sensory experiences in the animal kingdom, showcasing how evolution tailors the senses to the specific needs of each species. While our visual limitations might seem constraining, they are simply a result of the unique evolutionary path our species has taken. These differences in sensory perception provide a glimpse into the extraordinary ways in which life on Earth has adapted to its environment.

Key Vocabulary:
- **Ultraviolet (UV)**: A type of light beyond the violet end of the visible spectrum.
- **Photoreceptor**: A cell in the retina of the eye that responds to light.
- **Tetrachromacy**: The ability to see four primary colors.

- **Navigation**: The process of determining and controlling movement in a particular direction.
- **Perception**: The ability to see, hear, or become aware of something through the senses.

The Odd Reason Why Hot Water Can Freeze Faster Than Cold Water

It seems counterintuitive, but in some cases, hot water freezes faster than cold water—a phenomenon known as the Mpemba effect. This paradox was first observed by Aristotle, though it wasn't thoroughly investigated until the 1960s. The cause of this peculiar effect remains a topic of debate, with several theories attempting to explain it. One popular theory is that hot water evaporates more quickly, reducing the amount of water that actually needs to freeze. Another explanation involves the formation of supercooling, a state in which water below its freezing point remains in liquid form until disturbed. Hot water may reach this state faster than cold water, allowing it to freeze more rapidly once disturbed. The presence of dissolved gases in hot water may also play a role, as they escape as the water cools, potentially aiding the freezing process. Some scientists believe that the interaction between water and the container it's in can affect the rate at which it freezes, with hot water adhering more tightly to the surface than cold water. Though the exact mechanisms remain elusive, the Mpemba effect is a fascinating example of how seemingly simple physical processes can defy our expectations. Understanding this phenomenon might not just shed light on the mysteries of water but also provide insights into other nonlinear processes in nature.

Key Vocabulary:
- **Evaporates**: The process of liquid turning into vapor.
- **Supercooling**: The process of cooling a liquid below its freezing point without it becoming solid.
- **Mpemba Effect**: The phenomenon where hot water

freezes faster than cold water.
- **Adhering**: Sticking or attaching to a surface.
- **Nonlinear**: Not following a straight or predictable path.

Why Some People's Hair Stands Up Before a Storm

As storms approach, many individuals experience a peculiar phenomenon: their hair stands on end, a response known as piloerection. This is caused by an electrostatic charge building up in the atmosphere, which can affect the body's own electrical field. The hair follicles on the skin are sensitive to changes in electrical charge, and when a storm is nearby, the electrical tension causes them to contract, making the hair rise. This response is an ancient, evolutionary adaptation that helped animals appear larger and more intimidating to predators. In humans, however, it is less practical, though it remains a vestige of our fight-or-flight response. The increased static electricity in the air, due to the movement of ions, may trigger a physical reaction in some people, especially when a storm is accompanied by lightning. The sense of impending danger or discomfort that accompanies this hair-raising experience is deeply ingrained in our psyche, even though the response is mostly involuntary. While not everyone experiences this phenomenon, it is a fascinating example of how our bodies remain attuned to the forces of nature. Understanding this phenomenon can offer insight into the complex ways in which environmental stimuli can influence our physiological state.

Key Vocabulary:
- **Piloerection**: The process by which hair stands on end due to stimuli.
- **Contract**: To tighten or shrink in size.
- **Evolutionary**: Pertaining to the gradual development of species over time.
- **Fight-or-Flight**: The body's instinctive reaction to perceived danger.

- **Ions**: Charged particles that can create electric fields.

How the Brain Creates Illusions of Movement in Still Images

The human brain is adept at creating movement from stillness, a phenomenon known as the motion aftereffect. When viewing certain static images for an extended period, the brain compensates for the visual stimuli by "inventing" motion, a process that occurs in the visual cortex. This is especially true with high-contrast patterns or geometric shapes that create an impression of fluidity. The brain's response to these images is a result of its tendency to adapt to prolonged exposure to specific visual stimuli. In some cases, such as with rotating patterns, the brain perceives movement even though the image remains fixed. This occurs because the brain becomes less responsive to the static visual input over time, creating a kind of "motion fatigue" that is momentarily replaced by the illusion of movement. The phenomenon can also be influenced by external factors such as color or background contrast, as these elements can amplify the perceived motion. Such illusions of movement are not limited to visual art—they are present in films, advertisements, and even some forms of psychedelic experiences. These illusions reveal the brain's incredible ability to interpret and manipulate visual data, turning stillness into something dynamic.

Key Vocabulary:
- **Motion Aftereffect**: The phenomenon of perceiving motion after observing a stationary image.
- **Visual Cortex**: The area of the brain responsible for processing visual information.
- **Rotating**: Moving in a circular motion.
- **Psychedelic**: Inducing altered states of perception, often through sensory effects.
- **Compensates**: Adjusts or makes up for something, often as a response to change.

The Strange Science Behind Why Tears Have Different Compositions Depending on Emotion

Tears are not merely a response to irritation or pain; they have a complex biochemical composition that can vary depending on the emotional stimuli involved. There are three types of tears—basal, reflex, and emotional—each with distinct chemical makeups. Emotional tears, produced in response to joy, grief, or stress, contain higher levels of prolactin, a hormone associated with stress. They also contain more manganese, which is believed to play a role in regulating emotional responses. Reflex tears, on the other hand, are produced when the eyes are exposed to irritants like smoke or onions, and they serve as a defense mechanism to flush out foreign substances. Interestingly, emotional tears are thought to have evolved as a means of non-verbal communication, signaling distress or happiness to others. Studies have shown that when people cry in the presence of others, their emotional state can trigger empathy and compassion in those around them. This suggests that the act of crying may serve both a physiological and a social purpose. The composition of tears, therefore, is an intricate blend of biology and emotion, a reflection of the body's response to internal and external stimuli. Understanding this complex interaction provides insight into the fascinating relationship between our bodies and emotions.

Key Vocabulary:
- **Basal**: The basic or underlying layer of something.
- **Prolactin**: A hormone that plays a role in milk production and stress responses.
- **Manganese**: A mineral linked to a variety of bodily functions, including emotional regulation.
- **Empathy**: The ability to understand and share the feelings of others.
- **Compassion**: Sympathy and concern for the suffering of

others.

Why Whales and Elephants Can "Feel" Earthquakes Before They Happen

Whales and elephants are renowned for their ability to perceive seismic activity before it reaches humans, a phenomenon that has puzzled scientists for centuries. These animals are believed to detect vibrations and sounds traveling through the Earth, using their advanced sensory systems to pick up on subtle environmental cues. Elephants, for example, can sense low-frequency infrasound waves that are produced by distant earthquakes, enabling them to react long before the tremors reach the surface. Similarly, whales, with their exceptional hearing and ability to detect sounds over vast distances, may perceive these vibrations underwater, allowing them to navigate toward safer areas. Their ability to sense impending earthquakes may be linked to their heightened sensitivity to natural phenomena like storms, winds, and tidal changes. Some researchers believe that these animals use their acute hearing and vibration-detecting abilities to communicate over long distances, as well as to anticipate changes in their environment. While much remains unknown about this extraordinary skill, it serves as a reminder of the remarkable ways in which certain species interact with the world around them. The ability to feel earthquakes may provide these animals with an adaptive advantage, increasing their chances of survival in an unpredictable natural world.

Key Vocabulary:
- **Infrasound**: Low-frequency sound waves below the human hearing range.
- **Advanced**: Highly developed or sophisticated.
- **Vibration-Detecting**: The ability to sense vibrations in the environment.
- **Acute**: Highly sensitive or sharp in perception.
- **Adaptive Advantage**: A beneficial trait that enhances an

organism's ability to survive.

How the Human Nose Can Detect Over a Trillion Different Smells

The human olfactory system is a remarkable and highly sophisticated mechanism, enabling individuals to detect an extraordinary array of odors. Recent scientific discoveries confirm that the human nose can perceive over one trillion distinct smells, a revelation that underscores the remarkable sensitivity of the olfactory receptors. These specialized olfactory receptors—approximately 400 in total—are scattered throughout the nasal cavity, each dedicated to recognizing specific odor molecules. These receptors transmit signals to the brain's olfactory bulb, where they are processed and interpreted, culminating in the perception of a smell. This complex process forms part of a broader sensory phenomenon known as chemoreception, which governs both smell and taste, creating an intricate interplay between these senses. The olfactory system is particularly influential in shaping human emotions, as scents are directly linked to the brain's limbic system, the region responsible for memory and emotional responses. Through this connection, certain aromas can evoke vivid recollections or alter our mood. This olfactory ability may have evolved over time, with some researchers suggesting that humans once had a keener sense of smell, now somewhat diminished due to the primacy of other senses. Despite this, the human nose remains an underexplored frontier in sensory research, offering vast opportunities for further exploration.

Key Vocabulary:
- **Olfactory receptors**: Sensory cells in the nose that detect odors.
- **Remarkable**: Extraordinary; worthy of attention.
- **Chemoreception**: The ability to sense chemicals, such as odors or tastes.
- **Limbic system**: The part of the brain involved in

emotions and memory.
- **Underexplored**: Not sufficiently studied or understood.

The Invisible Forces That Keep a Bicycle Upright

The act of riding a bicycle is governed by a fascinating interplay of forces that are often invisible to the rider. The primary force at work is gyroscopic stability, generated by the rotating wheels of the bike, which resists changes in the orientation of the bike. However, this force alone is insufficient to explain the dynamics of balance when the bike is in motion. To maintain stability, cyclists must instinctively engage in countersteering, a process in which they steer the handlebars in the opposite direction of the lean. This action induces a torque on the front wheel, which, in turn, adjusts the bike's direction and helps right it. The delicate balance between gyroscopic forces, countersteering, and the rider's body creates a seamless feedback loop that stabilizes the bicycle. Scientists and engineers have employed mathematical models to analyze these complex interactions, demonstrating how minute alterations in speed or direction can influence the bike's equilibrium. Despite the simplicity of riding a bike, this intricate combination of forces exemplifies how the human body intuitively interacts with complex physical principles. The phenomena at play demonstrate the elegance of dynamic equilibrium, where multiple forces work together in harmony to maintain stability.

Key Vocabulary:
- **Gyroscopic stability**: The force produced by spinning wheels that resists tilting.
- **Countersteering**: Steering in the opposite direction to balance a bike.
- **Torque**: A rotational force that causes an object to rotate.
- **Feedback loop**: A system where outputs are fed back into the system, affecting future outputs.
- **Dynamic equilibrium**: A state of balance where forces are

constantly adjusting but remain stable.

How Animals That Hibernate Don't Get Muscle Loss

During the winter months, many animals enter a state of torpor, reducing their metabolic rate to conserve energy and endure the harsh conditions. Remarkably, these hibernating creatures, such as bears and ground squirrels, do not experience the debilitating effects of muscle atrophy that humans often suffer from prolonged immobility. This is due to the secretion of specialized proteins like atrogin-1, which play a crucial role in preserving muscle tissue by inhibiting the usual process of muscle breakdown. Hibernating animals also engage in protein turnover, a process that ensures the constant renewal of muscle proteins, preventing degradation despite long periods of dormancy. This preservation is further enhanced by the animal's ability to metabolize stored fat efficiently, providing the energy needed for survival without compromising muscle integrity. The reduced circulation during hibernation minimizes the use of muscles, which helps conserve energy. These fascinating biological adaptations have evolved over time, allowing animals to thrive in environments where food is scarce, and survival is contingent on physical preservation. The study of these mechanisms holds potential for improving our understanding of muscle degeneration and developing treatments for conditions like muscular dystrophy.

Key Vocabulary:
- **Torpor**: A state of physical inactivity and reduced metabolic rate.
- **Muscle atrophy**: The weakening or wasting of muscle tissue.
- **Atrogin-1**: A protein involved in muscle preservation.
- **Protein turnover**: The continuous process of breaking down and rebuilding proteins.
- **Physical preservation**: The act of maintaining physical

strength and integrity.

The Strange Connection Between Your Gut and Your Mood

The gut-brain axis is a complex and intricate system of communication between the gastrointestinal tract and the brain, profoundly influencing our emotional and psychological states. Within the gut, a vast colony of microorganisms, collectively known as the microbiome, plays a pivotal role in regulating mental health. These microorganisms communicate directly with the brain through the vagus nerve, affecting the production of neurotransmitters such as serotonin, a chemical integral to regulating mood, sleep, and appetite. Astonishingly, around 90% of serotonin is produced within the gut, making it a key player in our emotional well-being. Disruptions in the microbiome, caused by poor diet, stress, or illness, can lead to imbalances in serotonin levels, which are linked to conditions like depression and anxiety. Researchers are exploring the potential of probiotics to restore balance to the gut microbiome and alleviate mood disorders. Moreover, the influence of gut health on emotional stability underscores the importance of a holistic approach to mental wellness, recognizing the interdependence of mind and body. This emerging field of study has opened new avenues for treatment, where improving gut health may offer profound benefits for mental health. The gut-brain axis exemplifies the increasingly recognized connection between the body's internal ecosystem and emotional well-being.

Key Vocabulary:
- **Microbiome**: The collection of microorganisms living in the gut.
- **Vagus nerve**: A nerve that transmits signals between the brain and gut.
- **Neurotransmitters**: Chemicals that transmit signals

across the brain and nervous system.
- **Probiotics**: Beneficial bacteria that support the health of the microbiome.
- **Holistic**: An approach that considers the whole system, rather than just individual parts.

How the Position of the Sun Can Make You Feel Happier

The position of the sun relative to the Earth plays a significant role in regulating our mood and energy levels. This phenomenon is primarily linked to the secretion of serotonin, a neurotransmitter that enhances mood and well-being. When sunlight enters the eyes, it stimulates the brain's pineal gland, signaling the body to produce serotonin and, during the evening, melatonin, a hormone that induces sleep. The angle at which sunlight enters our eyes varies with the time of day and the season, affecting the intensity of light exposure. This explains why people often feel more energized and optimistic on bright, sunny days, while shorter days in winter can lead to feelings of lethargy and even seasonal affective disorder (SAD). Light exposure, especially in the morning, aligns our circadian rhythm, synchronizing our internal body clock with the external world, promoting wakefulness and overall well-being. Studies suggest that individuals living in areas with long winters or frequent cloud cover may experience a decline in serotonin levels, contributing to feelings of depression. Therapeutic light exposure, often used as a treatment for SAD, capitalizes on the healing effects of sunlight to restore balance. The intricate relationship between sunlight and mood underscores the delicate balance of biological systems that influence our emotional states.

Key Vocabulary:
- **Serotonin**: A neurotransmitter that affects mood and emotional well-being.
- **Pineal gland**: A small gland in the brain that produces melatonin and regulates sleep.

- **Optimistic**: Hopeful and positive about the future.
- **Seasonal affective disorder (SAD)**: A form of depression linked to changes in seasons.
- **Decline**: A reduction or decrease in quality or quantity.

Why Our Bodies "Jump" Right Before Falling Asleep

The sensation of hypnic jerks, the involuntary twitch or jolt that occurs as we drift toward sleep, is a mysterious but common occurrence. Scientists suggest this phenomenon is linked to the body's transition from wakefulness to the early stages of sleep, when the brain is still alert. One theory is that as the body begins to relax, the brain misinterprets this relaxation as a sign of falling, triggering a reflex that causes the muscles to contract suddenly. This startle reflex, as it is known, is thought to be an evolutionary adaptation designed to prevent injury or ensure that the body remains alert in vulnerable situations. Despite the discomfort these jerks may cause, they are typically harmless and can even be triggered by certain factors such as stress or caffeine consumption. The frequency and intensity of hypnic jerks vary from person to person, with some experiencing them more frequently than others. The phenomenon may also be influenced by the circadian rhythm, our internal biological clock that regulates sleep-wake cycles. Interestingly, hypnic jerks are often accompanied by a brief feeling of dread, as if one is about to fall. Though their exact cause remains elusive, these jerks are a natural part of the sleep process, reflecting the complex mechanisms at play during the transition from wakefulness to slumber.

Key Vocabulary:
- **Hypnic jerks**: Sudden muscle twitches or jolts during the transition to sleep.
- **Startle reflex**: An involuntary response to a sudden stimulus.
- **Circadian rhythm**: The body's internal clock that

regulates sleep-wake cycles.
- **Dread**: A sense of fear or anxiety, often about an impending event.
- **Transition**: The process of moving from one state or condition to another.

How the Brain "Edits" Our Memories Over Time

The human brain does not store memories like a recording device; instead, it constantly reconstructs memories, shaping them over time. This phenomenon is known as memory reconsolidation, where the act of recalling a memory alters the memory itself. When we retrieve a memory, the brain reactivates the neural networks associated with that memory, making it malleable and susceptible to modification. Over time, these reconsolidations can introduce distortions, adding new details or omitting others, thereby changing the way we perceive past events. This malleability is one reason why memories can become unreliable, with people often misremembering facts or events, especially as they are reinterpreted through the lens of present-day experiences. Emotional states can further influence the way memories are edited; for instance, feelings of regret or nostalgia can imbue memories with a sense of intensity or emotional weight that may not have been present at the time. This dynamic process highlights the fluidity of memory, as it evolves to fit the ever-changing narrative of our lives. Some researchers suggest that this fluid nature of memory may serve an adaptive purpose, allowing us to integrate new experiences and learnings. While this reconstruction process enhances cognitive flexibility, it also underscores the fallibility of memory as a source of objective truth.

Key Vocabulary:
- **Reconsolidation**: The process of reactivating and modifying a memory when it is recalled.
- **Malleable**: Capable of being changed or shaped.

- **Unreliable**: Not consistently accurate or dependable.
- **Intensity**: The degree of strength or emotion attached to a memory.
- **Learnings**: The knowledge or experiences gained over time.

The Unexpected Math Hidden in Nature's Designs

Mathematics is more deeply embedded in the natural world than many realize, often appearing in the form of symmetry, patterns, and proportions that govern everything from the growth of plants to the structure of galaxies. The Fibonacci sequence, for example, a series of numbers in which each number is the sum of the two preceding ones, can be found in the arrangement of leaves, the spirals of shells, and even the branching of trees. This sequence embodies the principle of golden ratio, a mathematical relationship often associated with aesthetically pleasing proportions. The golden ratio can be seen in the proportions of the human body, in the design of classical architecture, and in the spiral patterns of hurricanes. Beyond the visual, math also dictates the way animals move, such as the gait of a horse or the flight patterns of birds, which follow specific geometric principles. These recurring mathematical phenomena underscore a deeper order within the apparent chaos of nature. Scientists and mathematicians have long sought to understand how such patterns emerge and why they seem to follow mathematical rules. Some suggest that these patterns represent the most efficient solutions to biological and physical challenges, such as maximizing sunlight absorption in plants or optimizing the use of energy in animal movement. The hidden math in nature serves as a reminder of the intricate and elegant systems that govern the world around us.

Key Vocabulary:
- **Symmetry**: Balanced proportions or arrangement in nature.

- **Fibonacci sequence**: A series of numbers where each number is the sum of the two preceding ones.
- **Golden ratio**: A mathematical ratio found in many natural and artistic patterns.
- **Gait**: The manner in which an animal moves or walks.
- **Elegant**: Simple, effective, and aesthetically pleasing.

Why Some People Never Get Motion Sickness

Motion sickness occurs when there's a discrepancy between the visual input and the signals sent by the inner ear, resulting in a disorienting feeling of nausea. However, some individuals remain unaffected by this common ailment. This resistance is often due to differences in the vestibular system, the part of the inner ear that controls balance and spatial orientation. Some people have a more robust vestibular system that efficiently processes sensory information, preventing the confusion that leads to nausea. Others may possess a genetic predisposition that enhances their ability to adapt to different types of motion, allowing them to function without discomfort. Interestingly, studies suggest that habitual exposure to motion—such as regular travel or activities like sailing—can condition the brain to tolerate motion more effectively. This ability to adapt is linked to neural plasticity, where the brain rewires itself in response to frequent experiences. The phenomenon is further compounded by psychological factors; individuals who expect to experience motion sickness are more likely to manifest the symptoms. Conversely, those with high resilience tend to remain unaffected, possibly due to an optimistic or relaxed outlook on the situation. While the exact reasons some individuals are immune to motion sickness remain unclear, the relationship between the brain, inner ear, and adaptation is undeniably complex and fascinating.

Key Vocabulary:
- **Vestibular system**: The part of the inner ear that controls

balance and spatial orientation.
- **Robust**: Strong, resilient, or durable.
- **Genetic predisposition**: An inherited genetic trait that increases susceptibility to certain conditions.
- **Adapt**: To adjust or modify in response to new conditions.
- **High resilience**: The ability to recover quickly from difficulties or challenges.

How Dolphins Sleep with Half Their Brain Awake

Dolphins possess an extraordinary ability to sleep with one half of their brain at a time, a phenomenon known as unihemispheric slow-wave sleep. This unique adaptation allows them to remain alert to their surroundings, especially when swimming, breathing, and avoiding predators. During this type of sleep, one hemisphere of the brain enters a restful state while the other remains active, controlling essential functions. Dolphins need to be vigilant in their aquatic environment, as they must consciously come to the surface to breathe, even while resting. The brain's left and right hemispheres take turns entering sleep, ensuring that one side is always on alert. This process is believed to be an evolutionary adaptation that helps dolphins avoid danger while still allowing them to rest. Unlike humans, who experience full brain activity during sleep, dolphins have mastered the art of divided rest, maintaining a constant balance between rest and alertness. The ability to sleep with half the brain at a time reflects the complexity of the dolphin's cognitive and behavioral abilities. This fascinating trait is just one example of how certain animals have evolved unique survival mechanisms to thrive in their environments.

Key Vocabulary:
- **Unihemispheric slow-wave sleep**: A type of sleep where one hemisphere of the brain is active while the other rests.
- **Consciously**: With full awareness or intention.

- **Balance**: A harmonious or stable condition.
- **Complexity**: The state of being intricate or complicated.
- **Adaptation**: A change in an organism to better suit its environment.

The Physics Behind How Ice Skaters Spin So Fast

When ice skaters perform spins, they exhibit an extraordinary demonstration of angular momentum, a physical principle that governs rotational motion. As a skater pulls their arms in toward their body while spinning, they reduce their moment of inertia, the measure of an object's resistance to changes in its rotation. By decreasing their arm span, the skater's body becomes more compact, and according to the law of conservation of angular momentum, their rotational speed increases to compensate for the reduction in inertia. This is why ice skaters can spin so rapidly, achieving speeds that would be impossible without this physics principle at play. The energy required for the spin is conserved, and the skater's velocity increases as their mass is concentrated around the axis of rotation. The fluidity and grace of a skater's movements are not just due to skill but also to their ability to manipulate these forces through precise body positioning. The torque applied by the skater's limbs helps to initiate and sustain the spin, providing the necessary force to maintain the motion. As they reach the peak of their spin, the skater can adjust their body position to control the speed, demonstrating a remarkable understanding of both physics and biomechanics. The interplay of physics and athleticism in ice skating showcases the elegant ways in which the laws of nature govern our physical abilities.

Key Vocabulary:
- **Angular momentum**: The measure of the rotation of an object in motion.
- **Moment of inertia**: The resistance of an object to changes in its rotation.

- **Velocity**: The speed and direction of an object's movement.
- **Torque**: The force that causes an object to rotate.
- **Biomechanics**: The study of the mechanical laws relating to the movement of living organisms.

Why Some People Experience "Tingles" from ASMR Sounds

Autonomous Sensory Meridian Response (ASMR) is a phenomenon where certain sounds or visual stimuli trigger a pleasurable, tingling sensation, often felt on the scalp or spine. This sensation is thought to be caused by a neural response in the brain, specifically the release of endorphins and other neurotransmitters that promote relaxation and pleasure. ASMR videos, which feature soft whispers, tapping, or crinkling sounds, have gained widespread popularity for their ability to induce calming effects and alleviate stress. The tingling sensation is often described as a deep, soothing experience that some individuals seek out as a form of therapy. The triggers for ASMR can vary widely, with some people responding to particular sounds or visual cues more than others. Researchers believe that ASMR may have evolved as a form of social bonding, as many of the triggers mimic the soothing sounds of caretaking behaviors, such as a mother's voice or the sound of gentle brushing. Despite its widespread appeal, not everyone experiences ASMR, and some individuals may feel discomfort instead of pleasure when exposed to the same stimuli. The science behind ASMR remains relatively unexplored, but it continues to fascinate both scientists and enthusiasts alike, who are intrigued by the potential therapeutic benefits of this unusual response.

Key Vocabulary:
- **Neural**: Relating to the nervous system or brain.
- **Endorphins**: Chemicals produced by the brain that act as natural painkillers and mood enhancers.

- **Calming**: Making someone feel peaceful or relaxed.
- **Discomfort**: A lack of ease or pain.
- **Scientists**: Experts in the study of the natural and physical world.

How Certain Flowers Generate Their Own Heat

Certain species of flowers, such as the skunk cabbage and the titan arum, have the remarkable ability to generate heat, a phenomenon known as thermogenesis. This biological process involves the production of heat through metabolic activity, allowing these flowers to warm their surroundings in order to attract pollinators, even in cold environments. In the case of the skunk cabbage, the flower's spadix, the central spike of the bloom, produces heat that melts surrounding snow, making the plant visible to early-season insects. This warmth is also believed to release a pungent odor, which mimics decaying flesh, thereby attracting pollinators such as carrion flies. Similarly, the titan arum, one of the largest flowers in the world, is capable of heating up to nearly 98°F (37°C), a temperature that helps it release its distinctive foul smell and draw in the flies that are essential for its reproduction. The ability to generate heat is an evolutionary adaptation that increases the likelihood of pollination in regions where temperatures are typically low. This endothermic behavior demonstrates the extraordinary ways in which plants have evolved to survive and thrive in diverse climates. Despite the energy-intensive nature of thermogenesis, it is a survival strategy that proves essential for the reproductive success of these remarkable flowers.

Key Vocabulary:
- **Thermogenesis**: The production of heat within a living organism.
- **Metabolic**: Relating to the chemical processes that occur within a living organism.
- **Evolutionary**: Relating to the gradual development of

organisms over time.
- **Endothermic**: The ability to produce internal heat.
- **Spadix**: The central spike of a flower, often surrounded by a sheath.

The Strange Way Bubbles Always Pop in the Same Shape

Bubbles, despite their delicate nature, consistently pop in the same shape—typically a circular or oval form. This is due to the unique surface tension of the soap film that makes up the bubble. Surface tension is the result of the cohesive forces between water molecules, which causes the bubble to maintain its spherical shape while it is intact. As the bubble bursts, the molecules of the soap film quickly reorient themselves, releasing the trapped air and causing the bubble to collapse in a way that minimizes the surface area. The uniformity in the popping process can also be attributed to the fact that the force of the pressure inside the bubble is evenly distributed across its surface. When the bubble finally bursts, it does so with a rapid release of energy, sometimes causing the characteristic pop sound. The symmetry of the bubble's shape before and after it pops reflects the principles of physics at play, particularly the behavior of liquids under pressure. While bubbles may seem like simple toys or fleeting objects, their behavior is governed by the same laws of nature that govern much of our physical world, showcasing the underlying beauty in even the most ephemeral phenomena.

Key Vocabulary:
- **Surface tension**: The cohesive force that causes the surface of a liquid to behave like a stretched elastic membrane.
- **Collapse**: To fall or cave in suddenly.
- **Pressure**: The force exerted on an object per unit area.
- **Symmetry**: The quality of being made up of exactly similar parts facing each other or around an axis.
- **Ephemeral**: Lasting for a very short time.

THE JOURNEY OF VOCABULARY LEARNING

As we reach the end of this journey through fascinating stories and enriching vocabulary, it's important to reflect on the key themes we've explored. Throughout this book, you've encountered a vast array of stories from nature, history, space, science and more. Each story offered an opportunity to explore the world around us but also a chance to expand your vocabulary in context-rich ways. By learning words within stories, you've gained a deeper understanding of their meanings and applications, making them more likely to stick with you in everyday conversations and writing.

The stories in this book have shown us the power of language when it's connected to something engaging and memorable. Whether you were intrigued by the behavior of the pufferfish or learning about the cause of brain freeze, every story perhaps introduced you to some new words that may ultimately become part of your expanding vocabulary. This method of learning—through context—goes beyond memorization. It connects words to real-world events, helping them feel alive and relevant.

The importance of context in language learning cannot be overstated. Words take on richer meanings when they are tied to experiences, ideas, or phenomena that capture our attention. This is why learning vocabulary through stories works so well. It allows you to understand not just the literal definitions of words but also their emotional weight, historical significance, and practical use. As you continue to read, listen, and speak in English, you'll find that your growing vocabulary will naturally come into play, enriching your language skills and helping you communicate more confidently and effectively.

Now that you've completed this book, the journey of vocabulary learning doesn't end here. The world is filled with endless stories, each offering new opportunities to learn and grow. Continue to seek out stories—whether in books, audiobooks, podcasts, documentaries, or conversations—that introduce you to fresh vocabulary. Every new word you encounter is a key to unlocking deeper understanding, clearer communication, and greater connection with others. We hope you've enjoyed this book, and feel confident that you've learned a few things too.

www.ingramcontent.com/pod-product-compliance
Lightning Source LLC
Chambersburg PA
CBHW062006180426
43198CB00037B/2429